W9-CMJ-826

CHARITY COSTUMES

of children, scholars; almsfolk, pensioners

PHILLIS CUNNINGTON

CATHERINE LUCAS

BARNES & NOBLE
BOOKS
10 East 53d St., New York 10022
(a division of Harper & Row Publishers, Inc.)

Published in the U.S.A. 1978 by
HARPER & ROW PUBLISHERS, INC.
BARNES & NOBLE IMPORT DIVISION
ISBN 0-06-491346-5
LC 77-8742

9-20-78

Text set in 11/12 pt Photon Baskerville, printed by photolithography,
and bound in Great Britain at The Pitman Press, Bath

NOV 02 1978

CONTENTS

ACKNOWLEDGEMENTS

Dr Cunnington died following a car accident late in 1974 when plans for this book had already been made. *Publisher's note*

Simply because of their number it is impossible to do justice to those who have contributed with their special knowledge to this book. The local historians and librarians in many of the towns mentioned have given generously of their time and often put prints, photographs and unpublished documents at our disposal. In London, the libraries of Guildhall, of the University of London (palaeography section), of the National Maritime Museum, of County Hall, of the City of Westminster and those of the Boroughs of Islington and of Kensington and Chelsea have been particularly helpful in this way. We have had much assistance from the staff of nearly every institution dealt with in the book, notably the archivists at Christ's Hospital, the Thomas Coram Foundation and Dr Barnardo's Homes where we were dealing with exceptionally rich records. Besides many individuals mentioned in the text, Miss Janet Arnold, Miss Jean Swann and Mrs "Felix" Stone have contributed from their special knowledge and skills.

Mrs Susan Luckham's efficiency, watchfulness and patience in typing the book deserves a very special mention. Finally, our warmest thanks are due to Miss Sibyl Clement Brown, O.B.E. for much constructive criticism, to Major Alan Mansfield for his expert help over selection and technicalities, and particularly to Dr A. Walk, without whose invaluable advice and exhaustive editing of the manuscript and handling of proofs, the book might never have seen the light.

CATHERINE LUCAS

TO THE READER

In this book we have made an attempt to trace the history in England of clothing provided for poor people of all sorts by charity; that is to say clothing given in kind by a wide range of benevolent individuals and groups, but not including supplies given out as statutory relief, nor hand-me-downs from masters to servants.

The period covered is from late medieval times to the mid twentieth century.

It is unfortunate that in many cases, and increasingly with time, "that most excellent gift of charity" became debased into a cold and rigid system, especially when the inspired donor of a charitable endowment had been long since dead. Thus the word "charity" acquired pejorative overtones, and the outward garb of the recipients was subject to disparagement and even ribaldry. At the same time it is noteworthy, and even salutary, to see that in other cases, for instance in some schools, colleges and pensioners' institutions, the beneficiaries of ancient charitable foundations have advanced in social status, and indeed both uniform and foundation have eventually come to mark out the one-time objects of charity as an élite social group.

The three opening chapters analyse these and other social implications, after discussing the general characteristics of charity costumes and the problems of providing them. We give examples not only of donors' and recipients' attitudes (where possible in their own words) but also of those of the public. Reactions are further illustrated in the final chapter where it is shown how charity uniforms, whether individually picturesque or not, have been enjoyed as a spectacle when grouped together and have even been used for their decorative effect in many public parades and pageants. The introductory chapters, and the final one, may be read together – separately from the descriptions in the remainder of the book – as an essay in social history.

Chapters 4 to 14 are addressed more closely, though not exclusively, to the student and historian of costume. They give an account of the dress worn in a wide variety of institutions, many of whose histories go back several centuries and are of great interest in themselves. The attendant changes in costume, as well as the frequent fossilizations of ancient styles, are traced.

A diversity of sources has been used, including manuscripts, pictures, sculpture, surviving garments and badges. Many of the records that we have used describe features of attire that were not confined to charity costumes as such. These particulars have sometimes been included in the book for the sake of completeness, and because we hoped that they might be useful to those interested in the historic costume of the poor in general, a sparsely documented subject.

In the illustrations, only contemporary work has been used to exemplify costumes of the past; but it has to be remembered that the originals cannot invariably be taken quite literally – sometimes the artist's licence was too large or his information too little.

The institutions cited are to some extent arbitrarily chosen, but it is hoped that the selection is fairly representative of the vast field available.

> If ever thou gavest hosen and shoon,
> – Every nighte and alle,
> Sit thee down and put them on;
> And Christe receive thy saule.

From *A Lyke Wake Dirge*, set to music by
Benjamin Britten

CHAPTER 1

Problems and practices

ACUTENESS OF THE NEED

Living in the Western World in the late twentieth century we find it difficult to realize that lack of clothing was, in the past, a major cause of suffering for a considerable part of our own population. Acute poverty is associated in our minds with areas where malnutrition is the crucial factor, the climate rendering scantiness of clothing little or no hardship. But in Britain until quite recent times it has been almost as important for charity to clothe the poor as to feed them. Statuettes that decorated eighteenth-century charity schools (Fig. 1) often portrayed a boy with a scroll bearing the text "I was naked and ye clothed me" and this was scarcely an exaggeration. Rogers in his *History of Agriculture and Prices* . . . emphasizes that, for centuries, even shirts were "such valuable

1. Charity schoolboy, holding a scroll with the words "I was naked and ye clothed me". Statuette made for St Mary Abbots Charity School, Kensington, 1712, now on the primary school on the same site (Courtesy: Kensington Public Libraries)

articles that they are often the subject of charitable doles and . . . not un-
frequently . . . devised by Will''.[1]

The dissolution of the monasteries exposed the extent of poverty. It
was not long before the City of London was obliged to take measures.
Roused by Bishop Ridley, who also appealed to King Edward VI for
support, the aldermen and Common Council made a survey. The six
categories into which they classified the City's poor form a useful basis
for our own study, since in all of them it has been found necessary,
throughout history, to supplement the clothing. The list may be of
interest:[2]

Fatherless and other [destitute] Children	300
The Sore and Sick	200
The poor overburdened with Children	350
The Aged	400
Decayed Citizens [innocent unemployables and the handicapped]	650
Idle Vagabonds	200
	2100

Sir Thomas Bennett in 1616 left £24 per annum "for clothing poor
naked men, women and children wandering in the streets of London";[3]
and, if we choose children alone, it is easy to exemplify the destitution
that could prevail in town and country alike.* Thomas Anguish was
moved to endow by his will of 1617 a home and clothing for "Younge
and very poor Children . . . of Norwich, and specially suche as for
wante, lye in the Streetes, Vaughts, Doores and Windowes, whereby
many of them fall into great and grevious diseases and Lamenesses".[4]
Compare Fig. 117.

In the mid eighteenth century, many homeless boys were rescued by
Hanway's Marine Society (Chapter 10), and their need for clothing, in
particular, is shown by the Society's rule that on arrival "Their cast off
clothing are put into a large box till disposed of as rags . . . there is
only a very small part of it fit to be mended or which it is not *dangerous*
or *inconvenient* to use even after washing".[5]

It was the custom, in the charity schools that sprang up under the
Church of England's revival in Queen Anne's reign, to provide the
children with clothing although they attended only by the day. Here

---

* When the Foundling Hospital opened in 1741, the women disappointed of vacancies
for their infants were addressed by one of the Governors who actually "desired that
they would not Drop any of their Children in the Streets".[6] Exposure of the newborn was a
common practice.

2. "Transformation scenes in real life . . . before and after reclamation" at
East End Juvenile Mission, 1875 (*The Graphic*, vol. II, 64)

the advantage was not always just to clothe the naked but to obviate for the parents the necessity of sending a child to work to earn for itself what it wore. Even for children with some employment the clothing problem could be desperate, as the nineteenth-century ragged schools showed.

Dickens, in a letter of 1843,[7] describes the children in one of these: "there is no such thing as dress among the seventy pupils . . . I have very seldom seen . . . anything so shocking". One of the boys was clad only in "a bit of a sack". Dickens remarks that this school was in a "rotten house" like Fagin's in *Oliver Twist* and "on the same ground".

As late as the 1870s the homeless children rescued by Dr Barnardo could be thus described:

Their ragged garments had become so clotted and clogged through not having been removed for months that they had to be cut from their bodies. In one or two cases, where the garments were outgrown . . . there was no alternative but to plunge the children into warm water . . . and leave them to soak. Bit by bit the disgusting rags were cut, peeled or torn from their bodies.[8]

With charity schools the clothing of the children was aimed partly at giving them a decent appearance because the school was in the public eye. This is shown by the fact that in the Ratcliff Hamlet School, Stepney, where the charity could not clothe all the children, a rule had to be made in the 1830s that the "unclothed" must contribute 1d a week till they had saved half the cost of a pair of shoes. Thereafter, the charity having made up the difference, the child was never allowed to appear barefoot again. The existence of a London Poor Children's Boot Fund in the nineteenth century (later absorbed into the Shaftesbury Society) emphasized this need.

Truancy was often due to the embarrassment of parents. Mrs Trimmer, writing on charity Sunday schools in 1801, explains and advises:

. . . some decent parents are too poor to be able to make their children fit to appear . . . even of the children present, many are wretchedly clad . . . It would be a disgrace to humanity to profess kindness to these children, and not to do for them all that can be afforded. *Caps* and *Tippets* made of old cloth can at least be provided; and *young Ladies* can make them.[9]

It was not until the early twentieth century that most of the charitable institutions gave up providing clothes in kind. Then, what with national prosperity, a modicum of levelling, and the fore-shadowing of the Welfare State, such dire necessity receded and it became reasonably safe for the charities either to give money in lieu or to ignore the question of clothing altogether. This coincided with the

SAINT ANN'S SOCIETY SCHOOLS.

3. "Charity" with ragged urchins (*right*) and costumed charity boy and girl (*left*). The girl wears characteristic white tippet and apron. Both boy and girl have typical caps (Headpiece of dinner ticket of a City of London charitable society, St Ann's, 1827. Guildhall Library C.49.1)

trend, which was noticeable all through the period we cover and now reached its peak, whereby the institutions which began as aids to the poor were invaded by the middle classes. This naturally affected the charity costumes in ways we shall trace and contributed finally to their abolition as such.

COST AND CARE

Charity clothes would obviously as a rule be chosen with economy. If not the benefactors themselves, at least their trustees and/or management committees were generally business people, who were shrewd and would seek a good combination of cheapness and durability. A disadvantage was that until very recent times they were nearly always men, even when appointed to choose clothing for women, girls or babies. Certain charity schools in York seem to have been quite exceptional in the eighteenth century in having been administered and even founded by ladies.

Charitable institutions were occasionally presented with free or cut-price garments in kind, particularly when they first opened. This is

4. Barnardo boys making shoes (1883) and girl darning (1880). Note her pinafore with shoulder lappets (*Night and Day*, vol. VII, 20, and vol. IV, 85)

recorded for linen collars in St Anne's School, Soho, and cloaks for one in Clerkenwell.

Sometimes one charity helped another with clothing. In 1813 the head of the Royal Military Asylum for boys offered to the Foundling Hospital one thousand pairs of shoes, saying he would charge only one shilling a pair "which will be applied in retrieving the ... 2 guineas per week which we are obliged to pay the two men for teaching and assisting the Boys in making them".[10] Boys' mending was always done by the girls when a sister school or home existed. The Red Maids' School, Bristol, helped, from 1780 on, by the almswomen of Fry's House of Mercy, had to make shirts for the boys of the neighbouring but quite separate charity school of Queen Elizabeth's Hospital.

Aside from gifts and bargains, the rule was careful bulk buying. Two members of the Mercers' Company, Richard (Dick to us) Whittington and Ellis Davy, when they endowed almshouses in the mid fifteenth century (in London and Croydon respectively) both laid it down that "... clothing of the tutor [warden] and poure people ... to be ... of easy price cloth according to their degree" (i.e. the warden's better than the men's but all must be cheap).[11]

The Earl of Northampton's trustees (again shrewd Mercers) in 1615 went so far as to decree that the warden of Holy Trinity Hospital, his almshouse in Greenwich, "shall ... once euery yeare buy so much good durable cloth as shall serve to make eueryone of the poore men a gowne ... and he shall make this purchase of cloth in the best season of the yeare when and where he may have yt best cheape".[12] The warden's accounts show that this was faithfully carried out; for example in 1685: "26th January. To London to buy the wollen Cloth my selfe and two old men – boat hire 2s our dinner 2s spent 1s porter to carry two peces of Cloth to Tower Warfe."[13]

Great care was given to economical cutting out. The Foundling Hospital in 1753 worked out how many bibs should be cut from five pieces of "check" and how many nappies from eighty-one pieces of "Russia huckaback".[14] Men's and boys' suits and men's gowns were generally made by a tailor, but all other garments were made, from the cloth provided, by girl and boy beneficiaries or occasionally by their mothers. Even those were cut out by an expert, and in schools and homes this would be the teacher of tailoring and sewing.

Boys sewed only if they were meant to take up clothing trades or to go to sea, but they always knitted (they began it before they were five years old) and sometimes, as at the Military Asylum, they made shoes. Foundling girls learnt to sew and knit between the ages of three and five. At the Cripplegate-Within Ward School, opened in 1712, the girls must have spent nearly all their time sewing: it was not until 1777 that

5. London charity schoolgirl in typical dress, holding knitting needles and a stocking she has made. C. 1805 (John Page *Book of engravings depicting the costume of ... each charity school ... in the ... anniversary service ... in St Paul's*, Guildhall Library)

any of them were taught to write. At the Foundling in 1771 a minute records severely: "The Committee observing that many Stockings are bought for the use of the Girls . . . *ordered* that the Girls do in the future knit their own or go without".[15]

In *The Schools for the People* (1871) George Bartley notes that the Müller's Orphan School, Ashley Down, Bristol, gave "a training consisting entirely of bookwork" but even there the girls made their own clothes. We have it from one who was brought up in an orphanage in the 1890s that making their black wool stockings on a machine was a positive pleasure for the girls. "I loved it. Bang! Bang! Six stockings in a morning!"[16]

Durability of the clothing was of course sought, especially in footwear. At Christ's Hospital three pairs of mid-nineteenth-century boys' shoes are still preserved and one pair is studded all over the heels and soles with large projecting hob-nail heads. The minutes of the Clerkenwell School's Committee show how closely this matter of nails was gone into. In 1835, for example, it resolved "that the girls' Shoes have more nails in the heels and the Boys' Shoes be without iron heels but be well-nailed with sperables [sparrow bills – brads or headless nails with wedge- or beak-shaped ends] both heels and soles filed down flush . . ." Latymer Upper School still possesses a nineteenth-century boy's shoe, the heel of which is fitted with a steel rim, a third of an inch wide, like a horseshoe.

Stringent economy in the amount of clothing is most noticeable in outdoor wear, which was often omitted altogether until the nineteenth century. A nominal allowance for girls of a "new cloak or shawl every two years"[17] was seldom lived up to and at the York Grey Coat School in 1809 the cloaks in use were found to be thirty-seven years old. When clothing had been given out, it was still watched over by the authorities and subject to regulations. Even adults were not trusted with their best clothes. At Holy Trinity Hospital, Greenwich, under the statutes of 1615, it was the duty of the sub-warden to "Keepe the liuery gownes in the roome and presses [cupboards] made for that purpose and deliuer them every Sunday at eight of the clock to the rest of the brethren and receive them againe at night brushed foulded by them handsomely and lay them vp in the said presses".[18]

Clothes were conspicuously marked to prevent their finding their way into the pawnshop and seamen pensioners at the Royal Hospital, Greenwich, if caught "changing the colour or marks" of their clothing would be fined or imprisoned for three months.

The vested interests of those with power to place contracts were often a cause of inefficiency. On the other hand, constant vigilance

6. Block with which clothes were marked at the Grey Coat school, Westminster (*Parochial Charities . . . of Westminster*, 1890, published by parishes of St Margaret and St John)

would be exercised to circumvent the wiles of dealers. At the same hospital in Greenwich, for example, when supervision had temporarily grown slack in the late eighteenth century, an investigation revealed that "the pensioners' shirts were always becoming narrower and shorter; their stockings broke into holes when first put on, and their shoes, which were to last them 8 months were out in a fortnight, the inner soles being made of brown paper".[19]

The Foundling had a special sub-committee to deal with footwear who, in 1813, shrewdly resolved that the firm paid to *supply* shoes must be different from the one paid to *repair* them! Even girls' bonnets might saddle a careful committee with quite a lot of work and frustration. At Clerkenwell in 1828 the trouble seems to have been twofold: "The 6 large Bonnets are no use to the Charity and must be returned ... and if they [the makers] do not choose to accept the price of their own tender for the remainder, they will all be returned".[20]

Even more than might be supposed, used garments were handed down from one recipient of charity to the next. At death or departure, alms people, and even their warden, had to hand on their livery gowns (their specially designed outer garments) to their successors. When the retiring warden at Holy Trinity Hospital, Greenwich, broke the rule, in 1634, he had to tell the trustees that in view of the new warden's "kindness in letting me have away my old gowne I do crave your favour in making this [year] one of the two years that his gowne wilbe due to him". (Gowns were given only in alternate years.)[21]

From Victorian times right up to the 1960s this transmission applied to top hats which have been known to outlast three or four old men in succession.

There were other ways of using worn clothes. When any almsman at Holy Trinity Hospital, Clun, in Shropshire, had his best gown, which was blue, replaced after four years, it was "dyed to a sadder Colour" and he then had to have it cut up to make a "Suit [doublet and breeches] . . . to wear upon Sundayes".[22]

Labour being cheap, it was found worth while in the nineteenth century to have the bonnets of little charity girls "dyed and new-ribboned at Christmas"[23] or cleaned at 5s. 6d. a dozen (1841). Their tippets or little capes might be made out of tiny remnants of print (Fig. 7) or, for winter, out of overlapping strips of list or selvages of warm materials, sewn on to calico. At a charity industrial-cum-Sunday school in the 1790s even the girls' gowns were made of oddments "neatly joined together and dyed with logwood". When it was found that "to dye injured the texture", each gown was left as an overt patchwork of colours (and compared with Joseph's coat!).[24]

To avoid waste, the Foundling's steward was even ordered "to enquire what is given by Persons buying Pieces of worn out Leather"[25] from old shoes.

The need to conserve the funds was always conflicting with other claims. One of these – concern for the wearer's comfort and welfare –

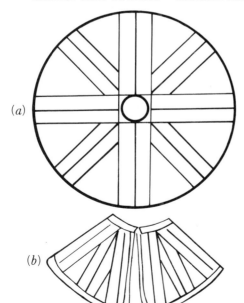

7. "An economical mode of making tippets for poor children or charity schools": (*a*) arrangement of remnants, (*b*) as made up (*Workwoman's Guide* by a Lady, 1838, Pl. 13 and p. 104)

8. A cheap form of stays for girls, made of shoe leather. *Left* Back view: vertical scoring to allow them to bend round the body. *Right* Front view: the leather is covered with fabric to act as a stomacher to the dress (Specimen in Bridewell Museum. Photo of back: P. Mactaggart. Courtesy: City of Norwich Museums)

is an aspect of compassion and is therefore dealt with in Chapter 3. But there was also, of course, the question of efficiency and durability. To take a small example, the matter of stays. Stays, or "a pair of bodies", in the eighteenth century were the stiff laced-up component of the bodice of the gown and, being believed to prevent deformity, were considered by most people as necessities for growing girls and working women. When charities supplied them, they were made of shoe leather about a quarter of an inch thick. P. and A. Mactaggart, in *Strata of Society*, write: "the fact that leather stays did not require stiffening [whaleboning, etc.] . . . resulted in their being cheap though very hard-wearing. These facts must have commended themselves to . . . the trustees of charity schools, amongst whose accounts most of the references to them occur".[26] We shall come across several instances of this.

It is sometimes moving to read the minutes of charity committees when they show what close attention could be paid by busy men to the practical details of their voluntary task. A member of several such bodies was that dedicated philanthropist, Jonas Hanway. In the third

9. Committee of the Marine Society, Jonas Hanway in the chair. Ragged boys (*right*) being rigged out (*left*) to go to sea: sailor-style wide trousers, etc. (Jonas Hanway *Three Letters on the Subject of the Marine Society,* 1758, frontispiece)

of his *Letters* (1758) about the work of his Marine Society in clothing boys for a life at sea, he writes:

It is hardly credible, how quickly *boys in general* wear out clothes, as those who have children know well; but *such boys,* in such an occupation, must require an uncommon vigilance on board ships, to prevent their being a disgrace to human society. As this clothing is to stand all weathers ... no reasonable expence should be spared to render it proper in its kind. It is a melancholy case when men suffer in this way, whether it arises from too great parsimony, or from the iniquity of contractors.[27]

The *quality* of the cloth used was a first consideration. Back in 1380 William of Wykeham stipulated that the piece of cloth bought with his endowment to make the livery of any three Fellows at New College must measure at least twenty-four yards *after* it had been "steeped in water, dried and sheared".[28] When all (charity) outer garments were made of inexpensive woollens, shrinkage was a major problem.

The coarse woollen fabric, kersey, was the natural choice but there were kerseys and kerseys. The Committee noted that quality was not proportional to weight: the fabrics that were coarsest, worst dyed, and least free from residual fuller's earth, were the heaviest and poorest in quality. They bothered to find out that one of the slopman's fabrics shrank one in every $30\frac{3}{8}$ inches. The value of pre-shrunk kersey was "double the value of kersey not shrunk" and they decided to buy the former direct from Halifax, to be made up by a tailor. Hanway even held that the jackets should be further shrunk after making; if not "they draw up very considerably when wet, and put the wearer in a miserable plight ..." He also advised strengthening the elbows of jackets, noting that "the King of Prussia's soldiers wear a bit of leather in the shape of a heart, sewn on the elbows of their regimentals".[29]

Then there was the question of dyes. Cheap blues were got from woad or logwood. But the Marine Society's Committee had an earnest discussion in June 1779 on some samples and estimates. They observed that the use of logwood resulted in a jacket soon becoming "whitened" so that it "looks shabby".[30] Taste not being what it is today, this was turned down in favour of unadulterated indigo, an expensive imported dye.

Committees often took much trouble to ensure consistency in the colour of the uniforms that they supplied over the years. The Clerkenwell Cloathing Committee was a good example of a conscientious body. This group of men, at the end of a long day (7 March 1838), minuted: "Three samples of Merino were sent in from Messrs Wilson but the Committee not being able to ascertain the Colour etc. by candle light they adjourned to Saturday morning next."[31]

Even a colour match did not always satisfy. A contractor who in 1842 supplied the Foundling Hospital with brown cloth had it all returned to him because it was not dyed in the wool.

The work put in by the Harpur trustees in the eighteenth century over the little boys' suits in their children's home at Bedford is testified, rather touchingly, by a scrap of blue twilled woollen fabric stuck into their minute book by a conscientious clerk.

An occasion when even governors themselves played a part was when the first lot of boys and girls were given outer clothing four days before the Grey Coat School (later "Hospital") opened in Westminster. The eight governors, who were leading tradesmen of the neighbourhood (none of them women), assembled on the evening of 5 January 1699 to see the clothes tried on and also to supervise a barber whom they had ordered to come and cut the children's hair.

The fitting of shoes was often a major object of concern. At Clerkenwell the Committee ordered sealed tenders and samples of

10. Boy of Grey Coat Hospital, Westminster: grey coat, white "band" (collar), knitted cap with tuft, sleeved waistcoat, buckled shoes (Statuette on the school, Greycoat Place, Westminster. 1701 or soon after)

shoes many months in advance, examined each pair (though there were about one hundred children) and often sent some back. At St Martin-in-the-Fields School in 1700 the shoes – of good leather – were actually made to measure. (The ready-made shoes of Edwardian times could be disastrous. See page 191.) Our Clerkenwell Committee in 1837 even specified that there should be "more nails in the centrepiece of the heel and the side seams should be straight".

The Foundling Committee made regulations in 1814 that are so careful as to be worth quoting in full. Each child was to have two pairs of shoes at 5s., including the binding, strings and sparrow bills (brads) on the heels:

One pair on the feet and the other on the shelves in the shoe room with a ticket on them with the name of the child.

Examination of the Shoes on the feet [was to be made] every Saturday at 3 oclock in the presence of the Steward and Sub-Matron.

That the cobler take away the Shoes every Monday . . . and bring the same back properly mended on the following Saturday before noon.

Boys to clean the shoes every Saturday.[32]

In 1860 at Clerkenwell, at the meeting of an *ad hoc* committee consisting of ten men, "two girls were dressed, one in the present style and one in the suggested alteration".[33] The new style was approved but the two girls were invited to parade in front of the General Committee before it was finally adopted. In the late eighteenth century, a doubtless shy little girl, seven-year-old Sarah Lightwood, from the Harpur Children's Home at Bedford, actually appeared before the august trustees themselves to model a new uniform.[34]

Such conscientious care was sometimes obligatory under the terms of a benefactor's will. An extreme example was when the trustees of John Driden's (the "Orange") School in Northampton ordered in 1819 that the uniform should be restored to its original colours, even noting that, in the boys' blue coats with orange facings, "the working of the buttonholes . . . shall in future be of an orange colour as directed by the Will [of the founder]".[35]

HEALTH AND HYGIENE

Obviously, when bringing up children, charity had the problem of clothing them so as to allow for exercise and growth without undue expense. Furthermore, dealing with the poor generally meant dealing with the unwashed. There were therefore health hazards in much of the work, from which we may select a few examples.

In the early days children in residential institutions were shockingly ill-provided with opportunities, and appropriate clothing, for outdoor exercise. In the eighteenth century the Harpur Trust Home was probably typical in not allowing the children off the premises at any time except for church on Sunday. The gate was locked and spiked.[36]

A change began in the nineteenth century as exemplified at St Martin-in-the-Fields School in 1846. The management then noted that "Frequent walks . . . cause the shoes and stockings to wear out faster, but they are very advantageous to the health of the children . . ." It was found "necessary to have new bonnets every year now that the children are desired to walk daily".[37]

Constricting clothes were a discomfort, if not a danger to health. At the Foundling Hospital the Surgeon reported in 1751 "that the Boys' Shoes and stockings were unfit for their wear by reason of the height of the heels and the turning up of the toes, the feet of their stockings and soles of their shoes were also too short which contracts and distorts their feet".[38] It was decided that "low heels and flat soles like the chairmans" should be adopted, i.e. like those of men who carried sedan chairs; also that Matron was to give the children "shoes and stockings of the full long size; and that, on Examination of the Boy John Herbert they find that by reason of his being crump-footed shoes must be made in a particular manner for him".[39] These reactions suggest the good health standard that prevailed at this particular home owing to the eminence of its early supporters (see Chapter 9). They were very advanced, in 1759, when they decided that the girls should not be allowed to wear the usual stays, and appointed "Mr Hanway" (Jonas himself) to see that the rule was observed. Matron helped by producing a pattern of "Bodice . . . made without stiffening except Buckram". A year later the Sub-committee "Resolved that as the Shape and fashion of the Girls Cloth[e]s seem not to be calculated for their holding up their heads, and their ease, this affair be further considered . . .".[40]

With so many babies in its care the Foundling Hospital was fortunate in having in his day the services of Dr William Buchan. Very advanced in his views, in 1769, in his book *Domestic Medicine*, he was decrying the use of swaddling clothes: "Rollers and wrappers applied to the baby's body as if every bone had been fractured at birth". He expatiated on the dangers of this and saw to it that no swaddling clothes were supplied to the Hospital.

Dirt and consequent infestations and infections were a constant source of worry. Hanway, once more, studied "the pernicious effects of filthy garments" in the spreading of lice on board ships (typhus, being lice-borne, was rife in the Navy) and we shall see in Chapter 10 how he dealt with this problem through his Marine Society's clothing department.

In almshouses cleanliness was difficult to control where only upper garments were supplied. A letter from the warden of the Holy Trinity Hospital, Greenwich, dated 1772, to an overseer of the poor in Bungay, concerning John Bass of Bungay, a resident in the almshouse, speaks for itself: "He has nothing but wrags about him, is a shame to the College and Swarms with Vermin in and about his . . . Body and

Cloaths . . . I hope . . . the Parish . . . will speedily send up some Money to Shirt and Cloath him from Head to Foot otherwise the Company will discharge him and send him down to your Parish."[41]

The contagious "Itch" (scabies) was spread by the clothing and at the Foundling was a frequent trial. Patients were put into cast-off clothes (afterwards burnt) and sent to the Infirmary. Their own least good garments were "kept in a heap in some hovel or place to be burnt or sold for old rags", while the better ones were "smoaked with Brimstone . . . and hung out in the Brewhouse Yard"[42] (1759). There was a risk in the handing down of clothes, but here at least it was a rule that "the Dead Children's bundles . . . be all washed".[43] Furthermore, with reference to garments made by the children (1775), "The Cloathes of [i.e. made by] such children suffering from the Itch be baked in the Oven after the Bread is drawn [and the Apothecary] to see that the clothes be delivered to the Steward who is to take care that the Baker put them into the oven for an hour".

A catch in the otherwise thrifty practice of calling for gifts in kind was revealed when scarlet fever raged through Dr Barnardo's Home at Ilford in 1879. There were 170 cases, all traced to a single infected garment that had been given by a ladies' working party.

Hair hygiene concerns us in so far as it affected hairdressing. A statute of Holy Trinity Hospital is typical of many elsewhere. In order

11. Foundling girls with cropped hair and long plain pinafores, 1898 (Courtesy: Thomas Coram Foundation)

12. Girls of Welsh Charity School, Ashford, Middlesex, at festival presided over by the Prince of Wales, 1867. Hair cropped for hygiene (*Illustrated London News* supplement, 9 March 1867, p. 237)

"that the poore men and servants of this hospital may be the better kept cleane from vermine and goe more decently" it was ordained that an honest and properly trained "barbour" should be appointed "who shall foure times every yeare . . . come to the said hospitall and trimme them, either in their chambers or in the common hall".[44]

The Marine Society gave printed instructions to the man who took charge of boys when they were brought in off the London streets: "When boys have foul bushy hair, which only serves to disfigure them, or to harbour filth, you are desired to see it cut off, and their heads wash'd with brandy . . . and you are to recommend to *all* the boys to cut their hair off".[45]

Except for a short experimental period in the 1760s the Foundlings, both boys and girls, always had their hair cropped close, and this was usual in homes and even in charity day-schools. At the home in Birmingham (a "Blue Coat School"), even in 1927, Matron would also give a punishment of "1000 lines" to a child found to have nits in the hair. Despite its superior status, the Red Maids' School insisted on cropped hair for girls under fourteen as late as 1911 (Fig. 59); at a time when bobbed hair was unheard of this must have been seen as something of a stigma.

CHAPTER 2

General characteristics of the costumes

EXPRESSION OF HUMILITY

The attire of "objects of charity" was originally, above everything else, designed to be what Mrs Trimmer in 1801[1] urged for charity school uniforms: they must be "in general *plain* . . ." The reasons are dealt with later – sufficient here to show how universally imposed was this mark of humility. Its clearest expression lay in the colour. This was often like that of the habits of monks or friars – men, women and children alike would wear black, brown, grey or white. William of Wykeham, disliking the association with monasticism, avoided naming these colours but insisted that the boys he supported at Winchester and his students at New College, Oxford, should wear a very dark colour without any relief. Whittington had the same rule for the occupants of his almshouses. The colour of charity uniforms was thus comprehensively defined as "sad colour" at least until the end of the seventeenth century, but it should be noted that here this meant "sober" (as witness that trustees would be instructed to appoint as a warden "some sad man"). Blue was the only cheerful shade often used and was common only for the women and children. As we have seen, some blue dyes were cheap and the colour had class significance, being characteristic of servants and es-chewed by the gentry in the seventeenth century.

When drabness was less insisted upon, the clothing must still be demure. The Ladies' Committee of the St Martin-in-the-Fields charity school noted in 1836 that the colour of the girls' cap ribbons had "created some displeasure".[2]

To look modest, in the sense of chaste, was, needless to say, strictly enjoined on the female sex. Charity girls had their necks covered with white tippets when other girls had them bare; and their hair was concealed under caps long after other girls wore it free.

Just as doffing the hat is a sign of respect in men and boys, so humility could be expressed by not having a hat at all, and this was the rule for Wykehamists, unless they were prefects, for a long time. In the eighteenth century fee-paying students might wear hats even with their gowns, but endowed scholars never.

New fashions were always frowned on as being immodest. Sharply pointed shoes, red or green garters and long hair were all forbidden at various times and places to youths receiving scholarships. The sword, which was the mark of a gentleman and was even worn by boys until near the close of the eighteenth century, was also prohibited. A resident master was specially appointed *c.* 1688 at Westminster School to discipline the foundationers after it was noticed that "the King's Scholars ... have openly and commonly beene seene in the day time out of College, walking about without their Gownes [uniform], drest up with Swords, laced cravats ... etc".[3]

Ornaments were equally disapproved of, for example, by some of the London charity schools even at their annual celebration in St Paul's Cathedral. One of these, in Highgate, called "The Ladies' Charity School", was considered "a model of strictness" on these occasions.[4]

The views, on the same topic, held by the Society for Promoting Christian Knowledge (S.P.C.K.), who inspired the foundation of most of these schools, were quoted by the Rev. T. B. Murray, together with his own, in 1851:

In April 1754 the use of feathers and ribands, as ornaments of the clothing, was objected to by the Society [S.P.C.K.], as improper and superfluous, occasioning vanity in the children ... there is much wisdom in checking these beginnings of personal display and it is to be hoped that the simplicity and modesty of the children's apparel which now forms one of the most pleasing features of the assembly ever be retained. "In their dress, in their diet, in their instruction and in their very psalmody there should be the same simplicity" (Bishop of Oxford, 1802).[5]

More personal ornaments were even worse. A regulation forbidding ear-rings at the Ratcliff Hamlet School, Stepney, resulted, in 1831, in the committee's reprimanding one of the mothers "by reason of her daughter Lavinia coming to school with earings [*sic*]".[6] The mother said the child had bad eyes and the rings were considered of benefit (the superstition that pierced ears improve eyesight is not wholly extinct even now); but the committee refused to yield unless a medical certificate could be produced.

The caustic Dr Gabell, headmaster of Winchester, 1810–24, would find it difficult to believe his eyes today. The story is told that, observing a ring on the finger of one of the scholarship boys, he put a question to the class: "What animal besides a charity boy wears a ring?"

One of the boys came up with the answer: "A pig, Sir".

"Quite right, go up", replied the headmaster.[7]

A secular trend can be noticed towards the easing of these puritanical rules in charity and other institutions. The change was very gradual, until twentieth-century social science nearly swept them away altogether. Up till then even small concessions to fashion or comfort stand out as striking exceptions. That is not to say that ordinary modifications of style which were universal did not make their appearance in charity clothes. About 1800 the committee of the Ratcliff School minuted, after some discussion, that the boys' coats should be allowed collars and their shirts made to button at the sleeve. About the same time a Captain Boulcott presented each one with a felt hat to the value of 5s. to replace the humble caps.

History was made at Christ's Hospital Girls' School when it was resolved in 1724: "in behalf of the Girles of the House that they may be allowed high heel'd Shoes in the Room of the Shoes they have been used to wear in common with the Boyes".[8]

Concessions were sometimes made when it was important not to deter the young from accepting charity. The uniform of the ex-prostitutes in the Magdalen Hospital was not meant to be quite as austere as it seems to our eyes. In 1917 H. F. B. Compston wrote of it as follows:

The Magdalen costume is one of the numerous signs of chivalry and discernment shewn in the treatment of the inmates. Some philanthropists would have prescribed a severe and quasi-funereal uniform. Not so the original committee [in 1758] and their successors. A girl is helped to realize ... her appearance is vastly better as penitent than as prostitute.[9]

It was in about the middle of the nineteenth century that a general relaxation was most marked. The *Illustrated London News* of 1842 foreshadows this, with heavy irony, in a discussion of charity schools.

In some instances, as in that of St Botolph [Aldgate] ... the more modern trouser of the boy, and the less rigid stiffness of the girl, bespeak a distant, a very distant, approach to modern taste, and argues the possibility of [the dress of] the children actually becoming in some degree fashionable, a century after it has ceased to be considered so ... we think a little improvement might be made in this matter, without the slightest danger of *too* much innovation or expense.

13. Contrast between two contemporary charity boys' uniforms, 1842. *Right* Typical, in eighteenth-century style. *Left* Somewhat "modernized". Contrast the neckwear and legwear. (One boy shows a circular badge on his waistcoat) (*Illustrated London News* vol. I, 44)

Dr Barnardo promoted this relaxation, writing in 1875 that his orphan girls should not be "clad in some dull uniform divested of all prettiness".[10]

Miss Nicoll, head of the Hampstead Reformatory, was another pioneer. In 1888 she allowed her girls "small divergencies of ornament" with their uniform and made a dig at some of the charity schools when she said "All hideous bonnets, cloaks, and dresses ought to be banished from the School – the uniform being one which ought not to draw particular animadversion to the wearer while in the street."[11]

In the early twentieth century drastic changes were made in nearly all charitable institutions in favour of more up-to-date and individual dress.

UNIFORMS

A feature of charity clothes that stands out as sharply as their humble appearance is the uniformity observed within each institution. It was not only in schools and orphanages but also in almshouses too that all the occupants were dressed alike. This chilling uniformity obtained until the late nineteenth century. Children tended to be distinguished

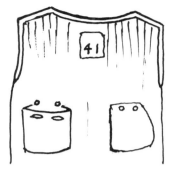

14. "Pinafore for National [Society] and other schools". Child's number *appliqué* and pockets for knitting (*Workwoman's Guide* by a Lady, 1838, Pl. 16, Fig. 9)

only by number. As late as 1838, "a pinafore for national [National Society charity] and other schools", as described in the *Workwoman's Guide*, p. 135, was "marked, in red or other tape with the number of the child. The child is generally called by her companions by the number . . . which is, in many ways, a great saving of memory, time and trouble".

Dickens, describing the enrolment of poor Mrs Richards's little boy in the "Charitable Grinders' School" writes: " 'The number of her son, I believe,' said Mr Dombey . . . speaking of the child as if he were a hackney coach, 'is 147.' "[12] (This number can be seen in Fig. 36.)

There were, however, many advantages in sticking to a uniform. In some circumstances its impersonal quality was actually desirable to the wearer (see page 55); in all cases a uniform promoted economy through mass production. Its other objects were to ensure recognition of the recipient as such, when he was off the premises; to remind him of his debt; and to promote egality, humility and *esprit de corps*.

The fact that a uniform marked an individual when out of doors was useful for the maintenance of discipline. This is clear from a rule in most schools under S.P.C.K. auspices: "That the children wear their caps, bands, and cloaths, and other marks of distinction every day, that the trustees and benefactors may know them, and see what their behaviour is abroad".[13] Bad conduct in the streets could be spotted and, as there was generally a metal badge with the child's number on it, the offender could be reported and punished.

Even almsfolk needed to be reprimanded at times, especially old men who frequented public houses, and their uniforms or badges thus served a similar purpose. At Emmanuel Hospital, Westminster, the old people as well as the children had (by statute of 1601) to wear their badges "soe apparently that they may be discerned thereby wheresoever they shall be come".[14] A fine of sixpence was charged for default.

The importance of distinctive school uniforms is emphasized by the fact that in the eighteenth and nineteenth centuries there were in Westminster alone charity schools popularly known as Grey Coat, Green Coat, Blue Coat, Black Coat and Brown Coat (the last derived from the Emmanuel Hospital); so that when, *c.* 1840, still another one sprang up, it had to be the "Drab Coat School".

Uniformity was again useful when, as so often happened, the endowed pupils of a school came, in course of time, to include some who were decidedly less poor than the rest. Jealousy was guarded against thereby. For example, at Christ's Hospital, when in 1758 it was found that some of the girls were paying to have their dresses trimmed, the authorities pronounced that gowns should no longer "be bound with galloon [braid] or ferret [ribbon] which the Nurses are paid for by the children or their Friends", since allowing this would "be of ill consequence, especially for those children who have no friends".[15]

As in a monastery, the impersonal garb in colleges and almshouses was intended also to promote self-forgetfulness and a dedication to the prayerful life. This last was expected of the old people in almshouses almost to the end of our period.

Another advantage of a uniform was sometimes the promotion of *esprit de corps*. In its highest expression the effect was seen, for example, in the statutes of Merton College (1274) and of Wykeham's New College, Oxford (1380). In each the Fellows and students were given liveries of the same cloth, as "a sign of unity and mutual esteem".[16] At Trinity College, Cambridge, it was expressly stated in 1546 that the unusual violet colour was chosen "to cause admiration of corporate qualities".[17]

15. Two pewter charity-school badges, St Andrew's, Holborn, bearing children's numbers and symbolic figure of St Andrew with cross. Eighteenth century (Badges lent by Society for Promoting Christian Knowledge)

Finally, the charm of a uniformed procession was for some institutions a means of attracting public interest and support. The children of Müller's Orphanage used to be paraded through the city of Bristol expressly for this purpose.

ADHERENCE TO TRADITION

A striking feature of charity uniforms is that they stubbornly resisted change and thus became "traditional". Those of Chelsea pensioners and Christ's Hospital boys are not exceptional but typical in this respect. The uniform at Christ's Hospital is ancient indeed. The flowing, ankle-length garments, suggesting an ecclesiastical connection, have been thought to hark back even to medieval days when the school was connected with a monastery. This is not so. In point of fact, they resemble what was normal wear for very young boys (as well as girls) in the period when the school was refounded after the dissolu-

16. Traditional costume: Christ's Hospital boy in Tudor-style coat, "petticoat" and cap. "Wings" to the coat are present at shoulders but are not clearly seen. Compare Figs. 17 and 45 (From print of 1827)

17. Typical dress of small
Elizabethan boy, for comparison
with Fig. 16. Under the long girdled
coat, with wings at shoulders, a petticoat. A ruff is shown because this is
not a *poor* boy (Brass effigy at Aveley,
Essex. After Fig. 46 of John Page-
Phillips *Children on Brasses*, 1970)

tion. The likeness is strongly suggested by two sixteenth-century
effigies of boys shown in Figs. 17 and 100. The full-length girdled coat,
having wings (wings resembled diminutive epaulettes), unlike any
ecclesiastical dress, and worn over a petticoat, was typical for little
Elizabethan boys. Certain it is that, whatever its precise origin, the
Christ's Hospital dress has changed scarcely at all, since the time of its
oldest known illustration, which is early seventeenth century.

Another almost Tudor figure, familiar to everyone until the present
century, was that of an old man wearing a loose black open gown,
again of ankle length. This was the garb of almshouse inhabitants,
dating back to the sixteenth or seventeenth century.

Within the illustration, in handwritten lettering on the wall:

London
as it is—
drawn and lithographed
by
Thos. Shotter Boys
90 Great Portland St

18. Typical London street boys of the mid nineteenth century. Two have white neck bands indicating charity status, confirmed by the badges on the left breast (Frontispiece of T. Shotter Boys *London As It Is*, 1842)

The boys in many of the more ordinary charity schools, those founded around 1700, went about for two centuries wearing a coat, waistcoat, breeches, and white neck "bands" like those of their predecessors in Queen Anne's reign. These bands are a relic we shall often notice. Derived from the collar of ordinary dress in Puritan days ("Geneva bands") they disappeared at the Restoration except for academic, legal and clerical wear. They were adopted for charity boys presumably because of this sober connection. (Originally they were tabs hanging from the collar or band; it was only in the nineteenth century that the tabs themselves came to be called bands.)

This mark of the charity boy was so typical that, when Shotter Boys drew a symbolic group of three poor schoolboys in London in 1842, two of them are wearing the white tabs (see Fig. 18).

Though to a rather lesser degree than in the dress of the boys and men, the dress of charity girls also showed echoes of the past. The *Illustrated London News*, also in 1842, described the dress of one of them, the School for Welsh children founded in Clerkenwell in 1737, as follows: "she still exhibits the mittens and close-plaited [pleated] cap of sixty years ago, and which, at that time, royalty itself did not disdain to wear. West's portraits of the young princesses, daughters of George

19. Charity girl in already very old-fashioned uniform: cap, tippet, sleeved mittens, etc., 1842 (*Illustrated London News* vol. I, 44)

III, at Hampton Court, appear thus habited". (See Fig. 19.) With girls, just as with boys, one of the marks of traditionalism was the neckwear. For example, the white tippet which started in the eighteenth century was seen in the twentieth century at Red Maids' School, Bristol, and the Blue Coat Schools of York and Birmingham.

Such "Conservation" has many causes, some of which operate with any uniform, while others are peculiar to charity costume. First, as we have already suggested, to be old-fashioned in dress is associated with being humble, since the styles of the lower classes tended, until recent times, to be many years behind those of the upper.

Secondly, and bound up with the first cause, was the association of many charities with religion, where this same principle of dress operated, i.e. humility was expressed. The headwear of charity girls and nuns had much in common and the neckwear of charity boys and clergymen was identical (see Fig. 94).

A third cause was a loyalty to the originators. Mrs Trimmer puts it thus, speaking of London charity school uniforms (and mentioning incidentally the status factor too):

The adherence in many of them to the *Old English Fashions*, gives those who still receive education and maintenance, through the bounty of our pious ancestors, a pleasing distinction, by marking, at once their rank in society, and the antiquity of their respective schools ... and it certainly is a very proper tribute to the memory of the deceased benefactor or benefactress [Mrs Trimmer was a feminist] to preserve the very appearance which they delighted to behold.[18]

Finally, deliberate conservation was also encouraged by the fact that most people enjoy looking at fancy dress. This will be illustrated in Chapters 3 and 15.

Traditional dress was sometimes preserved for its associations alone, quite apart from being picturesque. Charles Lamb, himself an "Old Blue", said of the Christ's Hospital boy: "his very garb, as it is antique and venerable, feeds his self-respect" and "never may modern refinement innovate upon the venerable fashion!"[19] It is remarkable how often that particular uniform was emulated, causing others to become "traditional" side by side with their model. George Wickham declared that, except for the colour of the coats, the uniform of the Green Coat Charity School in Hertford was a plagiarism of the Christ's Hospital preparatory school close by.[20] He remembered resenting this when he was there in the 1820s.

At Queen Elizabeth's Hospital, Bristol, the founder, John Carr, had actually stipulated in his will in 1586 that the boys should be uniformed "like Christ's Hospital nigh St Bartholomew's in London".

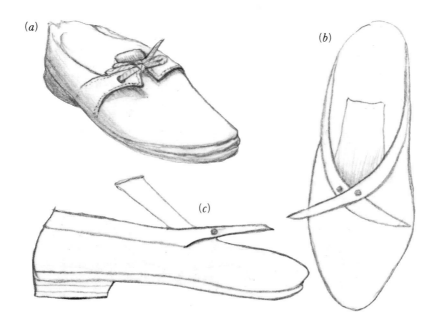

20. Nineteenth-century boys' shoes made in late seventeenth- or early eighteenth-century style. Compare Fig. 37. (*a*) from Christ's Hospital, made in 1850s. (*b*) and (*c*) from Colchester Blue Coat School, made 1880–90; showing eyelet holes for laces. (*a* After photo: N. Plumley. Courtesy: Christ's Hospital. *b* and *c* After drawings by V. Mansfield. Courtesy: Holly Trees Museum, Colchester)

Even more striking is the fact that when the Royal Wolverhampton School was established for the orphans of a cholera epidemic in 1850, these boys too were given the ankle-length coats made venerable by Christ's Hospital.

Traditional dress sometimes lingers on simply because the choosers are not the wearers and so may have little incentive for change; but it often results from a vague nostalgia on their part. The men and women at Sackville College, East Grinstead, supported by the second Earl of Dorset's bequest since 1609, at some point in history began to receive a dress allowance instead of garments, and so to dress as they pleased. The twenty-second warden, in 1913, thought this a deplorable neglect. He had the men put into carefully designed calf-length black coats like early almsmen's gowns, and the women into cloaks and bonnets one hundred per cent "traditional"; Sackville badges were made *de novo* for all.

In view of its charm and its often very unpractical form, it is perhaps not surprising that charity costume in many institutions, eventually took on a ceremonial role. At Liverpool Blue Coat School the girls' everyday tippet was converted in 1907 into a special feature of Sunday dress. And the workaday pinafore was elevated at the Royal Masonic School for Girls (see Chapter 6) to a garment for formal wear. Even in Stepney, for its bicentenary celebrations in 1910, the Ratcliff School dressed up the head boy and girl in replicas of its eighteenth-century green costumes and immortalized them in a coloured postcard. They were even worn there on Prize Day in 1976.

Again, in most almshouses that still possess uniforms (and we shall see there are a good many) these garments are nowadays cherished in mothballs and worn once a year for Founder's Day.

As an epilogue, it may be pointed out that the evolution of costumes has much in common with Darwinian evolution in nature. Thus the antiquated garments seen in modern times might be compared with the "living fossils" which are occasionally found still walking the earth today; and furthermore, curious resemblances can sometimes be explained in terms of common ancestry. Why else do almsmen at Guildford wear what seem to be academic gowns and almswomen at Castle Rising a "Welsh" hat and cloak? (See Chapter 12 and Figs. 135 and 147). Not conscious imitation in these cases, but preservation of a single inheritance is the cause.

Each costume has seldom fossilized *as a whole*. In its present state it is more like a collection of fossils from successive strata, since its different parts may represent old fashions not all of the same date. If we refer again to the nineteenth-century Christ's Hospital uniform, the main garments recall the sixteenth century, the bands the seventeenth century, and the ornamental shoe buckles the eighteenth. In the same way, an almsman often wore in the twentieth century a gown that was Tudor, with a top hat that was Victorian.

Thus a present-day costume cannot represent any extinct one as a whole, but it may throw sidelights of historic interest on the component garments individually.

COMMEMORATIVE SYMBOLS

An interesting function of any style of dress that was peculiar to a given endowment was the opportunity it afforded to commemorate the giver and remind one of the debt – like a flag on a charity flag day, but with the wearers' roles reversed. To the false modesty of the present day it is almost shocking to find how often a donor or his trustees stipulated in writing that the beneficiaries should be labelled as such. Motives will be discussed in Chapter 3; suffice it here to show how costumes could commemorate.

At All Saints' Church, Northampton, is a memorial tablet to two charitable sisters, Mrs Beckett and Mrs Sergeant, who in 1738 founded a school for teaching and clothing poor girls (Chapter 6). It depicts, carved in stone, one of the pupils wearing her uniform (Fig. 63).

But for many, a walking reminder was better than a static one. A simple reminder was through distinction of colour. At Frome Blue Coat School (1728) the original twenty boys had red tassels to their caps; but when the brothers Stevens endowed twelve more, these were marked out with white ones. Then in Birmingham and Northampton Blue Coat Schools, as we shall see, later benefactors who wished their scholars distinguished from the originals ordered that they should be dressed in green. At Northampton eventually there were boys attending one and the same school wearing blue, green and orange respectively, to mark three separate endowments.

The colour was not always an arbitrary choice. Henry Greene of Melbourne, Derbyshire, made it a condition, under his will of 1679, that the recipients of his charity should be dressed in green because of his name. Thomas Gray of the same town was not to be outdone. Under his will of 1691 the trustees must buy every year six waistcoats of *grey* cloth for poor women and three coats of *grey* cloth for men.[21] Melbourne thus had unmistakable memorials to two of its dead in a form specially useful in illiterate days.

Donors belonging to armigerous families made use of their often very decorative crest, or the somewhat simpler badge (derived from this or their other armorial bearings) such as would be worn on their servants' livery. Poor folk had their dull garments brightened with this

21. Silk embroidered badge for beneficiaries of Robert Dove (d. 1612) in Merchant Taylors' almshouses: a silver dove (Courtesy: Merchant Taylors Company)

badge, typically worn (like their heart?) on the sleeve, in medieval style. Alternatively, the design might appear on their buttons. Edward Hastings, Lord Loughborough, in 1573, stipulated that his almsfolk in Stoke Poges should have blue broadcloth gowns "and a bull's head on the sleeve". A "bull's head, couped, or" was the Hastings badge. A great variety of beasts and birds thus adorned charity costumes, sometimes punning on the donor's name: white rabbits (coneys) for Coningsby's old men and, in the Merchant Taylors' Almshouses, doves for the almsmen established there in 1605 by Robert Dove. Stow's *Survey of London* tells us (1618 edition) that Dove maintained "12 poor Almes-men in gowns of good cloth; well lined, with a silver Dove upon each man's left sleeve". The badges were embroidered and Fig. 21 shows one that was worn in quite recent times.*

The famous schools associated with the name of Edward Latymer began in a small way as a result of his will dated 1624. Eight boys were to be clothed and sent to a local school and six poor men given a cassock or coat annually. As there were no buildings provided, it was all the more important that the beneficiaries should be marked out and Latymer laid down that all should wear a "Latymers cross" cut out of red cloth and sewn on to the left sleeve. This specially shaped cross (Fig. 22a) was one of the charges in the Latymer arms. A portrait of an old man of Hammersmith of the early nineteenth century still exists, in which the cross shows up clearly. The buttons of the men and boys were also marked (Fig. 22b).

Special clothing for the men ceased in 1878 but today the boys of the Lower School wear the red cross in their caps, and those of the Upper the entire Latymer arms.[22]

Mrs Montagu (née Elizabeth Robinson), whose family crest was a buck, was staying at Allerthorpe, Yorkshire, in 1742 when she wrote the following to a cousin: "In this parish Dr Robinson, our . . . uncle has founded a school and almshouse . . . I saw the old women with bucks upon their sleeves at church and the sight gave me pleasure; heraldry does not always descend with such honour as when charity leads her by the hand".[23]

Where the donor was not the happy possessor of armorial bearings, his beneficiaries were often marked with his name. Fig. 23 shows the girdle-buckle worn by those boys at Christ's Hospital who benefited under the will made in 1724 by Samuel Travers. Again, when a Mrs

---

* The Company's records show that from 1605 to 1610 nineteen dove badges were bought at 4s. each (personal communication from the Clerk to the Merchant Taylors Company).

22. (a) Badges of a boy endowed by Edward Latymer in the school he founded: "cross fleurie" taken from Latymer arms; "94" is the boy's number. (b) Latymer School buttons showing foundation date "1624". (c) Latymer School boy, 1868–70, wearing school buttons and badge, typical bands and flat cap (a and b after William Wheatley *Edward Latymer and his Foundation*, 1953, c Courtesy: Latymer Foundation)

Leech in 1799 endowed places in the existing charity school of St Mary Abbots, Kensington, the words "Mrs Leech's Charity" were to be clearly marked on their cuffs and these must be always worn.[24]

The donor's initials were more usual than the whole name and certainly more convenient. We shall meet with many examples of their use; it is enough here to cite two. At Shepton Mallet, the brothers Sir George and William Strode established, by a deed of 1639, almshouses for four women. "Every two years on the Feast of Ascension the poor widows should have . . . a new gown of blue broad cloth, of 20s. price and upon the right sleeve of each gown should be set these letters S ".[25]
G   W

Another member of the Strode family later added some labelled old men (see page 248).

23. Silver buckle for girdle, as worn by Christ's Hospital boys who were beneficiaries of Samuel Travers. Antique (and bent) specimen in museum at Christ's Hospital (Photo: Nicholas Plumley. Courtesy: Christ's Hospital)

An example where the wearers were children is afforded by Queen Elizabeth's Hospital, Bristol. Soon after its foundation by John Carr, in 1586, it received funds from various directions for the maintenance of more boys, and these were distinguished by the initials of their respective supporters. The minutes of the managing committee in 1620 show the purchase of flannel for cutting out the letters to be sewn on the boys' coats.

Eight children had the badge "I.C." for John Carr, six "C.B." for City of Bristol (see Fig. 44), six "M.R." for Lady Mary Ramsey (widow of a one-time Lord Mayor of London; she also endowed and took much interest in Christ's Hospital), three "W.B." for William Birde, late Mayor of Bristol, and one "R.D." for Robert Dowe, the Robert Dove mentioned previously.

In 1836 handsome silver badges were issued, each embossed with a benefactor's initials, and having on the back the city arms. By this time five more donors were being commemorated. The use of badges ceased, in the 1870s, but the idea was revived; since 1922 prefects have

24. White metal badge of Sir John Cass School, with repoussé design of his armorial bearings and description "S[i]r John Cass K[nigh]t Ald[erman] of Port[soken] Ward 1710", nineteenth century (Museum of London, Acc. No. 24616)

all worn a Carr badge. The school still has a full collection of the badges.

There are a variety of other tokens intended to keep memory green. Of such are the sprigs of oak worn by Chelsea pensioners on Oak-apple Day (29 May – see page 265) in memory of their founder, Charles II. More curious is the red quill to be seen in the caps of Sir John Cass schoolgirls. The history and the badges of this school are of special interest. Sir John Cass, a City magnate and a member of Parliament, knighted by Queen Anne, was a man of shrewdness with an interest in education. In 1710 he erected in Aldgate a building to serve the triple purpose of shops, burial vault and, on the top floor, a day school for the poor. By the time of his death in 1718 there were ninety pupils being taught and clothed. His will, which he did not live to sign, provided for the upkeep, and after a lapse, and much litigation, the school was refounded in 1748.* The children were then given typical charity school uniforms of the period, in blue, and wore metal badges handsomely engraved with the founder's arms, name and style (Fig. 24).

* The statuettes now on the Foundation's building in Duke's Place, Aldgate, appear to be a little earlier than 1748 and perhaps belonged to Sir John's own time. The costume is typical for charity schools of the period 1700–1730, and no badges are worn.

25. Red quills worn by Sir John Cass schoolgirls on Founder's Day, 1973 – see text; also a version of the original school badge embroidered in their caps (compare Fig. 24) (Photo: Keystone Press)

But the most remarkable memorial is that still worn by the pupils of this flourishing school on the birthday of their founder, namely a red feather in the cap. Sir John, on his deathbed, before he could quite complete his will, was seized with a fatal haemorrhage; and the quill pen with which he was writing was stained with his blood. Thus a red feather was adopted to symbolize the eternal gratitude of his legatees.

It is not unknown for someone's dress to act as a memento, not of his own benefactor but of a person the latter revered. George Fentham of Birmingham, in 1690, left £10 a year "for the providing . . . [of] 10 as good coats as . . . might be without fraud had, for 10 poor widows", each of whom should "continually wear in some visible place upon her coat the capital letters G. and B. . . . in the memory of Goodyth Burridge, widow deceased" – a woman who had been Fentham's own benefactress.[26]

At the actual death of a charitable person it was normal for his beneficiaries to be plunged into mourning – at the expense of his foundation or estate. Thus it was fitting that the Chelsea pensioners should mourn for Queen Anne, in 1714, since their Hospital had been founded by her uncle, Charles II, and depended on royal patronage.

We know that "black padua silk" was bought for all of them, doubtless to make a weeper for each man's hat and/or a scarf over his shoulder.[27]

Very humble in his bequest of mourning for himself was William Gregory, "Citizen and Skynner of the Citie of London", who died in 1465. One of his many charities was a quaint provision that reflected his customary thrift. His executors were to buy "xij yards of blak clothe, price the yerde iijs iiijd" to serve both as a pall for himself and mourning for others: "And after my 'terment fullfilled I woll that the same xij yerdes of clothe be gyfen and departed [divided up] among iiij pore men or wommen . . .".[28] The four were to be chosen from those most in need, who would be glad of anything to wear, and they must pray for his soul in return.

Even small children were put into mourning when their patrons died. The little girls of the Royal Masonic Institution would have "black crepe round their arms and in their hats" or "black ribbons in their Hats and black gloves";[29] in the early nineteenth century this happened three times in fifteen years.

A Westminster philanthropist, the Rev. James Palmer (a frugal man, who is said to have slept in the steeple of St Bride's Church where he preached), putting his "Hospital" in the hands of trustees in 1677, ordered: "these Boys to have black Gowns and Caps which they are to wear when they are to attend at the Funerals of any of the Governors of this Hospital".

Similarly Thomas Anguish had ruled, sixty years before, that the children in his Hospital in Norwich, at all governors' funerals, should "in their habits go before the corpse in a decent manner . . .".[30]

After all this, let it not be forgotten that anonymity instead of commemoration was sometimes sought by the benevolent. Sir Stephen Fox, who did so much to establish the Royal Hospital, Chelsea, also, in 1682, founded an almshouse at his birthplace, Farley, Wiltshire. He refused even to have it named after him and chose as its motto "*faire sans dire*".

CHAPTER 3

Attitudes towards the costumes

It is impossible to study our subject without wanting to enquire into the human motives and responses involved. Though we are unqualified to do this in any depth, it seems worth while to record some of the attitudes that people held towards charity costumes as expressed in their own words and actions or in the costumes themselves.

DONORS' ATTITUDES

COMPASSION

Taking first the attitudes of donors and trustees, one finds, of course, a tangle of motives behind their charity. First and foremost there is compassion, without which little would have been done. Major examples were noticed in Chapter 1 under the general headings of need and of health. The small concessions to dictates of fashion, which we saw were occasionally made, are examples where a special kind of sympathy enters in; so was the opposition to uniformity of dress pioneered by Dr Barnardo. But concern over physical discomfort was the sort of compassion most often shown. To provide and conserve warmth cheaply was the principal aim as a rule, especially where old people were concerned, and we notice how frequently it was insisted that their garments should be lined with wool. But children are subject to chilblains and a truly compassionate attitude appears in the words of Emery Hill, that imaginative philanthropist of Westminster. Not content with founding almshouses and a grammar school, he made a bequest in 1677 to the Green Coat School of Westminster (the so-called King Charles's Hospital) where he doubtless knew the prevailing conditions. The money was for extra coal "and that the poore Children there have Rostmeat and Plumporridge every Christmas day to put the poore Creatures in Mind of that extraordinary good provided for their Soules on that Day and that they may have green Mittens every time they have new Cloth[e]s . . ."[1]

The compassion which produced largesse to the troops in 1793–4 was thus expressed in the morning papers:

LADIES SUBSCRIPTION

Several Ladies, with a humanity peculiar to the Fair of this Happy Island, having set on foot a Subscription for providing Flannel Waistcoats for the Gallant Soldiers serving on the Continent under the command of his Royal Highness the Duke of York, which must prove a most comfortable accommodation to them in the approaching season of inclemency, are desirous of giving their fair country women an opportunity of contributing to a scheme which needs only to be known to meet with universal approbation . . .[2]

Comfort in clothing is sometimes less important than dignity, even with the very poor. William of Wykeham had this partly in mind when, in 1380, he made provision for the Fellows' clothing at his New College, Oxford: "lest they blush for lack of clothes or appear shameful to other scholars of the aforesaid university and suffer from excessive poverty".[3]

And even the dignity of the dead could be a concern. For a funeral the corpse needed not only a shroud but also a covering pall. For the decent pauper this was lent by the parish, but not for the outcast. Stow tells us that adjoining the lands of the Prior of St John of Jerusalem, near Charterhouse, was a plot called "Pardon Churchyard" which "served for burying of such as desperately ended their Lives or were executed for Felonies. Who were fetched . . . thither usually in a close Cart . . . bayled over and covered with blacke [the pall], having a plaine white Crosse thwarting, and at the fore end a St John's Crosse."[4] In true compassion, the St John's Order (whose cross we shall see gracing other good works) provided this rather beautiful pall to cover the humblest of all, at their ignominious end.

RELIGIOUS CONNOTATIONS

Deo et pauperibus is the motto inscribed over the door of Hall's almshouses in Bradford-on-Avon. Religious houses were often endowed by the charitable in order that monks or nuns should offer prayers and help pilgrims, the poor and the sick on behalf of the donor. In a sense therefore the dress of the nuns in our Fig. 26, cloak,

26. Nuns being served by the deceased through whose endowments they are clothed and maintained, 1426 (Miniature in Lydgate's *Pilgrimage of Man*, British Library MS Cott. Tib. A VII fol. 97v)

habit, pleated barbe and veil, was a charity costume. This is explained in the allegory, *Pilgrimage*, which the picture illustrates: the two people serving the nuns at table represent the dead who:

> Made the foundation
> Of this eke same house
> And gave unto [the] religious
> Meat and drink of good intent
> And lynclode [clothing] competent
> Of purpose sooth for to say
> That they should for him pray.[5]

When houses or hospitals were founded for lay brethren and sisters, often with prayer as one of the purposes, they too had a somewhat monastic-looking uniform, hooded capes with a religious badge, which, for example at Armiston, Northants, founded in 1231, depicted a pastoral staff. Often they were tonsured and sisters had short hair, for instance at St Nicholas Hospital, York.

A remarkable establishment which bore many resemblances to a monastic hospital was St Katharine's (now chiefly remembered in the name of St Katharine's Dock). Founded by Queen Matilda in 1148, it was refounded by Queen Eleanor in 1273. There were then to be three priest-brethren, three nursing sisters, ten bedeswomen, kept in return for their prayers, and six poor scholars or clerks.

Queen Philippa in 1335 gave additional support and made the following rules on dress for the men:

the said Brethren shall wear a strait coat or clothing and over that a mantel of black color, on which shall be placed a mark signifying the sign of the Holy Katharine [wheel and book] but green cloaths, those entirely red, or any other striped cloaths or tending to dissoluteness, shall not at all be used. And that the Brethren and Clerks shall have their heads shaved in a becoming manner.[6]

The St Katharine's wheel is an example of the many symbols marking the wearer's debt, not to a direct benefactor, but to Christianity itself. The commonest was of course a cross. Besides those we have already noticed, a favourite was the red cross, the sign and seal of the Knights Templars since 1145, but used by many followers. An early fifteenth-century example of this was at Ewelme, Oxon., where the bedesmen's tabards had a red cross on the breast. The Hungerfords in 1472 gave it to their almsmen in Heytesbury, Wilts., who still wear it on their blue coats. In a medieval house at Alkmonton, Derbys., the almsmen had the unusual T-shape of the *tau* cross. As a post-Reformation example we find that at Shenley, Bucks., in 1607, the almsmen had a typical red cross on the sleeve.

A black cross was perhaps a sign of penitence. At the Hospital of St John Baptist and St John Evangelist, Northampton, which had been founded in 1138, its patron, the Bishop of Lincoln, in 1395, having uncovered some abuses and neglects on the part of the brethren, laid it down that they should wear "a uniform and humble dress of one colour with a black cross upon it" and should not go out except in this dress.[7]

The rosary was so much part of the pre-Reformation almsman's attire that his very name "bedesman" reminds us of it. His wearing of it indoors and outdoors (see Whittington's College, Chapter 12) was a striking sign of the religious attitude of his benefactor. The rosary was even used symbolically by folk when seeking charity. Stow in his *Survay of London* (1598) tells us that between Aldgate and Bishopsgate there had been some cottages, built by a neighbouring priory, for bedridden sick. (He deplores their demolition by "development" during the sixteenth century.) "In my youth, I remember devout people . . . were accustomed oftentimes especially on Fridays . . . to walk that way purposely there to bestow . . . alms". Each poor sick person would display on his windowsill "a clean linen cloth and a pair of beads to show that there lay a bed-rid body unable but to pray".

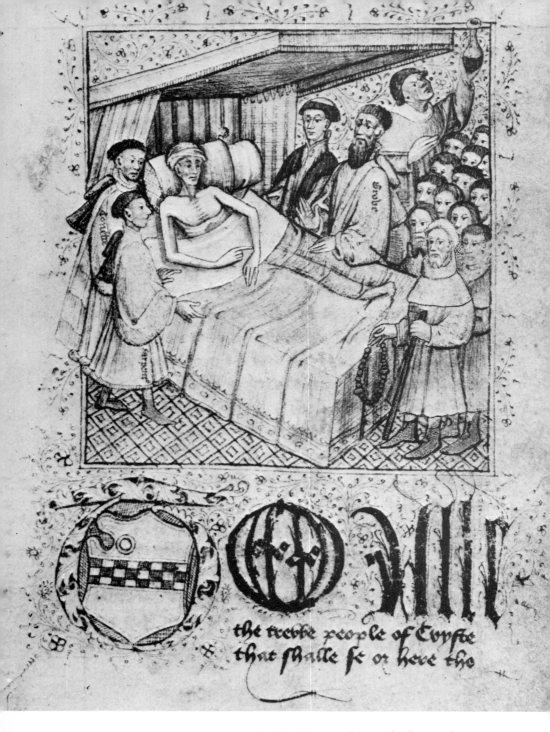

the trewe people of Cryste
that shalle se or here the

27. Richard Whittington on his deathbed. *Right* Thirteen bedesmen he endowed. One, with white hair, holds rosary in hand. They wear the caped hoods of the peasantry, in contrast to the fashionable *chaperons* slung on the shoulders of the executors. C. 1430 (Illumination in Mercers' Company MS.– Ordinances of Whittington's "Goddeshouse or Almeshous"–probably drawn by an artist named Able)

In institutions new clothes were nearly always distributed at the great Christian festivals, Trinity Sunday (e.g. at Holy Trinity Hospital, Greenwich), Whitsun, Christmas and most of all Easter. Furthermore Christ's Hospital was made a bequest in 1670 to buy the boys gloves to wear at the Spital Sermon in Easter week, and each was to "have upon his gloves a paper with these words printed . . . HEE IS RISEN". The spirit of this unpractical instruction was followed right up to 1877, but latterly the legend was embroidered on silk and pinned on the breast.

The religious motive was of course reflected in a general way by insistence on a humble appearance in the people's dress.

MORAL CONNOTATIONS

A moral sanction was applied in the provision of reward and punishment clothes. The award of better or less depressing clothes was often offered as an incentive to good behaviour or accomplishment. Those at the York Spinning School (see Chapter 10) are a striking example of graduated rewards. Under the influence of the same pious and practical women, the York Grey Coat girls received prizes as follows:

First (top) Form "Best washer and Ironer – A muslin Handkerchief, value three shillings".

Second Form "Best line Spinners – A muslin Handkerchief value two shillings".

Fourth Form "Best and quickest Knitters – A pair of cotton Mittens".[8]

At the Foundling Hospital, where the brown uniform was replaced by a more cheerful green for some of the older girls, we read that in 1790 "Matron would be glad to give a green gown to Alice Bright as an encouragement for her assiduous behaviour".[9] In the Marine Society in the earlier days, boys who had qualified to go to sea were rewarded with a "cap assimilated to that of the Royal Navy". In 1877, by which time all the boys wore these caps, one of the prizes given on the *Warspite* was a "pea-jacket for the winter".[10]

An interesting enterprise at Colchester Blue Coat School was to send the older children, probably aged fourteen and fifteen, as pupil teachers in the new National school; in 1813 eleven boys and thirteen girls were given a pair of shoes each "as rewards for their assiduity and attention as teachers".

But, alas, there were punishment clothes too. The severity of some of the children's chastisements is startling and those for adults still more so. A comparatively mild one for bad behaviour at the Ratcliff School was to deprive the children, perhaps for the rest of their school career, of the clothing they were accustomed to receive. For the least serious offences they were made to wear their weekday clothes on Sundays, a disgrace particularly hated by the girls.

Other ways of embarrassing a culprit were approved by Catherine Cappe, again at the York Spinning School in 1800. "If a child spin thick, or be idle, or waste her wool, it may be useful for the Mistress to turn her bedgown [inside out] or to pin some of the thick-spun wool to her shoulder threatening that if she be not more careful, she shall be exhibited to her Patronesses . . ."[11]

More severe were the punishments at the neighbouring Grey Coat School in the eighteenth century. "Every girl who goes out without leave of the Matron, shall, for the offence have a jacket put on with a red R upon it, for one day; those who go out twice, have the jacket put on and [are] handcuffed for a day . . ."[12]

Later, it was directed that a clog for the legs should be put on, even for the first offence of this kind.[13]

Similar horrific restraints were inflicted on the boys of the Royal Hospital School, Greenwich, even up till 1851; they might suffer "confinement of the arms by a straight waistcoat".[14]

Charles Lamb paints a grim picture of how an incorrigible Blue Coat boy would be dressed up for his flogging, in the presence of the whole school, on the day he was expelled (1780s):

The culprit . . . was brought forth . . . arrayed in uncouth and most appalling attire – all trace of his late "watchet weeds" [the blue uniform] carefully effaced, he was exposed in a jacket resembling those which London lamplighters formerly delighted in, with a cap of the same.[15]

Lamplighters were apt to wear a vividly striped jacket[16] – the boy was to be made horribly conspicuous.

Yellow, as is well known since Nazi anti-semitism, is the colour of disgrace (compare the San Benito garment of the Spanish Inquisition). In 1771 at St Martin-in-the-Fields School it was "Order'd That a coat be made with Yellow Sleeves and a Slip of Yellow down the back Seam to be wore by such Boys who shall play Truant or commits any such Offence . . .".[17]

Even old men were not exempt from such punishments. Erring pensioners at Greenwich Hospital had to wear, even on Sundays, a coat with yellow sleeves, or an entirely yellow coat, depending on the gravity of their offence.

SECONDARY MOTIVES

Before the Reformation caused chantries to be abolished, a leading purpose of many endowments was, as we have seen, to secure prayers for the donor's soul. Charities were further looked on as indemnities for sin, and it therefore seemed extra appropriate that bedesmen and women should be sombrely dressed – an ascetic attitude, however, that contrasts with that of the poetess Anna Wickham, whose metaphor is worth quoting:

> Fashion me a garment of repentence
> Lovely as the colour of my sin;
> For the livery of God is beauty[18]

An ulterior motive of many charities was to promote the interests of the public in general. The object was then what Hanway frankly called "Policy". He assured subscribers to the Marine Society: "Your gifts of clothing are a means of indusing many stout land-men to enter the sea service who would not otherwise come . . . they often stand in need of others to think for them".[19] The Society emphasized, in a patriotic appeal in 1779 ("when our coasts are daily threatened"), that the resulting recruitment to the Navy was a prime advantage of the work. And there were others. The Society extended the bounty to felons who were sent aboard by magistrates, and here especially it served to "prevent their communicating to others, with whom they must immediately intermix, those infectious stenches which are the constant companions of filthy garments".[20] The general effect of the "Policy" on the Navy was very marked.

Another national advantage of charity was in the care of girls. Here the secondary motive was to control prostitution, for it was felt that providing fallen girls with a respectable garb would make them both look and feel more suitable people for proper employment. Not only was public morality protected but, as was often pointed out, the middle classes found a source of domestic servants.

A further very practical aim was to clear the streets of beggars and thieves and, as we shall see, it was Sir John Fielding's experience as a Bow Street magistrate that inspired much of his noble effort to get the juvenile poor both clothed and housed.

PATERNALISM

There is no doubt that feelings of ownership and paternalism were rife, even in some of the best of people, at least until social psychology came on the scene not a century ago. Charity children, in Georgian times, were "dressed" almost as though they were the bountiful ladies' dolls. The evils of this were inveighed against without effect by Bernard de Mandeville in his pamphlet on charity and charity schools called *The Fable of the Bees*. In an addendum to the 1723 edition, speaking of the pleasures taken by the parish at the sight of its charity children in their donated uniforms, he says (italics ours): "In all this there is a shadow of *property* that tickles every body . . . especially those who actually contribute and had a great hand in advancing the pious work". As he remarks, rather cruelly, "There is a Melodious Sound in the word 'Governor'".

A morally superior attitude seems to have been openly admitted. St Ann's Society aided "legitimate children, particularly those of respectable parents". When boys left the Foundling Hospital to be apprenticed they were given a parchment to keep, bearing maxims and advice. In the opening paragraph were the words: "You were . . . quite helpless, forsaken, poor and deserted. But of charity you have been fed, clothed and instructed".[21] One can only hope that this was meaningless to a boy who knew only children in the same boat.

Class consciousness was quite as much in evidence as moral superiority. The frankness of its expression is sometimes almost refreshing in these days of bogus egality. Samuel Harmer, in 1642, wrote of charity children belonging to "the lowest social classes": "The very garments that in some places are given them to wear, and their maintenance in all of them by Charity, are the constant badges and proofs of their dependence and poverty; and should therefore teach *them humility* and *their parents* thankfulness".[22] Almost a century later, Isaac Watts in his *Essay on Charity Schools* (1728) puts it equally bluntly: "The clothes which are bestowed upon them . . . are of the coarsest kind and of the plainest form, and thus they are sufficiently distinguished from children of the better rank . . . There is no ground for charity children to be proud of their rayment when it is but a sort of livery".

At St Anne's School, Soho, for the pupil teacher to wear a hat instead of a bonnet, in the late nineteenth century, was actually a "punishable offence".[23] It would certainly have breached the code recommended by Mrs Trimmer, who wrote in 1801: "The mention of servants brings to my mind what I think may be ranked among *female virtues*, I mean *propriety of dress* . . . it would be a kind office in Ladies, to endeavour to inspire girls of the lower ranks with the laudable ambition to appear *neat* rather than *fine*, and to be always dressed in character".[24]

PRIDE

The idea that the clothes are the man and that each man had a station in life to express in his clothes died hard: still harder the notion that dependency must not go unannounced. There were, of course, the silent minority of benefactors whose own humility mattered more than the humbling of others. The tender-hearted Thomas Anguish of Norwich in bequeathing in 1617 a new-built house as a home for "Children that be very poor, and have not Friends to helpe them" declared that he did so "in Compassion and great Pitye, in a good Conscience, although I doe acknowledge my Self the weakest among many Other in Abilitye, having many Children my self, or in Wisdom, to direct for the keeping and bringing up of poor Children, not-withstanding as a beginning to my small Power . . ."[25]

For the most part, however, a donor's condescension was mingled with a not unnatural pride in those he had rescued and clad. This was one of the factors imposing special costumes and badges. The use of these as memorials has already been discussed. Suffice it here to give one example. Henry Smith, an alderman of London, left large sums to assist the poor in many parts of England and in his will of 1627 he ordered that, where the money was not otherwise spent, it should be "disposed in apparel of one colour, with a badge or mark denoting the same to be the gift of the said Henry Smith". And sure enough, two centuries later, the Charity Commissioners reported that at Thetford, Norfolk, the Smith trustees saw to it that each spring seven poor men's coats were made "having the letter S engraved on the buttons".[26]

Pepys leaves few aspects of social life quite untouched. He wrote a few words to our purpose on 21 June 1660 when he went to see "the Great Wardrobe". This was a house attached to the office of Master of the Wardrobe, to which Pepys's then superior, Lord Sandwich, had just been appointed. The house, having been unclaimed by the latter's predecessor, had been put to a highly incongruous use. "With my Lord to see the Great Wardrobe, where Mr Townsend [deputy to Lord Sandwich] brought us to the Governor of some poor Children in tawny clothes, who had been maintained there eleven years . . . the children did sing finely and my Lord did bid me give them five pieces in gold".[27]

The position of these children seems to have been perilously near to that of squatters and was now apparently hopeless. But even here one senses that the governor was proud of his little charges, and their uniform evidently enhanced their effect when he showed them off.

For groups of charitable people the opportunity to gratify their pride arose when they had an annual meeting. The Philanthropic Society, which in 1792 founded an industrial school in Southwark for "children in the high road to vice" and "the offspring of felons", was one of these. At the Society's annual dinner in the following year: "The children under the Society's protection walked in procession round the room . . . The decent appearance and orderly demeanour of the

children filled the minds of the spectators with the most pleasant sensa-
tion ... contemplating the happy change".[28]

The Benevolent Society of St Patrick, which provided schools for Irish
children in London, must have had the same sort of proprietary feeling
at their annual fund-raising dinner at a tavern in the City (Fig. 28).

In the same period, but on a very different social level and at a very
grand dinner, the little girls of the Royal Masonic Institution used to
be paraded before a great company of formally attired freemasons. In
the painting commemorating one of these occasions their founder
leads in the little uniformed procession with very evident pride (Fig.
29).

The ladies of the Friendly Society for working girls in York showed
their pride in a rather democratic manner. In 1794 they resolved that
the "whole Society, Honorary [ladies] as well as General Members
[girls] should attend Divine Service at the Cathedral ... distinguished
by a green Ribband placed in their hats ..."[29]

The Marine Society found a direct and amusing way of advertising
their clothing work at their first anniversary. A procession of the lads
from headquarters to a City church carried a banner bearing on one
side the motto "Charity and Policy United" and on the other the figure
of a boy brandishing in his arms a charity coat.

An example where the beneficiaries shown off were men occurred in

28. Members of Benevolent Society of St Patrick, attending annual dinner at a
tavern, watch procession of children from the school they founded. Boys in
charity flat caps and girls in typical aprons, sleeved mittens and tippets. 1844.
(Press cutting, Mansell Collection)

29. Children of the Royal Masonic Institution for Girls shown off at annual dinner of Freemasons: girls in blue uniform dresses with white neckerchiefs. Freemasons wear traditional masonic aprons. 1808–9 (Detail of coloured print after Rowlandson and Pugin in R. Ackermann's *Microcosm of London* vol. II, inspired by Stothard. Compare Fig. 66)

the seventeenth to nineteenth centuries. Thomas Jordan in *London's Glory* describes how poor men were dressed up to gratify their patrons when the Lord Mayor was a Merchant Taylor, in 1680:

> Many poor pensioners that march i' the Rear,
> With gowns and caps, Standard and Banners bear;
> A numerous Troop of Persons that are poor,
> In Azure* Gowns and Caps one hundred more,
> With Javelins and with Targets [shields] are all Actors [participants]
> And bear the Arms of their good Benefactors.

It is interesting that the pensioners were wearing the almsman's gown and thus resembled, through the remote common origin of that gar-

* It is known that, in 1655, when the Mayor was a Mercer, the poor men wore red (personal communication from Miss Jean Imray, quoting the Mercers' Company Minutes).

ment, the members of guilds in the same procession who were wearing the gowns of their own Livery.

What seems to have gratified friends of the poor more than anything was to see their protégés having a meal; and there again the fact of their being dressed in donated clothing enhanced the pleasure. The print in Ackermann's *Microcosm of London* (1808–9) showing the Lambeth Asylum with its uniformed orphan girls (Fig. 101) is described in the text by William Combe as

a representation of the objects of this benevolent institution at their repast in the presence of some of their guardians [subscribers] who seem to contemplate the good order . . . and comforts of their little wards with all that interest and delight, that luxury of fine feeling [etc., etc.] . . . gratified by the conviction that their virtuous endeavours are crowned with success.

To parade one's beneficiaries at one's own funeral was a frequent expression of pride: the spectacle was enjoyed in imagination if it could not be at the time. Before the Reformation there were many wills like that of Sir John Gilliot, 1509, who made provision for black gowns to be given to 113 poor men, of whom thirteen must "bear torches" at his funeral.[30]

Mrs Newcomen of Southwark gave precise instructions in her will of 1675. Twenty poor women were to receive: "A Cloth Petty Coate and Wastecoate [i.e. skirt and jacket] with head Geare of twenty shillings value . . . yearly, but their first to be against the funerall and with them [i.e. wearing them] they are to attend my corpse to the grave".[31]

30. Almswomen in mourning gowns and veils at funeral of Lady Lumley, 1578 (British Library MS Add. 35324 fol. 19)

31. Foundling Hospital girls watching a procession in celebration of return to health of Prince of Wales, 1872. Favours on their tippets (Contemporary print, Mary Evans Picture Library)

IN RELATION TO PUBLIC EVENTS

The bountiful sometimes regarded those whom they helped as, in a manner, an extension of themselves. They might therefore dictate such people's behaviour in relation to public events, and on at least two sorts of occasion this involved details of dress. A pleasant way, for example, of expressing patriotism was to have one's beneficiaries attend national celebrations, decking them out with trimmings appropriate to the occasion. An opportunity came in 1872, when Queen Victoria emerged from her retirement for a service at St Paul's in thanksgiving for the recovery of the Prince of Wales from a serious illness. Three hundred Foundlings were sent to watch the procession. "In long rows at the shop windows sat the little maidens" and a "scarlet, white and silver favour"[32] decorated the white kerchief of each one (Fig. 31).

Examples of happy public occasions where charity people were actually organized so as to contribute to the spectacle are given in Chapter 15.

There were also times when beneficiaries were put into mourning, not for anyone to whom they were specially indebted, but simply to reflect the loyalties of the donor or his trustees. Sovereigns were mourned with black armbands and ribbons, even in the poorest of charity schools, and there were other public figures whose deaths had to be lamented by charity folk. In 1722 the Chelsea pensioners were put into mourning for the Duke of Marlborough, and his funeral was attended by "out-pensioners . . . to the Number of 73 (answerable to the years of his Grace's age) in mourning gowns with the Badge of his Grace on one Arm".[33]

We have not come across examples where a donor's party politics were expressed in a recipient's garb, unless we count a leek (Fig. 75). Indeed it is interesting that the Governors of the Green Coat School, Camberwell, thought it worth while to prohibit, in 1721, "the use of badges or marks of party distinction on days of publick rejoicings or thanksgivings", a wise precaution against affrays. On the other hand it appears that under William and Mary the royal cipher was deliberately placed on the backs of corporals, drummers and all lower ranks of Chelsea pensioners; this is thought by C.G.T. Dean possibly to have been aimed at eliminating men with Jacobite sympathies.[34]

32. Funeral of Duke of Marlborough, 1722. Second and third lines show seventy-three Chelsea pensioners in mourning cloaks and with crepe draping their hats and staves. The last one shows best the Duke's badge, which all have on their cloaks (Contemporary print, British Museum)

RECIPIENTS' ATTITUDES

SATISFACTION AND GRATITUDE

It is difficult to know just what a recipient felt about the clothing he was given, for his views were rarely recorded. Obviously there was often pleasure, and sometimes gratitude.

Hanway, speaking of the Marine Society's effort to clothe poor men for a life at sea, had had encouragement: "It is not to be conceived with what pleasure and advantage, the soberer part of these men received their clothing . . ."[35] In 1778 the Society was minuting: "the design [of the clothing] is so gratefully salutary that some ordinary Seamen have been induced to accept the bounties of Landsmen and pass as such, for the pleasure of making a clean, Maritime appearance".[36]

With women, reactions were usually mixed, but even at the Magdalen Hospital the better-class* girls liked the anonymity of the uniform (as we saw), and the others were sometimes glad of its respectability. Compston tells us that on attempting to leave one of the girls was shown the clothes she had arrived in and would have to wear again if she went: "the old hat, and the shabby ulster, and the leaky worn-out boots which had seen such hard service as their wearer tramped the streets in search of the wages of sin".[37] That did it. She opted for the uniform.

Poor children naturally sometimes registered a real joy in new clothes, and Mary Carpenter, in her study of *Reformatory Schools* (1851), puts the obvious point that with the very poor and disreputable even a uniform may be "conducive to what is a matter of no slight moment to the elevation of a child", namely "improving its personal appearance . . . and thus promoting its self respect". When thousands of charity children assembled in St Paul's for the annual thanksgiving – the girls all in their freshly starched white linen – a columnist in 1842 suggested, surely with some truth: "Must not each girl feel honestly proud of her station in society", which, humble though it was, "commands respect . . . from the crowd of richer countrywomen who surround her" owing to the girls' "propriety of manner and appearance".[38]

When an institution which began as a modest charity became, as so many did, renowned, then positive pride could be felt in belonging. Leigh Hunt in his autobiography (1850) writes of his old school:

---

* Horace Walpole records in a letter (January 1760) that one of them was "Sir Clement Cotterel's niece".

I love and honour the School ... it is one of those judicious links with all classes ... Christ's Hospital is a nursery of tradesmen, of merchants, of naval officers, of scholars. It has produced some of the greatest of their time ... I am grateful to Christ's Hospital for having bred me up in old cloisters.

Charles Lamb shows how pride in this same Alma Mater became associated with its uniform:

The Blue-Coat boy has a distinctive character of his own ... His very garb, as it is antique and venerable, feeds his self-respect ... He is never known to mix with other boys ... all this proceeds, I have no doubt, from the continual consciousness ... of the difference of his dress from that of the rest of the world; with a modest jealousy ... lest, by over-hastily mixing with common and secular playfellows, he should commit the dignity of his cloth.[39]

A far cry, as Lamb remarks, from "feeling a charity boy": a sense of fellowship conferred by the dress could tip over into a feeling of shared superiority.

HUMILIATION

But unhappily charity clothes frequently inspired neither gratitude nor pride but only a sense of humiliation. We shall see how often it brought down the public's contempt or ridicule. The wearer's embarrassment is easy to illustrate.

D'Arcy Wentworth Thompson, Sen., recalling his feelings as a boy at the school from 1837 to 1849, complains that the coat, "opening in front, disclosed the ridiculous spectacle of knee-breeched yellow-stockinged legs".[40]

Generally the trouble was that the uniform as such was a social stigma. The reality of this is shown by the fact that Camberwell "Green Coat" charity school made a concession whereby, when the children left, if they had been well behaved they might be rewarded by having their uniforms *dyed black* to prevent recognition.

Dickens would have understood all these feelings. When the Charitable Grinders' uniform which her little boy would have to wear was described to Mrs Richards, "a vision of Biler with his very small legs encased in the serviceable clothing ... swam before Richards' eyes and made them water".[41] Humiliation was going to be felt on both counts: for the sequel see page 60.

A costume that seems to have been specially shaming was the kind bearing a badge with the donor's name or initials. John Merryweather was evidently aware of this for, when he left money in trust, in 1632, to provide "upper garments" for poor people in Wokingham, he directed that the recipients should wear "the letters I.M. made fair with red

33. Inmate of a penitentiary in her humiliating garb, e.g. a straight skirt at a time when crinolines were at their largest (Anonymous pamphlet *Penitentiaries and Reformatories*, 1865)

cloth upon the breasts and stomach, and that if any should refuse to wear them, the garments should be taken away and given to some other person who would . . ."[42] Whitehead, of Kirkland, Cumbria, was not so far-sighted. He made a similar bequest in 1712, but without the proviso, and the Charity Commissioners in the nineteenth century found that "the coats which the founder had directed should have his initials 'P.W. in red cloth upon the left arm' were discontinued on account of the objection to wearing the letters, and instead thereof 7s. used to be given to each of the poor persons towards furnishing a coat".[43]

There were sometimes extra reasons for preferring obscurity, as when Bridewell boys left to take up a job. The clothing provided was a uniform and had overtones of delinquency and even of prison, and, as we shall see (pages 195–6), the lads adopted ruses to make it less recognizable. Again, Bartley tells us that the Jews' Free School, Bell Lane, London, a worthy charity set up for Jews in 1817, offered every child a suit of clothes each spring. "Some request to have boots alone, as they are too proud to appear in the clothes". However "they are not allowed to have any portion of the gift, unless they undertake to wear the whole dress".[44]

If charity clothes brought shame on their wearers, it must not be

forgotten that the tables could be turned – witness the rule that a
"Magdalen" who was dismissed from the hospital and had nothing of
her own had to be given fresh clothes at considerable expense so that
her subsequent bad behaviour did not disgrace the uniform.

OTHER DISLIKES

It need hardly be said that many charity garments were cordially disliked by their wearers for reasons other than their power to humiliate.
Suffice it to glance at the hardship for two boys, one girl and a man. At
Christ's Hospital, many felt (and feel) that the coat is cumbrous and,
before the days of special kit for games, it was hated as a hindrance to
exercise. All its drawbacks are well put in "A begging Letter from a
Blue Coat Boy" in *Punch*, 7 May 1864.

Please, Sir, Mr Punch, will you . . . have a shy at our old Governors, and make
them change our togs and dress like other fellows, and not go about like girls
in those old stupid stuffy gowns, which stick so to our legs that we have to tuck
'em up whenever we play football . . . And then in summer time you know our
gowns are beastly hot and heavy, and cling about one so that of course one
can't play cricket . . .
    I remember you once made a sketch of one of us in Crinoline, which you
thought the Governors perhaps would recommend for us, if they meant that
we should dress more in the style of modern fashions . . . I think if we wore
Crinoline, our gowns would look so foolish that the Governors would let us
take to wearing coats and jackets the same as other fellows, and then perhaps
we might leave off those bands, which make us look like sucking parsons, and
those beastly yellow stockings which we all of us so hate . . . Juvenal says that

34. Skit on Christ's Hospital
uniform. See text (*Punch*,
7 May 1864)

35. Greenwich pensioner in
cocked hat, 1828
(Lithograph published by
Enlgemann, National
Maritime Museum)

poverty makes chaps look ridiculous, and if he had but seen our gowns and
yellow stockings, I'm sure he would have said that charity does the same . . .

Augustus Blobbs

P.S. Couldn't you make a picture of one of our old Governors togged out in
our school uniform, and trying to play leapfrog . . .

At Westminster it was the coarseness of the material in their gowns that
the boys disliked and those who could afford it sometimes even had them
copied in better materials.[45]

As an example of the many items that must have been disliked by
girls we have the white pinafore of the Royal Masonic School, which in
the twentieth century was "detested" for being so unpractical.

Finally, it is sad to learn, of Chelsea pensioners, that "The old
soldier damns his cocked hat". That very becoming tricorne is hard
dealt with by Edward Howard in *Heads of the People* II (1841):

Most of the pensioners are old and infirm men, requiring protection from the
variations of our climate. Now, the only good of the cocked hat is to hold hail,
rain and snow in the upper part; it does not protect the face and eyes from the
sun, the dust or the wind. It hurts his forehead, and lets in the cold behind.

In the days of wigs (which is where the hat belonged) the latter draw-back did not arise. But now

there is no excuse for it. The pensioner hates his cocked hat; he calls it a smoke-jack. He has petitioned several times to have a round hat instead; but with no avail . . . the veterans generally sell their last year's cocked hat for eight pence to the coal heavers.

Few wearers of charity costumes have had so eloquent a spokesman, but even his words remained unheeded for many years.

ATTITUDES OF THE PUBLIC

RIDICULE, CONTEMPT, AND THEIR MITIGATION

A common reaction of the public was that of scorn for the dependent person and hence for the costume. The recipient's shame, already exemplified, illustrates the point. To follow the small boy, Biler, a little further, we have a heightened picture of what Dickens had doubtless seen. The child was rigged out in the charity school uniform, the coat having startling orange facings, the stockings being red and the cap yellow (an outfit scarcely different from the one actually worn, for example, by the "Orange boys" in Northampton).

. . . Biler's life had been since yesterday morning rendered weary by the costume of the Charitable Grinders . . . No young vagabond could be brought to bear its contemplation for a moment without throwing himself upon the unoffending wearer . . . He had been overthrown into gutters; bespattered with mud . . . His legs had undergone verbal criticism and revilings . . . Entire strangers to his person had lifted his yellow cap off his head and cast it to the winds.[46]

Christ's Hospital's revered costume could itself be ridiculed (as seen in *Punch* above), and even be greeted with insulting words and behaviour, accompanied by shouts of "Charity! Charity!" This is declared in 1877 by that nonetheless loyal Blue Coat boy, W. H. Blanch. He also says:

. . . small London boys make game of the dress and country lads open wide their mouths at the sight of it . . . It was a common remark with town boys that we had dipped our legs in the mustard pot: that we had a yellow stomach and a blue skin.[47]

Charles Lamb, in 1813, despite his eulogies, declares "While the coarse blue coat and the yellow hose shall continue . . . the sons of the aristocracy of this country, cleric or laie, will not often be obtruded upon this seminary".[48]

36. Charity boy being jeered at for his uniform. Note his shoulder badge, numbered "147". *Right* his horrified mother (Illustration by Phiz in Dickens' *Dombey and Son*, 1847–8)

However, the tendency to look down on those clad by charity and to mock their clothes was mitigated by a sympathy for their feelings which seems to have increased with time. A group of people in advance of their period were the Amicable Society in Rotherhithe, who recognized the pain that might be inflicted by the stamp of charity clothing, when they founded a school in 1739. A specially strong reason was given for avoiding any stigma here.

The Children they make choice of are mostly Descended from such as have liv'd in a Reputable Manner . . . for which reason the Society never Intended to put on them any Mark or Badge of Distinction such as Cap, Band etc. nor should any of us be willing a Mark should be set on our [own] offspring [should they ever need assistance].[49]

It was in the 1870s that a marked change of attitude is noticeable, coinciding, perhaps significantly, with the move towards universal education and resulting in the modification or disappearance of many insignia of charity. In 1870 an inspector said of the Birmingham Blue Coat School's uniform (which, however, outlived his remark by half a century): " . . . the children still wear a costume better suited to 1724 than the present, and I question the expediency of retaining an antique and ugly dress".[50]

In 1871, the *Spectator*, wrote about the ancient Emmanuel school in Westminster: "To the child, admission to the School is no boon . . . he . . . is compelled to wear a ridiculous dress . . . humiliating conditions surround his childhood".

RESPECT, ENVY

There had long been several big exceptions to the public's supercilious attitude towards charity clothes. Certain institutions (we have seen it happen with many schools) became, for one reason or another, renowned; then not only were the recipients proud of the uniform but the public grew to respect it. Sometimes this was largely because of its antiquity and associations. Thus W. H. Blanch assures us that, although the ignorant boys might jeer at a Christ's Hospital uniform, yet "in the City it is a sure passport to favour" and "everybody who knows anything about the School" respects the uniform.[51]

The change of attitude also occurred towards schools of less romantic association but where a good education was consistently given for a long time. What happened at the Greenwich Royal Hospital School occurred in many charity schools in the nineteenth century: a Royal Commission appointed in 1859 pronounced that by that time, far from being "a Charity School professing to bestow a limited education on the children of pensioners and poor seamen, the curriculum became so extended as to make the education an object of desire for the children of parents of higher social position". If not the "aristocracy" mentioned by Lamb, certainly the middle classes muscled in, and the uniforms gained respect. In universities and the best schools competition for scholarships became so keen that the holders of them were even envied and their distinctive dress coveted. In the eighteenth century the fee-paying undergraduates at Oxford and Cambridge petitioned to be allowed to wear the square caps that were prescribed for dependent scholars.

While the intellect conferred prestige on scholars' garments, it was character and life-work that gave it to ex-service pensioners' uniforms. W. H. Pyne's *Costume of Great Britain* (1808) refers to the dress of Chelsea pensioners in words curiously like Blanch's: "The dress worn by these, who are clothed by public bounty, far from appearing a mark of reproach becomes the passport to every good man's esteem".

PLEASURE IN THE PICTURESQUE

A happy element in the public's attitude was the pleasure it often felt simply in the sight of charity uniforms. As we have noted, they were "picturesque" individually because of being antiquated; most people, if they were neither the wearers nor the bullying boys, found the costumes appealing – and the more outdated and quaint, the better. Charity children's uniforms have been immortalized in paint, lead, stone, engravings and photography. The boys in George Müller's orphanage, founded in Bristol in 1836, were even thought a worthy subject for a coloured china figure. The whole of the *Illustrated London News* article "London Charities" in 1842 emphasizes the uselessness and charm of the garments worn, citing for example the Charterhouse boy's gown with its "long hanging sleeve never intended for use, but which adds considerably to the picturesque appearance of the wearer". Even a French journal, *L'Illustration*, in mid nineteenth century carried drawings of "*Costumes des Jeunes Garçons et des Jeunes Filles du Foundling Hospital.*"

The old people could be a pleasurable sight too. The *Illustrated London News* in April 1844, in an article on Easter entertainments, recommends a visit to Greenwich. The superannuated sailors, "the 'old Pensioners' as they are somewhat irreverently termed by light-hearted holiday folk", wearing their striking traditional dress were "great personages in the amusements of Easter week". Edward Howard (loc.cit.) had much the same attitude, despite his understanding of the pensioner's standpoint: "Let us view him with his three-cornered hat – his quaint, old-fashioned, yet age-becoming coat, with its patches of gold lace here and there – his full-dress smalls, 'all too loose for his shrunk shanks' – his worsteds, and shoes with their huge buckles . . .''

One of the visually attractive effects of charity costumes is so outstanding as to merit separate treatment, and to this we will devote our final chapter.

CHAPTER 4

Introduction to schools;
Blue Coat schools

There have always been those who saw lack of education as the chief deprivation of the poor and, until the State began to take over in 1870, poor children depended entirely on schools established and maintained by private or group charities. These aimed at teaching reading, writing and religion and often trained for future work or apprenticeship. All this was useless without attention to the children's physical needs: in many cases clothing, board and lodging were wanted as well. Institutions that were primarily homes will be dealt with in Chapter 9. We begin with schools proper and classify them as follows, despite some inevitable overlapping. Chapters 7 and 8 are concerned with typical charity schools, i.e. parish and ward schools, mainly supported by local public subscriptions, generally founded in the eighteenth century and nearly always day schools. The present chapter and the two following deal with more ancient and well-known schools, the majority founded and endowed by individuals. These are mainly boarding schools; many of them are "public schools", a term which is familiar but ambiguous. They were originally homes with free schooling, for the poor only, but, as the standard of their education rose, better-off parents began securing admission for their sons, often on payment of fees. This led to enlargement of the school, further rise in standards and status and an increase in the proportion of boys staying on after the usual leaving age. Thus the home-and-school for pauper children became the famous boarding "public school" of today. Fee-paying pupils were usually distinguished from the endowed "scholars". The scholars at Westminster, for example, were differently dressed from the "town boys" as well as being separated from them by a curtain during lessons.

Of the schools that survived the Charity Commissions of the nineteenth century and particularly the educational changes of the

1870s, some abandoned traditional uniforms at about that time. The Rev. W. Clare, to whom we owe some of what follows, contributed *The Historic Dress of the English Schoolboy** in 1940, in the hope of discouraging any further erosion of tradition.

BLUE COAT SCHOOLS

So important has uniform been that its colour has given a popular name to many schools of different types. Blue Coat schools in England were particularly numerous, especially from the sixteenth century on, the best known being Christ's Hospital. The term includes both typical charity day-schools and certain public schools. In some of the latter the uniforms remained almost unchanged for centuries and became historic monuments to the past. Why blue should have been a favourite colour for charity children is probably because in the sixteenth and seventeenth centuries it was the colour obtained from a cheap dye and worn by apprentices and servants. It was avoided by gentlemen and the aristocracy (see page 20). Blue-dyed** materials were thus originally economical and also implied a humble status.

A selection of Blue Coat public schools follows, starting with several that have a Tudor style of dress. Two others follow, founded about 1700, where the uniforms are more like those of the many charity day-schools that arose at about that time.

CHRIST'S HOSPITAL OR BLUE COAT SCHOOL

This famous school occupied at first the buildings of the dissolved Grey Friars' Hospital*** in London and formed part of the scheme for

* Some of the illustrations appear to have been done from life but this is not stated. Some are from imagination. The sources of the few that are copies of earlier works are not given.

** Shades of blue called "watchet", "plunket" or "blew", according to the depth of dye, were obtained from woad, which was European, whereas many other dyes came from the Far East and later from America.

*** The children were often called "the children of Grey Friars" for this reason. Infants were nursed in the country and in the later eighteenth century the girls and the youngest boys were housed in schools in Hertfordshire. A pair of statuettes of the boys, made in 1721, still stands at Hertford, at the gates of what has become Christ's Hospital girls' school. The entire boys' school was moved to Horsham in 1902.

aiding the poor recommended to Edward VI by Bishop Ridley. At first it aimed to provide not solely education but complete maintenance for destitute children and infants as well as out relief for the aged. The Hospital was entirely supported by the citizens of London and by a royal grant; Edward VI on his deathbed signed its charter in 1552. For a time only orphans were admitted to the school and by about 1560 there were some six hundred, of whom William Camden is thought to have been one.

In 1666 Charles II became a second royal founder when the school had to be rebuilt after severe damage in the Great Fire. It was now that education was considered paramount and the age of entry was raised to seven. The King chartered and partly endowed a department, the Royal Mathematical School, in the hope that its pupils, called "the King's Boys", would eventually go to sea.

The very first uniform of the Hospital was not blue but brownish, being made of the fabric often worn by the poor called (and generally coloured) "russet". "On Christmas day [1552] when the Lord Mayer

the Children Educated in x.ª Hospitall
the kings Royall gift & Foundation

37. Christ's Hospital "mathemat", belonging to Charles II's foundation and wearing its badge on his school uniform (see text). Note the bib-shaped collar which preceded the tabs shown in the next illustration, also the cap before its size was reduced. *C.* 1670 (Contemporary print.) Courtesy: Radio Times Hulton Picture Library

and Aldermen rode to Paules, all the children of Christ's Hospital stood in array, all in one livery of russet cotton [a coarse woollen with the surface raised to give it a nap], the men children with red caps, the women children kerchiefs on their heads". This is the description given by John Stow in his *Annals or General Chronicle*... (edn. 1592). He adds that in the next year, 1553, the children duly appeared in blue. They have continued so ever since, and in fact the well-known uniform seems to have survived almost unchanged for over four hundred years. Its origin was discussed on pp. 26–27. Stow's *Survey of London* in the 1720 edition describes it as follows:

a long Coat of Blue warm Cloth, close to the Arms and Body, hanging loose to their Heels, girt about their Waste with a red leather girdle, buckled; a loose Petticoat underneath, of Yellow Cloth, a round thrum [rough wool] Cap with a red Band, Yellow Stockings and Black Low heel'd Shoes, their Hair cut close, their Locks short.

The coat used to be even longer for the seniors, called "Grecians", to give them extra dignity. It was fastened down to waist level with hooks

38. Scholar of Christ's Hospital, probably a "button Grecian", 1816. Bands (tabs) and small cap (Print in *History of the Colleges of Winchester, etc.*, published by R. Ackermann)

and eyes in 1638; but certainly by 1706 a set of brass buttons had to be supplied yearly. In 1758 it was decided that these should be of white metal embossed with the head of King Edward VI. The most distinguished boys of all have a specially conspicuous set and are called "button Grecians".

The girdles of leather, which are no longer red, have for many years been of two kinds. Those of the seniors are broad, nicknamed "broadies", and in the early years were often stamped with various devices, the head of the young King Edward being conspicuous. Those of the juniors were plain and narrow and called "narrowies". The yellow "petticoat" was worn in cold weather until 1865. This was a sleeveless waistcoat reaching at first to the ankles and nicknamed "the yellow". An existing specimen at the school is open in front, tied from the waist up with three tapes. A curious reason was given for this yellow colour. In January 1638 it was decided that "the linings for the Coats shall be dyed yellowe as well as ye petticoates to avoid vermin by reason the white cotton is held to breed the same".[1]

Breeches were not provided until 1736, when leather ones were allowed to "sick and weakly children". By 1760 breeches, called brogues in the nineteenth century, had become part of the uniform. They were made successively, at different dates, from leather, Russia drab,[2] corduroy and, as knickerbockers, black serge.[3]

The shoes supplied in 1637 were of two kinds, large sizes of "neats leather" (ox hide) and small sizes of calves' leather. They were made at first by the school cobbler, but in 1735 were bought from Northampton, and a good fit obtained. Later in the century they acquired a fashionably large buckle and retained it for many years. Stockings of yellow worsted were, and are, always worn and were nicknamed "mustard pots".

The characteristic neckwear was probably preceded in the sixteenth century by an ordinary shirt collar* but the familiar eighteenth-century white bands have long been essential. They are a pair of rectangular tabs, which were derived from a square-cut, fairly wide collar (see page 29. Compare Fig. 176). By the eighteenth century, the collar had narrowed and developed the pendant tabs in front, these being secured

---

* The ruffs shown on the boys in the above-mentioned Charter picture are probably a fancy of the painter who lived a century after the event. Ruffs were not worn by the poor. At Queen Elizabeth's Hospital, Bristol, the illumination in the Elizabethan Charter (Fig. 45) shows the boys with turned-down collars, not ruffs. When the "tabs" began is uncertain. The boy statue, now at Horsham, has a wide, almost bib-shaped, collar without tabs.

39. *Left* Christ's Hospital boy with badge of Royal Mathematical School, 1975. *Right* Boy in "half-housey" dress, i.e. without coat, 1975. Note the superimposed bands worn by both (Photos: Nicholas Plumley. Courtesy: Christ's Hospital)

at the neck with pins. (It is on record that the matron in 1736 stole 207,082 pins valued at £10 7s.) The tabs used to have to lie side by side in the usual manner (Fig. 38) but it is now *de rigueur*, at Christ's Hospital, that they should be neatly superimposed. Happily pins are a thing of the past. There is a specially constructed shirt with a strategically placed button.

Each foundationer in the Mathematical School still wears a large metal badge to show whose beneficiary he is. The King's Boys, who soon became an élite group, wear an emblem depicting three goddesses of Mathematics and these badges, at one period, would

40. "Queen's Scholars" of the Royal Mathematical School of Christ's Hospital presenting their work to Queen Victoria, 1873 (After drawing by A. Hopkins, *Illustrated London News* vol. LXII, 468)

guarantee their owners for the rest of their lives against forcible impressment – no mean advantage of being a charity boy.

Twelve younger boys are supported from a bequest by Henry Stone in 1688 and their badge is different. It portrays three "Stone" scholars at work with mathematical instruments. Like the King's, this badge is worn on the left side of the coat. Stone left the money for the benefit of the Mathematical School in general and it was Pepys, as a governor, who finally settled how the fund should be disposed.

A third badge (Britannia with ships) distinguishes two future naval cadets on the foundation of John Stock, 1780. This is worn on the

41. Badge of Christ's Hospital mathematical boys endowed by Henry Stone, depicting boys at their work. They are wearing the badge but, oddly enough, on the right. Possibly the disc was designed from an engraving which would reverse the original drawing. Below is embossed "EX MUNIFICENTIA HEN: STONE ARM:" (Photo: Nicholas Plumley. Courtesy: Christ's Hospital)

right. All these badges were at first, as they are now, of silver. In between times, copper or pewter were sometimes used.

Sons of naval lieutenants, endowed by Samuel Travers in 1724, formed a special group in the Mathematical School and wore a silver commemorative buckle on the girdle (Fig. 23). This buckle is now awarded to the best mathematicians of their year.

Except in the eighteenth century, the round black cap, originally red, was too small – "about the size of a tea saucer"[4] – to wear comfortably on the head. Usually carried in the hand, it was worn on state occasions only; from the 1860s the boys went bare-headed at all times. The initials of each boy were marked with yellow worsted inside his cap. A cap in the school museum is a flat cap about four inches in diameter with a tiny brim of the same circumference. It is of knitted wool but feels dense, like felt (purposely shrunk). George Wickham[5] remembers that in the preparatory school at Hertford in the 1820s the little boys would use superannuated caps as bedroom slippers.

No child was allowed to wear any other dress than that provided by Christ's Hospital, nor any addition thereto, on pain of expulsion. Furthermore, until 1721, boys who wanted to visit the city and were allowed out, had to wear a brass ticket tied to their coats.

When freedom of movement was required, as for football or hockey in modern times, the long blue coat had to be adjusted accordingly. George Wickham, referring to sports and pastimes, wrote:

In the pursuit of our games our greatest annoyance was the the blue coat which in running would catch us between the legs and throw us down; this we remedied by tucking the ends in our girdles behind, buckling them as tight as possible.

Another plan was to fold them up on our back which presented the appearance of a soldier's knapsack . . . The last named plan was termed *making a roller* and, before the commencement of any game, "Who'll make us a roller?" was the favour asked by the players of each other.[6]

The boys had gym or running shoes for all games in the late nineteenth century, and also jerseys, but football matches had to be played before breakfast, as only then were they allowed to wear these.

Reactions to the standard uniform were many and various, as we saw in Chapter 3.

42. Christ's Hospital boys playing in the cloisters of the London building, wearing long petticoats, 1823 (Drawn and engraved by J. and H. S. Storer, detail)

Within the illustration: FIVES IN THE · OLD PLAYGROUND · HOCKEY IN 'THE GARDEN' · FOOTBALL IN THE HALL PLAYGROUND · AT THE TUCK SHOP DOOR · FRANK GILLETT

43. Management of coats for games, 1902 (Print after drawing by Frank Gillett, Guildhall Library)

The connection between the boys' and the girls' Christ's Hospital schools remains very close, and an anecdote by Pepys linking the two is quoted on page 104. The girls' school is discussed in Chapter 6.

QUEEN ELIZABETH'S HOSPITAL, BRISTOL

This school was founded by John Carr, a Bristol soap manufacturer who became a member of Parliament. On his visits to London he became interested in Christ's Hospital which had come into existence a generation earlier, and in his will, dated 1586, he stipulated that his Bristol school should be governed exactly like Christ's Hospital and wear the same uniform. It is a striking fact that the two schools have retained to the present day the oldest style of dress in any public school. The Queen Elizabeth's Hospital boys have always worn an ankle-length, belted blue coat, exactly like that at Christ's, except that its lining never underwent the change to yellow, and it was changed to blue in 1914. The breeches and yellow stockings are the same, and originally there was also a petticoat. Bands have been worn since the seventeenth century.

The cap has always been a blue flat cap, but it never diminished to the absurd size of the Christ's Hospital one and continued to be worn for a century longer. (The Sixth Form were privileged to go without it from 1961.) It had a yellow band and yellow tuft on top.

The Christ's Hospital uniform was so much respected that in 1843 the governors resolved that "buckles be in future substituted for strings in the boys' shoes", thus harking back to a fashion of fifty years before because it had been retained at Christ's. The experiment of putting the boys into ordinary suits with trousers in 1877 was quickly reversed, despite jeers from the local press.

The bands or tabs at the neck have probably had the same history and have become narrower with time in the same way. To help us judge what preceded their introduction in the seventeenth century, we are fortunate enough to have a picture of the boys painted at the very beginning of the school's history – earlier than any picture at Christ's Hospital. This is the illumination of the charter itself, signed by Queen

44. Statuette of Queen Elizabeth's Hospital boy, early eighteenth century. Coat, bands and cap as at Christ's Hospital. "C" and "B" badges indicate City of Bristol endowment. Note the skirt of the coat appears to be tied as well as belted. Compare tied girdle in the next illustration (Painted statuette at the school. Courtesy: Queen Elizabeth's Hospital)

45. Boys of Queen Elizabeth's Hospital at its foundation in 1590. See text. Coats are blue. Note the ordinary collars at this date (Illumination in the charter signed by Queen Elizabeth in 1590, detail. Courtesy: Queen Elizabeth's Hospital)

Elizabeth in 1590, and it seems likely that it is true to life. The boys wear neither ruffs nor bands but turned-down shirt collars like other working-class children at that time. This picture is full of interest. It shows that the belt, which is still called "girdle", was preceded by a girdle tied round the waist. Hanging from it each boy has an ink-container and pen-case.* The hair is close-cropped and remained so in the school until the 1940s.

Knowing the contemporary costume makes one see the point of some of the injunctions given to schoolboys in *The English Schoolmaster* by Edmund Coote, 1596–7:

> Lose not your bookes, inkhorne, or pen,
>   nor Girdle, garters, hat or band;
> Let shooes be ty'd, pin shirt-band close.

---

*These are the symbols of a schoolboy. Compare the brass effigy at Little Ilford of a fourteen-year-old boy reproduced in J. Page-Phillips *Children on Brasses* (1970), Fig. 17.

In the mid nineteenth century a "playground" or "yard" jacket was introduced to facilitate games (contrast Christ's Hospital here). Gloves, and "umbrellas instead of capes" were recommended – there was still, in the mid twentieth century, a stock of waterproof capes that boys could borrow. Mackintoshes seem to have been unheard of in both schools.

The tradition that clothing should be given free still holds for selected individuals.

CHETHAM'S HOSPITAL, MANCHESTER

This school was founded in 1656 by Humphrey Chetham for the sons of poor but honest inhabitants of Manchester. Although opening a century later, its uniform was again modelled, at Chetham's wish, on that of Christ's. Two details in an illustration of about 1939 show that even minor changes which had occurred in the latter were being copied: for example, the bands are superimposed instead of side by side and the shoes have very large buckles.[7] The only difference was the much larger and more obviously Tudor bonnet-shaped cap.

In 1875 the uniform was changed to Eton jackets and corduroy trousers, but the subsequent triumph of tradition was complete, as at Queen Elizabeth's Hospital. In Manchester it took another twenty years to come about.

Although the uniform has long since been abandoned, and moreover the school is now the coeducational Chetham's Hospital School of Music, the boy scholars still wear "the Tudor Clothes" on festival days.

Two other Blue Coat Schools that wore "Tudor" costume until recently are Bablake's in Coventry, an Elizabethan foundation, and Colston's in Bristol, founded in 1708 by a Governor of Christ's Hospital who had its uniform copied deliberately.

There follow two famous Blue Coat Schools which came into existence in the same period as Colston's. They were part of the wave of charity-school foundations encouraged by the Church of England after the departure of James II, most of them in the opening years of the eighteenth century. These two, unlike most of the others, were boarding schools from the start and gradually rose to the status of public schools; hence their position here rather than in Chapter 8.

WESTMINSTER BLUE COAT SCHOOL

There can still be seen in Caxton Street, Westminster, a statuette of a boy representing this school on the building put up for it by a local brewer in 1709. It was founded for poor boys in 1688, sponsored by Protestant parishioners in reply to the founding of a seminary in Westminster by the Jesuits. It preceded the Society for Promoting Christian Knowledge by ten years.

The uniform of 1709 is beautifully portrayed in the statuette. The boy's blue coat is, in style, typical of its own period, showing no influence by Christ's Hospital: it reaches only just low enough to cover the breeches, buttons all the way down and has no belt. The white neckbands are indeed like those of Christ's Hospital but these were worn by practically every charity school that arose in the next hundred years. The absence of any headgear is unusual.

There was still a distinctive dress, and twenty pupils were still being clothed on the foundation in the 1890s, when the school, as a separate institution, came to an end.

46. Statuette of Westminster Blue Coat boy, 1709, on former school building, Caxton Street, London. Contemporary style of dress except for bands (Courtesy: National Trust)

47. York Blue Coat School Sunday uniform, 1971, normally worn with white neckbands. Piping on the blue coat is yellow (Photograph of John Howard. Courtesy: Mrs Barbara Hutton)

YORK BLUE COAT SCHOOL

This, again a publicly supported charity school, was opened in 1705 for forty poor boys. As well as the three Rs, some training in spinning and weaving was given. In Yorkshire the woollen industry had prime importance.

The original clothing, supplied annually, comprised a blue coat and ordinary working-class clothes. The charity-school features were the white bands and the flat cap or bonnet; peculiar to York were the yellow facings of the coat and yellow edging to the blue cap.

Probably in the 1820s, the style of the suit was changed in favour of trousers and a smart square-cut tail coat. So it remains, for Sundays, still worn with the white bands, to the present day. The coat is finely piped with yellow and the cap still has its yellow edging, so that the uniform is both traditional and unique.

CHAPTER 5

Other boys' schools

THE KING'S SCHOOL, CANTERBURY

This school, founded as a cathedral school by St Augustine c. 598, ranks as the oldest in England. It was for general education, but cathedral choristers had preference. The qualifications for entry were, first, the ability to pass an examination and secondly poverty. Despite the latter stipulation the school was not free for all pupils until the sixteenth century. In 1541 it was entirely reorganized under Henry VIII and came to be known as the King's School, with at least fifty "King's Scholars" who were mostly boarders. Cloth of two qualities, to be made up into gowns for pupils and masters respectively, was issued every year before Christmas "to the intent that with new garments and new Spirits they may celebrate the birth of our Lord Jesus Christ".[1]

In 1665 the Dean and Chapter made the following rule:

That ye Ks [King's Scholars] shall have gowns of ye same colour i.e. of purple, or ye like. Without which gown (as well as his surplice) what boy so ever shall come to church shall be reputed absent ... it is required yt their surplices should be so timely washed and dried in the week time, as they may be ready for their use on Sundays.[2]

Between the years 1859–1873, the days of Dr Mitchinson, the King's Scholars were divided into three groups. Juniors were distinguished from probationers by a red tassel, and seniors wore gowns like those of Oxford scholars but with sleeves open from the shoulders down. From this time some licence was allowed at games: a portrait of a football team, 1882–3, shows players in striped vests, woollen caps and white trousers tucked into long stockings.

D.L. Edwards tells us that in 1886 the Headmaster, Field, "being a believer in symbols, introduced the first school uniform, a straw hat".[3] This was the only concession made to public school custom at the time, but today all wear conventional black trousers and black jackets or blazers with the school badge. Surplices, however, are still worn by some of the boys, since the school plays a considerable part in the cathedral services as it has done from time almost immemorial.

WESTMINSTER SCHOOL

In 1179 Pope Alexander III, reaffirming long-accepted practice for promoting education, made the maintenance of a school obligatory on all cathedral and monastic establishments. (The example of Canterbury was already centuries old.) The present Westminster School, which stems back to the fourteenth century, may owe its origin indirectly to this decree. The education was general, although some of the boys sang in the Abbey choir; all were fully maintained. Some accounts for the year 1307–8 record: "Cloth bought for the Master and boys with the shearing [a process of smoothing off the nap] of the same – 50s. and for fur for the master – 22d".[4]

The kind almoner occasionally provided kirtles (dresses) for the masters' wives. The gowns of the Singing Boys, and perhaps of all the scholars, were made of russet fustian [brown "mock-velvet", a fabric of coarse wool] lined with yellow. In 1479 the Singing Boys became a separate establishment.

After the dissolution of the Benedictine monastery the school continued, but the boys on the foundation came to be called "King's" or "Queen's" scholars. Some fee-paying "town boys" were admitted from 1543 onwards, but they were always kept to some extent apart and wore no distinctive dress. The school was formally refounded by Queen Elizabeth I. The livery at that time, given out every winter, consisted of a gown of "sad newe color" or of "London russet" (the cheap woollen fabric also used for Christ's Hospital's first uniform); under that was a doublet of sackcloth [coarse linen much used by the working classes] lined with canvas, and either Hampshire kersey "uper hoose" (the breech portion of what we call trunk hose) or – perhaps for best – "a payre of scabylonyans", which were fashionable close-fitting breeches. There were also a hat and shoes.

In the reign of James I the Bishop of Lincoln, who was Welsh, endowed four scholarships for boys who were natives of Wales or of the diocese of Lincoln. These were known as "Bishop's Boys" and were

48. Scholar of Westminster School, 1816. Special black gown with medieval-style hollow hanging sleeve tapering to a point at ground level. Mortarboard (Print in *History of the Colleges of Winchester, etc.*, published by R. Ackermann, 1816)

distinguished by wearing plum-coloured gowns until 1847 when this arrangement terminated.

A change in costume came at the very end of the eighteenth century, when trousers replaced breeches. This was in advance of most schools, as trousers were only just coming into fashion for men, though worn earlier by sailors and little boys. The gown, by now black, had probably changed little over the years. The mortarboard has clearly been taken over, in the eighteenth century, from the universities (Chapter 11). Scholars were never allowed out without this dress, and no added fripperies were permitted. Strict conventions still hold regarding its use.

WINCHESTER COLLEGE

What the Bishop of Winchester, William of Wykeham, brought into being in his magnificent buildings in 1394 was a large collegiate body incorporating the earliest English public school after King's, Canterbury. The Warden and ten Fellows, really chantry priests, were to lead a religious life in many ways like that of a monastery, but to be wholly independent of the monastic orders. The attached school differed from a monastic one in that education was to be the primary rather than a secondary object of the establishment as a whole. It was, in fact, intended from the beginning as a nursery for Wykeham's other foundation, New College, Oxford; and after the Reformation resident Fellows declined in numbers while the school grew.

The boys were to be the sons of parents of good social standing but in straitened circumstances, rather than those of the poorest class.[5]

There were to be only two schoolmasters, some of the older boys taking part in the teaching. There were also three chaplains, three lay clerks and sixteen choir boys (called "quiristers" to this day) for the chapel services. These last were working-class boys who waited on the Fellows, and even on the scholars, until the mid nineteenth century.

The whole establishment depended for everything, including clothes, on the founder's munificence, except for a handful of "commoners" who paid fees to the schoolmasters for the privilege of the education. The number of commoners grew slowly until it outstripped that of the "college boys" or scholars (earlier called "children") and formed the body of the school from the nineteenth century on. But the status and attire of the two groups were always distinct, the scholars being tied by ancient regulations while the commoners enjoyed less honour but a more fashionable dress.*

The livery of all the foundation members was prescribed in detail by Wykeham himself. It was never to be sold or pawned, or even given away except within the college, and then only after five years' wear. He did not want any ordinary "impecunious citizen to disport himself in the moulted plumage of scholars and Fellows".[6]

The amount of cloth allowed to each member varied strictly with status. The Warden, though surely not always the largest, received twelve yards, while the Fellows got eight yards each and a mere lay clerk only five. Scholars, who must indeed vary in dimensions, were each to have "enough for a gown and hood".

We are most fortunate in the survival to this day of a drawing[7] of the whole collegiate body made about 1463 by Thomas Chaundler who had been successively Warden of Winchester and of New College,

---

* But in 1571 sumptuary restrictions (as elsewhere at that time) were imposed from outside the College and these applied to scholars and commoners alike. There were to be no "great hose" (extravagantly distended "trunk hose" or breeches) nor must collars and ruffs be "wrought with silk or gold". Even "tutors and governors" must not "bye any gay apparel" (H. C. Adams *Wykehamica* ... (1878) p. 106).

49. Members of the College of Winchester in surplices, *c.* 1463. Founder, William of Wykeham, centre, wears an almuce of squirrel fur. Fellows, standing, have almuces probably lined with lambskin. One on right shows two pendant tails of fur. Scholars, the kneeling boys, have heads close shaven, some tonsured. (MS. C. 288 fol. 3. Courtesy: New College, Oxford)

Oxford (see Fig. 128 for his drawing of New College). The Winchester assembly is shown in chapel array, all wearing surplices. Many show the tonsure which, in fact, was statutory except for choristers and first-year scholars.

The Warden, being a priest of eminence, wears the almuce or cape for which he was allowed the best grey squirrel fur, thus resembling high dignitaries such as canons of cathedrals (who were nicknamed "grey amesses"). The Fellows and Headmaster wear hoods, with capes. These capes are unusual in that they lace up, but some of them show hanging in front the pair of fur "tails" which was so characteristic of ecclesiastical almuces. We know that the Fellows were granted annually a "*furrura*",[8] probably the humble lambskin, for use as a lining to these almuces.

Clearly no extra warmth was allowed to the remainder of the college, whether men or boys. Over their gowns (high-necked, with sleeves visible at the wrist) they have nothing but the surplice.*

The exact shape of the gowns was never described. But if the brass effigy of a scholar who died in 1434, while still a schoolboy, can be relied on, the gown took a form that was quite usual for civilian wear in the later fourteenth and early fifteenth centuries, except for its length (Fig. 51).** The sleeves are bag-shaped and, unlike those of today's scholars, long and closed at the wrist. Certain it is that the gowns of all the boys, quiristers included, were distinctly clerical in being ankle, or even heel, length (they were called *togae talares*). The Church Councils of London in 1342 and of York in 1367 condemned the wearing of short gowns by clerics and were very severe with those who wore them tucked up behind or open in front.

For the scholar the full-length gown persists to this day, though it has long been worn open in front and, if tucked up, evokes ridicule rather than reprehension. It remains the prime mark distinguishing him from commoners and is still presented to him in kind. So steeped was the school in tradition that even at the end of the nineteenth century the college tailor's apprentice announced deliveries of garments to scholars by calling out "*Togae, togae*"![9]

The sleeve of the gown changed, probably in the eighteenth century, from a full-length one to a unique, puffed-out, elbow-sleeve. A sleeved waistcoat of special design is worn underneath. This distended sleeve, gathered into a band, is described by Rich in connection with the college boys' habit of "bagging" each others' belongings: "the sleeve of our college gown . . . seemed really to have been made on purpose to hold contraband goods. From a loaf to a cup, nothing came amiss to it."[10] The objects were thrust in through the arm hole and held by the binding at the elbow.

"Contraband" indeed was what the future naturalist, Frank Buckland, once used the sleeve for, when a scholar, about 1840. He was

---

* The boys' outer garment has been taken by some writers for a gown, not a sur-plice—e.g. T. Kirby in *Archaeologia* vol. LIII, 231—but Leach (op. cit.) has no doubt it is a surplice and the same is implied by M. R. James (quoting the authority on academic dress, E. C. Clark) in his monograph on the manuscript itself (Roxburgh Club, 1916). Moreover, since the Warden and Fellows are dressed for chapel, it is unlikely that the boys are not.

** In early fifteenth-century brasses, where this type of gown is frequent, it is generally drawn short enough at least to show the ankles. Compare J. Page-Phillips *Children on Brasses* (1970) Figs. 9, 11, 16.

50. Scholar of Winchester, *c.* 1949. Gown with special puffed sleeve (After photograph facing p. 156, J. D'E. Firth *Winchester College*, 1949)

not above a bit of poaching and one day was obliged to swim the river to escape from the water-meadows keeper. "The sleeves of our college gowns", he wrote, "acted as pockets and I had two trout in one sleeve and one in the other." So secure was the bag that although the trout "came to life again" in the water, he landed without losing his fish.[11]

For Buckland the college waistcoat also had a special use and we are told that he never learnt his lessons better than when a dormouse or a snake was twisting and wriggling inside it.[12]

As regards the gown's colour it is interesting that Wykeham precluded black, white, russet and grey to avoid any resemblance to monks' and friars' habits. He also forbade variegated colours, which might look frivolous, but the gowns must be *colorati*; there is no evidence as to what was chosen. However, by 1563 "cimmerian", a very dark colour, almost black, had become the rule, and soon it was quite black and has remained so ever since.[13] The waistcoat, seventeenth century on, was also black.

Pantaloons or trousers had taken the place of breeches for scholars by 1829, but a good many years after they had been adopted by "commoners". These last followed the fashions of the day and imposed their own conventions; for example, a twelve-year-old new boy in the 1830s had to appear in the grotesquely high and spreading starched collar worn by contemporary beaux.[14]

For foundationers, even underwear was taken care of. There is a record of the cost of linen supplied to two brothers, "founder's kin" scholars, for making their shirts and pants in the years 1397–9.[15]

As to headwear, in the Middle Ages the Fellows and scholars had cloth hoods such as were worn by everyone in the fourteenth century and by humble people in the fifteenth. The Warden, being an eminent ecclesiastic, would wear a soft black cap, the *pileus*, ceremonially (Fig.

49). After the hood disappeared, there was, until at least the close of the seventeenth century, no headgear for the boys at all; indeed hats were forbidden. But in 1778 hats, for a time, became compulsory for "leave out" or going to "hills" and "mead" for exercise, perhaps because gentlemen were never without a hat out of doors, now that wigs were out of fashion. In the nineteenth century it was a top hat, if any, and in the twentieth the same persists for Sundays. On weekdays straw hats, boater-style, are *de rigueur* all the year round for going into the town, and some interesting conventions are recalled by Dr Kenneth Hutton[16] about their trimming. A wide black band was worn in the first year, a wide coloured one in the second and third, a narrow coloured band in the fourth year and a narrow black band in the fifth. Prefects have always had sartorial privileges. They may go without these hats and may even wear coloured ties and double-breasted waistcoats!

An interesting branch of the school is composed of the quiristers. The founder laid down that they were to be "poor and needy . . . under twelve . . . of honourable conversation . . . able to sing".[17] At first they were supplied with surplices, but for gowns depended on the cast-offs

51. *Left* Scholar of Winchester in long gown, 1434 (Brass effigy of John Kent, Headbourne Worthy, near Winchester). *Right* Arms of Winchester College. Shield bears Wykeham's own arms with the red rose as worn in quiristers' caps today (After design by Kruger Gray, twentieth century)

of other members of the college. Then in 1420 a generous local worthy arranged that they should have gowns like those of the scholars. In 1450 quiristers' gowns were of "blue or green medley" cloth and in the seventeenth century settled down to "cimmerian", once more like the scholars'. In about 1760 quiristers were again differentiated, wearing coats instead of gowns. What they scored in convenience they lost in charm. The nineteenth-century uniform, as worn up to the 1860s, was recalled by A. K. Cook[18] as "quaint reddish brown suits with swallow tail coats and brass buttons" and it was later changed to an "ugly serviceable grey" relieved only by silvered buttons bearing the college arms. It sounds a little like a servant's livery, which in a sense it was. There was a waistcoat and trousers, a peaked and braided stiff cloth cap and, until 1878, the usual top hat for Sundays.[19]

This outfit was updated in 1906, changing to a navy blue Norfolk suit. "The dress is a uniform but does not proclaim itself as such".[20] The headgear was either a straw hat like the scholars' or a blue cloth cap of the usual schoolboy type, but bearing now the bit of heraldry that once belonged to the buttons – a rose, extracted from Wykeham's arms, as a lingering memorial of the great founder.

ETON COLLEGE

Founded on the lines of Winchester in 1440 by King Henry VI, Eton College, by its statutes was to include seventy boys on the endowment who had to be of good character, "poor and needy". There were also to be some others, not fully maintained, called "oppidans", most of whom were fee-paying.

The statutes stated that the scholars and choristers should be supplied with ale, clothing and bedding. As at Winchester, in medieval times all were expected to enter the church and each scholar received yearly a suitable black gown and a hood. In a period of abuse in the seventeenth century there were complaints that the gown was "coarse and short". According to L. Cust, long before this, the oppidans had ceased to wear gowns at all and the garment "became the mark of a King's Scholar, who was hence styled 'togatus'". His sobriquet "tug" may or may not be connected with this word.[21] The gown was later restored to its full length and then had what may well have been its original form. The full funnel-shaped sleeves ended just above the elbow in front, but fell to about knee level behind (Fig. 52). This had been a fashionable sleeve in the early fifteenth century but by 1440 was scarcely worn except by the working classes. By the seventeenth century it had an academic connotation.

52. Scholar of Eton College, 1816
(Print in *History of the Colleges of
Winchester, etc.*, published by R.
Ackermann, 1816)

Little else is known about the costume until we come to a description
by that lively observer, Carl Philip Moritz, in his *Travels in England* in
1782:

Just before I got to Windsor, I passed Eton College, one of the first public
schools in England, and perhaps in the world . . . I suppose it was during the
hours of recreation . . . I saw the boys in great numbers walking and running
up and down. Their dress struck me particularly. From the biggest to the least,
they all wore black cloaks, or gowns (over coloured cloaths) through which
there was an aperture for their arms. They also wore besides, a square hat or
cap that seemed to be covered with velvet, such as our clergymen in many
places wear.

By the nineteenth century the gown was probably the only garment
normally given as such to the scholars. But another distinction held,
for a time, among the older boys; oppidans wore trousers or pantaloons as soon as these were fashionable, but the "collegers" or

scholars continued until 1814 to wear knee breeches, tied with fine cord and fastened at the knee with gilt buttons.

The famous Eton jacket, worn from about 1798 by all the boys below a certain height, was originally blue or red but was changed to black in 1820 when the boys went into mourning at the death of George III. They have stayed there ever since. The turned-down starched Eton collar, smart compared with the earlier soft band, came in at about the middle of the nineteenth century.

A tall hat was introduced in 1820, when it replaced the mortarboard so aptly described by C. P. Moritz. The silk top hat was essential for a gentleman at this time, and the social status of the school was already very high. The mortarboard had been taken over from the universities.

In the eighteenth century, Cust tells us, the collegers (the younger ones at least) "had many of the degradations of a charity school" and occupied a "position of inferiority in the opinion of oppidans".[22] But nowhere is the rise in status of endowed people better illustrated than at Eton, where it was meteoric. In the later nineteenth century the oppidans had so far increased in numbers as to leave the scholars in a small minority, and then in 1876 new statutes decreed that the scholars should be chosen for intellectual ability and not poverty. Thus they became "naturally the élite of the school"[23] and indeed often grew up to be among the élite of the country as a whole. The gown became a symbol of this dignity.

"The playing fields of Eton" are famous but we hear little about suitable clothing for games until the nineteenth century. Even for break (that is what Moritz witnessed) the boys sound uncomfortably clad in his day, since collegers were obliged to keep on their gowns. For play hours, however, the nineteenth century saw improvements. The costume of the cricket players in 1820 was described as "a white jean jacket, fitting easily to the figure with the blue tie of Eton; nankeen shorts and ribbed silk stockings, with socks tightly folded over the ankle and the white hat jauntily put on".[24] Sports clothes would only be supplied free if beyond the purse of the boy's parents.

Eton was a college in the same sense as Winchester. Besides the school there were Fellows and chaplains and thirteen bedesmen, all of whom were gowned through the endowment fund. These have all long disappeared. But despite the abolition of the old statutes in 1869, the scholars themselves are still given their gowns and, in the words of one of the masters in 1974, it is pleasing "to find a decorous tradition kept up without the need of a mandate".

CHARTERHOUSE SCHOOL

Founded by Thomas Sutton in 1611, Charterhouse was at first a hospital for eighty poor men as well as forty "children or poor men who wanted means to bring them up". It was built on the land formerly occupied by the Carthusian monastery in London, but the school was removed in 1872 to the neighbourhood of Godalming. About forty men are still retained on the original site.

Free scholars were nominated by the Governors. After fee-paying pupils were also admitted, the free scholars were known as "Gownboys" and the twelve junior Gownboys were "basinites". The scholars' costume underwent little important change for two centuries. "Every Gownboy, however senior, was supplied with a straight-cut jerkin or short jacket of black cloth which could be buttoned up in front in cold weather."[25] (Its large collar, which could be turned up, was probably a late addition.) Knee breeches were worn until at least 1832. The gown (a specimen is preserved in the school museum) was of black cloth with sleeves which, below the armhole, hang down into a slender point like those of a Westminster scholar, the tip being bound round with strong thread. Low shoes called "gowsers" were worn and a hat (of unknown shape), which was changed in 1805 for a cap.

Example was followed by the introduction of Eton collars for the Under School. Oddly enough the mortarboard was adopted for the Upper School at some time in the nineteenth century, while at Eton it

53. Scholar of Charterhouse, 1842 (*Illustrated London News* vol. I, 44)

had already been given up in 1820: hence the academic appearance which struck the *Illustrated London News* in 1842. In an article on London's charities it speaks of Thomas Sutton, "the munificent founder of the Charterhouse whose memory is worthy of all reverence" and continues: "The boys of his school are perfectly collegiate in their appearance. They wear the cap and gown of the university, with the long hanging sleeve."

In 1872, coinciding with the move to Godalming, the usual relaxation of dress occurred. The whole school went about bare-headed and the scholars no longer wore gowns. The uniform became a conventional black jacket and striped trousers for all. The choice of scholars by nomination and their free issue of dress came to an end and, as the school's historian E. H. Jameson puts it, " 'Gownboy' remains no more than a hallowed name".

DULWICH COLLEGE

In founding Dulwich College in 1619, Edward Alleyn's provisions are worth quoting:

Each poor scholar was to have every year (at Easter) and oftener if need be, one surplice of white calico, one upper coat of good cloth of sad colour, the bodice lined with canvas and the skirts with white cotton, one pair of drawers of white cotton, two canvas shirts with buckram bands to them, two pairs of knit stockings, shoes as often as need shall require, two round bands, a girdle and a black cap.

The girdled "upper coat" was doubtless a long one like that at Christ's Hospital; we know that in the nineteenth century this was its style. Apparently the "petticoat" was already dropping out of schoolboys' dress in 1619. The antiquated uniform was abolished in 1857, earlier than in most public schools.

GREEN COAT SCHOOLS

Much less common than blue as a colour for uniforms was green, held by some to be an unlucky colour. Sometimes it was chosen as the personal taste of a founder, but there was a variety of other reasons, as we shall see.

William Shelton's wish that the children of his free day school in St Giles-in-the-Fields, London, founded 1672, should be dressed in green, like his almsfolk, is mentioned in Chapter 12. At that time there were no Blue Coat schools close by and we can only suppose that Shelton had a liking for that colour. The scholars were to have a green coat at 6s every year and the Master a green gown at 20s. The tradition held in this small school until it closed in 1815.[26] The founder's name is commemorated in Shelton Street, St Giles.

Other such schools up and down the country had green uniforms arbitrarily chosen, but some resorted to this colour to distinguish the children from those in other local schools. In Westminster, for example, Blue and Grey Coat Schools were already in existence when the Green Coat was founded there in 1622. As this began as a children's home it is discussed in Chapter 9.

The Green Coat School, Greenwich, was a free boarding school in the parish of East Greenwich, established in 1672. It was founded by one of the "Clerks of the Green Cloth" to Charles II, and it seems possible that the colour green was chosen here, in allusion to the founder's office.

William Sladall's will, dated 1801, left money in trust for establishing and supporting a Sunday school in Kirkby Kendal in the former County of Westmoreland, now Cumbria. The thirty-five boys were to have green coats and the twelve girls green gowns and bonnets. "If any surplus should remain, this was to be laid out in buying green baize to be made into waistcoats or small clothes [breeches] for the most necessitous of the boys".[27] Here, the material for the coats was doubtless the locally made, coarse woollen cloth, chosen on economic grounds. It was often dyed green and called "Kendal green".

Touches of green were often used to distinguish the dress of boys who had a particular status in a school where the uniform was blue, for example at the Blue Coat Hospital, Chester (now a famous boys' public school). When day boys were admitted there, they were distinguished by the green colour of their caps, and they constituted what was known as the "Green Cap School."

NORTHAMPTON BLUE, GREEN AND ORANGE COATS

We conclude this section with the Northampton schools, since the town had not only Blue Coat, but also Green Coat, Orange Coat and even Brown Coat boys, and the interrelationship of the first three is interesting. Moreover the history of their uniforms over nearly two centuries can be pieced together from various sources.

The Corporation Charity School was founded *c.* 1753. The uniform provided being blue, the school was known as the "Blue Coat".

In 1761 one Gabriel Newton contributed a sum for the clothing and education of twenty-five poor boys in this school, who were to be picked out in green and called the "Green Coat" boys.

54. Lead statuettes from Northampton Corporation Charity School, *c.* 1761. *Left* Probably a Blue Coat boy; he holds a peaked cap. *Right* Probably a Green Coat boy in same school. See text (Courtesy: Northampton Central Museum)

The first written record regarding the clothing seems to be a minute by the Corporation (as trustees of this and other charities) made in 1796: "Ordered that the Charity School Boys and poor Men clothed on the 29th of May have in future good ground Lamb Leather* Breeches not exceeding fourteen shillings a pair, and that they be clothed in good Cloth at 3s. 6d. a yard and flat yellow Mettal Buttons thereto."[28]

More detail is given in the form of two statuettes of boys, now in the Central Museum, Northampton. They were taken from niches in the school building put up in Bridge Street in 1811. The two figures are identical in form except for their arms and what they carry. Made of lead, they appear to have been turned out of the same mould except for these parts. They are typical of the charity-school statuettes dis-

* Probably leather from lambskin, ground with a grindstone to give it a finish, like shammy.[29]

cussed in Chapter 7 and show the now almost obligatory white bands. The style of their coats suggests a date in the 1760s and they were doubtless made for the old building and moved to the new. As 1761 was the year when the Green Coat boys were added to the school, it seems almost certain that one of the two figures represents the Blue Coat boys and the other the Green. Unhappily, after repaintings and deterioration, the present brownish colour of their coats is no guide (they are reputed to have both been red in the late nineteenth century!), but confirmation lies in the headgear that the boys carry under their arms. One has the typical charity-school style of round flat cap with a tuft. The other, having a sort of jockey cap with a peak, which was unusual, must surely be the Blue Coat boy. L. W. Dickens, an Old Boy of the school, states in an article, in 1967, that within living memory "the Blue Coat boys wore longish blue coats, long trousers, red waistcoats with brass buttons, blue *peaked caps* with a red ribbon and a red tassel on top".[30] Except for the trousers the description could well apply to this eighteenth-century statuette. In 1898 the uniform and even the boots were still made to measure.

Green Coat boys had ceased to be distinguished by the 1890s, but the blue uniform persisted until the school came to an end in 1921. However, a tinted photograph[31] taken in that year shows that there had been two modifications, evidently made in the nineteenth century, besides the introduction of trousers. First, the cap had been turned into a flat sailor cap, reflecting the current liking for a nautical appearance in boys, without losing the peak. Secondly, the coat had been altered to a morning coat with tails and a red stand collar.

With this Victorian outfit the white neckbands were still worn in 1921 and provide one of the most striking examples of their survival.

The Driden (later Dryden and Herbert) Free Charity or Orange School was founded in 1709 for the clothing, educating and apprenticing of about twenty boys. John Driden ordained in his will of 1707 that the boys' uniform should be picked out with an unusual colour: "A blue coat faced with orange colour, with brass buttons, a knit cap and a pair of stockings of orange colour".[32] This scheme was adhered to except for a temporary lapse which was corrected in 1819. The trustees seem to have been extra conscientious, and the fund extra flush, when they ordered:

that the following alterations and additions to the Clothing of the Boys be made when they are next cloathed, namely that the facings of the Coat, waistcoat and breeches, the working of the buttonholes and the stockings shall in future be of an orange colour as directed by the Will instead of Red as they now are. That each Boy shall be allowed yearly one waistcoat one shirt and

55. Boys of Northampton Corporation Charity School, 1921. *Left* "Blue Boy". *Right* "Orange Boy". See text (Tinted photos. Courtesy: Northampton Central Museum)

one pair of stockings in addition to what they now have and that the sleeves of each Boy's coat shall be lined and one pocket made to the same. That the allowance for the shoes for the Boys shall be 4s 6d a pair instead of 3s 6d as now allowed. That the allowance for the coats, waistcoats and breeches shall be at the rate 3s 6d again instead of 3s 2d as now allowed, and that sufficient additional cloth be procured for making each Boy's waistcoat.[33]

In 1854 the Corporation School, having spare accommodation, offered to take in and teach the Orange boys. From then on, the Orange boys joined the Blue and Green, although the respective charities were still separately administered.

The Old Boy's article quoted above shows that there was a contrast in style as well as colour between the Orange boys' uniforms and the others'. The writer even remarks that the Blue Coat boys wore boots and the

Orange boys shoes. His description of the uniform agrees almost exactly with what was worn in the school's last year, 1921, as evidenced by the tinted photograph of an Orange boy, fellow to the one already mentioned showing the Blue. The orange facings, and even orange button-holing, were adhered to, also the blue waistcoat. But instead of trousers the Orange boy still wears breeches (blue with brass buttons), and instead of a sailor cap he sticks to the tam-o-shanter style (orange with red tuft).

Blue Coat boys were mainly selected from tradesmen's sons, while the Orange Coats were still genuine "poor boys".[34] Bands, in the twentieth century, were perhaps so closely associated with Christ's Hospital and its public school status that they had an élitist connotation. Thus while the Orange boy wears an ordinary collar and black tie, the Blue Coat boy has bands. Otherwise the Orange boy is the more old-fashioned, his breeches giving him a plebeian appearance.

The contrast between the two uniforms, worn in the same school at the same time, must have rubbed in the class distinction in an unforgettable manner.

CHOIR SCHOOLS

An interesting class of endowed school was that attached to a cathedral for the training and general education of its choir. (Its relation to the "cathedral school" varied. Compare King's School, Canterbury.)

The choristers were always provided with their surplices by the ecclesiastical distributors of charity constituting the "Almonry" and were often entirely clothed thereby. Since many such schools existing in England were run on the same lines we have arbitrarily chosen the Salisbury Choristers' School as an example.[35]

Bishop Simon of Ghent in 1314 founded this Song School for the choristers of Salisbury. Their gowns, supplied annually, were coloured blue. One account calls it "marbelon blod", "blod" meaning blue and "marbelon" marbled, streaked. Marbled materials were much used for servants' liveries, perhaps cheap because they could be woven, like "mixed cloth", of oddments of wool. Each gown had a "lamb-skin hood" attached. This medieval, warmly lined hood, usually worn out of doors, would be needed in an unheated cathedral.

In the Middle Ages the boys had to be tonsured and a barber was employed.

After a decline in the intervening period, the restoration of Charles II in 1660 brought a revival of ceremony in church and consequently of the status of the choir. The boys were given quite elaborate waist-

56. Chorister of St Paul's Cathedral
Choir School in Eton suit, Eton
collar and mortarboard, 1930s (After
illustration in Wallace Clare: *The
Historic Dress of the English Schoolboy* [1940])

coats and smart new livery coats, probably of the usual knee length, each even displaying a shoulder knot. This was a bunch of ribbon loops ornamenting the right shoulder, a decorative fashion of the time.

In the early nineteenth century the choristers' suits were changed again to comply with fashion. Every Whit Sunday each boy received a new suit which now consisted of a claret-coloured tail coat of broadcloth, very smart with brass buttons; a waistcoat, trousers, shoes and white socks; also a black satin cravat, a white linen neck frill or ruff and a tall black beaver hat. At Christmas in alternate years he got an overcoat with shoulder capes.

In 1853 the outfit was changed yet again. Eton jackets replaced the tail coats and were sometimes chocolate coloured instead of claret. Flat-topped peaked caps of the same colour replaced the beaver hats, and "pepper-and-salt"* trousers were worn. The frills continued in use and became a distinguishing mark of the Salisbury choristers until 1935, after which they were worn only in the cathedral. Perhaps because they were in the public eye in church, choristers tended to be

* Speckled, the general effect being grey. This was fashionable for country wear.

rather well dressed at all times compared with other boys of their age. Those of King's College Chapel can still be seen in the streets of Cambridge, walking in line, with top hats and rolled umbrellas. Thus the Eton suit, which was correct wear for gentlemanly young boys until the First World War, lasted until long afterwards in choir schools. It neatly combined conservatism with smartness.

CHAPTER 6

Girls' schools

As has already been seen, many schools of early foundation included girls as well as boys, but the girls were generally, if not always, taught separately. In course of time some of these schools split into two, and other schools for girls only were also founded. We shall deal here with the girls' school of Christ's Hospital and with a few striking examples of girls' schools in the main category.

CHRIST'S HOSPITAL GIRLS' SCHOOL

"Christ's Hospital" always included girls and, in the oil painting at the boys' school depicting the presentation of its charter by Edward VI, the sexes are shown in equal numbers.

At first the girls lived in separate wards of the London school but gradually, with a move into the country, they became nearly autonomous and they now flourish as a famous girls' secondary school at Hertford on the site of the school which in the eighteenth and nineteenth centuries they shared with the small boys.

As we have seen, their first gowns, in 1552, were of russet cotton and they wore a kerchief, doubtless white, which must have looked humbly medieval compared with the headdresses usual at that time. When their dresses, called "coates", were changed to blue, the skirt was open in front in the style of the time and so exposed a yellow underskirt, the petticoat. Thus they neatly matched the boys, except that they wore an apron which was white, blue or green.

The headdress at an early but uncertain date has been described as a "coif and peak".[1] The coif would be a close-fitting white cap and the peak a triangular piece of white linen fastened so as to point over the

57. Christ's Hospital girls, depicted at ceremony of presentation of charter by Edward VI. See text. Bishop Ridley is kneeling, Governors have staves. A schoolmistress stands on right (Detail of engraving by Augustus Fox for William Trollope's *History of the Royal Foundation of Christ's Hospital*, 1834, after a painting at the Hospital by an unknown artist, probably second quarter of the seventeenth century)

forehead. It is not shown in any known picture. This had been a fashion in the fifteenth century, when unmarried girls wore a peak over their otherwise uncovered loose hair. The seventeenth-century "widow's peak" was similar but black.

Both the "charter" pictures (middle and late seventeenth-century) show the girls in the plain white caps with side lappets that were common at that time for humbler people. At the neck is what looks like a very large plain white collar but was probably called a handkerchief. This was a usual garment in the seventeenth century and was especially, when quite plain, worn by Puritans.

In the Edward VI charter picture the dresses are blue open gowns, over green underskirts – possibly the artist confused the underskirts with the aprons, which were often green and which he omits altogether. Sleeves are turned up with red; the long gloves are brown.

Brown

Blue

Green

58. Statuette of Christ's Hospital girl on the school built in Hertford in 1778 (After photo. Courtesy Miss E. M. Tucker)

B.C.Phillipson 1977

As the Rev. William Trollope remarks in his *History . . . of Christ's Hospital* (1834), the girls were trained "for the humbler walks of life wherein they may be expected to move" and, as we have seen, there was inevitably a lot of sewing. It is not surprising that aprons were always a feature of the uniform. In 1717 the Governors of the Hospital noted the need for "a sufficient supply of green say [serge] to be made into aprons for the use of the Maiden children at Hertford" and in 1759 it was decided they should have three new blue aprons every year.

They were then still receiving "Three Peaks" and "Three Coifs" annually; the peak must have distinguished the Christ's Hospital girls from all others for over a century.

A painted statuette of a girl in uniform was mounted on the new building in Hertford in 1778 and happily still stands there. Unlike their brothers the girls had been freed from anything Tudor in their dress (the gown even has the Polonaise form so fashionable at the time) and they had at last been allowed to abandon the peak. The outfit is like that worn at the time in charity schools of eighteenth-century foundation (compare Chapter 7), for it features a very plain white cap, a wide white collar* and an apron. But the colours are those of Christ's Hospital – blue for the gown and brown, as an approximation to yellow, for the underskirt; the apron is green and this came to be its standard colour.

Probably about the turn of the century the collar was replaced by a "tippet", again like that of a charity girl (compare pages 136–7). In about 1832 a pupil, Susannah Holmes, aged about fifteen, sat twice for her portrait to Arthur Oliver. The paintings now hang in the school showing exactly what her uniform was like. Over her dark blue dress she wears the green apron and now, up to the neck, a white, starched cape, the tippet. This one does up at the back and has a two-inch ruff at the neck. The plain white cap is shaped like those in Fig. 90.

Nightcaps were discarded in 1834, except when specially recommended by the medical officer. Tippets and day caps were not given up until 1874[2] at which time the committee decided that, while preserving the colours as before, "a neat useful dress, uniform, but more assimilated to that of the day be introduced". The dress was still nearly foot length with a high neck and long tight sleeves.

Some interesting formalities arose over aprons. In 1899 senior girls were distinguished by wearing black aprons, not an unusual garment for ladies, while juniors had the white pinafores that were popular for small girls. But the traditional green apron came back. The following particulars are worth recording for what they reveal both of changing attitudes and of attachment to tradition in 1975.

The green apron today is worn by all members of the Sixth Form. Until July 1974 this was earned by merit in the course of the Sixth Form but since September all the Sixth Form share equally the privileges and responsibilities and wear the green apron for doing jobs about the place and for meals. Junior girls wear blue pinafores and Fifth Formers earn a black apron by good behaviour.[3]

The social and educational standing of the school rose rapidly in the nineteenth and twentieth centuries but the uniform is still a free gift. And, when in 1921 the now liberated girls went into blazers, these were in the "school colours" of blue and yellow, to recall the coats and petticoats of long ago.

---

* The collar and bodice have been more correctly painted recently than they were a little earlier.

An amusing story recounted by Samuel Pepys, who was Vice-President of Christ's Hospital, 1699–1703, is worth quoting:

Two wealthy citizens are lately dead and left their estates, one to a blue-coat boy, and the other to a blue-coat girl in Christ's Hospital. The extraordinariness of which has led some of the Magistrates to carry it on to a match, which is ended in a public wedding – he in his habit of blue satin, led by two girls, and she in blue with an apron of green and petticoat yellow, all of sarsnet, led by two of the boys of the house through Cheapside to Guildhall Chapel where they were married by the Dean of St Pauls she given by my Lord Mayor. (Letter to Mrs Steward, 20 September 1695.)

59. Uniform of Red Maids under the age of fifteen, 1910: white tippets over their red dresses and short hair (Detail from painting by William Titcombe at the school. Courtesy: the Headmistress)

RED MAIDS' SCHOOL, BRISTOL

John Whitson founded and endowed this boarding school for the daughters of "deceased and decayed freemen and burgesses of Bristol",[4] by his will dated 1634. He ordained that the girls should be "new clothed once in two years with red clothes and receive other apparel; and that there be provided for them in decent manner linen, stockings, shoes and sheets, with other necessaries as often as there shall be occasion".[5] The girls have been dressed faithfully in red uniforms from that day to this.

Over the red dresses they wore a bibless white apron and a white neck handkerchief, this being a triangular linen covering for the shoulders and bosom with two corners in front and one behind (compare page 138). In the nineteenth century the handkerchief took on the

60. Red Maids, boarders, in formal dress *c.* 1970. Two in centre, being Upper VI girls, wear fichu instead of round tippet. Dresses shortened in concession to fashion (Courtesy: the Headmistress)

more fashionable name of "fichu" but remained fundamentally the same. However from late Georgian or early Victorian times it was retained only for the girls who stayed on at school after the age of fourteen. For the others it was replaced by the increasingly popular charity girl's garment, the round white tippet.

Red was a very rare colour for charity dresses and may well be explained by the "Bristowe red" dye for which the city was famous (compare Kendal green used at Sladall's School, Chapter 5). The girls also had red cloaks, but these were common for women in many country districts. What is remarkable is their persistence at the Red Maids' School, where red or red-and-black-check cloaks have been worn nearly continuously up to the present day. After a change in favour of red coats for about fifty years, the cloaks were actually brought back for the sake of old times in 1959, for boarders.

In the 1850s the girls' handwork still included carding "nippins" (waste wool) for petticoats.

The past is honoured in our own time not only in the everyday red uniform but in the finishing touches that have become ceremonial wear. These are confined to the boarders, in recognition of the founder's original intention, and they wear full traditional dress on Founder's Day and other state occasions. It comprises, for all, a white apron over the red dress, and a Victorian straw bonnet with blue ribbon and white frill. For most there is also a white tippet, but the Upper VI has inherited the even more venerable fichu, proper to the older girls. Thus the costumes, individually and collectively, recall more than one period of the past, but they undoubtedly have a very attractive appearance in modern times.[6]

SCHOOLS IN YORK, WOKINGHAM AND READING

Established in 1705, the Grey Coat School for Girls in York was one of the spate of charity schools founded in the early eighteenth century by public subscription, the majority of which are dealt with in Chapters 7 and 8. It is placed here because it was rare in being a boarding school and for girls only.

The uniform was grey; the following is a list of clothes supplied to each girl in 1786, the time when Mrs Cappe and other ladies had reorganized the school:

3 pairs of Stockings	1 Day Cap
2 pairs of Shoes	2 Pockets
2 petticoats	2 Gowns
2 shifts	2 Bedgowns

2 pairs of Stays	2 Blue and White aprons
2 Nightcaps	2 Aprons
2 Blue and White Handkerchiefs	1 Band or Sunday Handkerchief
[Neckerchiefs]	1 Cloak
2 Hats	2 Pocket Handkerchiefs
1 pair of Garters	1 pair of Worsted Mittens[7]

The bedgown was a hip-length jacket bodice worn with a petticoat (i.e. a skirt), a common working-class style of dress. The pockets were small bags which were tied on round the waist under the dress and were usually reached through a placket hole.

The girls had to learn the usual textile skills and also knitted mittens and quilted their old gowns into petticoats.

The ten oldest girls had a green stuff dress, instead of the usual grey, and the girl who superintended the wool-spinning was allowed a scarlet cloak and a white apron to be worn when going out or at church.

In the nineteenth century all the girls were at last given outdoor cloaks and with these went straw bonnets. White aprons for all became the rule, muslin in the later years; also white frilled caps and white

61. Girl at Grey Coat School, York, ?1905. The triangular tippet, with its front points tucked under the apron, has tiny collar and white bow. (Photograph in *Bicentenary Souvenir of Grey Coat School, York, 1705–1905*)

triangular tippets like those of many other charity girls. All three garments were still worn on special occasions in 1929 but, as a concession
to fashion, the Regency bonnets were changed for hats in 1881.
These were probably the stiff straw hats which were one day to become
an equally outdated symbol, that of upper-class boarding school girls.
The punishment clothes used at this school were startling enough to be
included in Chapter 3.

For comparison with the York Grey Coat, there is the Palmer charity at
Wokingham, Berks. In this and the next three schools most of the lessons
were practical. Martha Palmer in 1713 left the wherewithal for running a
small industrial school, the "Maiden School", Wokingham. Her
detailed scheme must have given considerable job satisfaction to the
girls. The shifts they made and wore, the stockings they knitted and wore
were made respectively from the flax and worsted, provided free, that
they themselves had spun.[8]

Nearer in date to the Grey Coat, and like it in being a public venture
and in having ladies on the governing board, was the Green School,
Reading, founded 1779. The actual uniform shown in Fig. 62 is of un-

62. Reading Green School uniform
made and originally worn by a
pupil, 1903–7. Dark green dress,
white tippet, apron and sleeved
mittens, black bonnet (Uniform in
Reading Museum. Abigail Tucker,
as model, photographed by her
father. Courtesy: Reading Museum
and Art Gallery)

certain date but its survival in its entirety is of considerable interest as it exemplified charity school outfits as they would have appeared in the eighteenth century. A photograph in Reading Museum, of a pupil in Edwardian times, shows a similar attire, with the white cap that was still worn indoors.

An account of the school written about 1800[9] enumerates the garments provided when a girl was apprenticed out. The list is remarkably like that given to the school leavers in York in 1786. The main difference is that bonnets were given instead of hats – a reflection of change in fashion; once begun, bonnets persisted in the school itself until it ended in 1922.

DAY SCHOOLS

As examples of country day schools endowed by the local aristocracy we might take one in Hertfordshire and one in Wiltshire, each founded by a Lady Bountiful partly for the purpose of providing a source of preparatorily trained domestics.

A Countess of Salisbury in 1732 founded a charity school, the Countess Anne, Hatfield for forty poor girls, not far from her own very stately home. Twenty of them, whom she would choose herself while she lived, were to be paid for and clothed by her endowment. They were to be given once in two years a "gown and coat" (the "coat" being an exposed underskirt) of coarse brown linsey wool, a cap, a band and gloves, stays, stockings and shoes. This humble uniform was in typical charity style of the time and, as recorded in a contemporary sampler, was almost exactly the same as that seen in Fig. 78.

Countess Anne's underlying motive was clear. The girls were to be "taught on the Foundation to Read, Sew, Knit and Mark in order to fit them for Service".[10] The best foundation scholar was to be rewarded, on leaving, with a voucher for £3 for "draperies" with which to start her life as a servant; the money must be spent in the local shops.

A century later than Countess Anne's, but again founded by a lady of the local aristocracy to promote a supply of servants, was the Park School at Wilton, Wiltshire. Immortalized as it has been by Edith Olivier, we can do no better than quote her words. She recalls watching, as a small girl in the 1880s, a little procession going to church at Wilton,

composed of the Park School girls. They came from the Pavilion in the park, which Lady Georgiana Herbert [daughter of Lady Pembroke of Wilton House] . . . some time in the eighteen-thirties, had converted into a school for the daughters of workmen on the estate. In winter these girls wore cloaks made of lovely warm crimson cloth, and in summer they had little grey shoulder capes . . .

Needlework was their craft and the making and marking of the Wilton house linen was their duty. When they left school and each received her grown-up outfit packed in its own little travelling trunk, they were much in demand . . .[11]

BECKETT AND SERGEANT SCHOOL, NORTHAMPTON

Many of the girls' schools, like those for boys, had blue uniforms and were therefore called Blue Coat schools. For instance one was established at Greenwich in 1752 and another in York in 1786. The one in Northampton is an interesting example. Like the foregoing, this was a privately endowed charity day school for girls. Though closely associated with All Saints Church it was not a church school. It is interesting in that the development of its costume is epitomized in three pleasing works of art.

Two sisters, Mrs Sergeant and Mrs Beckett, were pioneers, for they set up their Blue Coat school for thirty girls in 1738 before Northampton had even got a Blue Coat school for boys. Their girls' school was to give a "practical" education with stress on domestic subjects but, as

63. Plaque representing a girl of Beckett and Sergeant Blue Coat School, Northampton, in 1740s (Stone carving in Central Museum, Northampton, closely related to the plaque on the founders' tomb, dated 1747, in All Saints Church)

64. Statuette on Beckett and
Sergeant School, Northampton,
newly built in 1862 (Courtesy:
Northampton Museums and
Art Gallery)

at the York Grey Coat, the education became gradually more
academic, while the clothing remained "charity costume".

The uniform was always a blue dress, with white neckwear and cap.
Two records of its style have been preserved in stone. In All Saints
Church the plaque, dated 1747, to the founders' memory, is ornamented by a figure in relief showing one of the beneficiaries of their
charity. She displays to us a scroll bearing the words "Go thou and do
likewise". Her clothes are like those at Countess Anne's school except
for the addition of a long bibless apron. Her dress has the bodice
typical of the period, laced over a stomacher; her apron, the close-
fitting little indoor cap with small frill, and her wide collar tied with a
tiny bow are all characteristic of charity girls of the mid eighteenth century. (Compare Chapter 7.)

The second record is an exceptionally fine statuette. This still stands on
the building that was put up in Kingswell Street to rehouse the school in
1862 and is probably of that date.

The chief changes are that the girl now wears a large tippet with a
little collar (compare Fig. 86f) and a tall-crowned cap tied under the
chin. Her skirt is clear of the ankles – a recent concession. She is
wearing undersleeves which are probably detachable. (Compare Fig. 85.)

65. Portrait of a Beckett and Sergeant schoolgirl wearing navy-blue dress with tippet and cap of early Victorian charity-school style, in 1920s (Painting by Sarah Rand, Central Museum, Northampton)

In the 1890s, we are told by one who could remember it: "Summer dress for the girls ... included bonnet, tippet and apron. Everything that could be starched was stiff and spotless, the whole providing a pleasing contrast in blue and white. Their winter dress included a long thick brown cloak".[12]

A portrait in oils by Sarah Rand, made in the early 1920s, is our third specimen. The picture makes the details clear; for example, one can see distinctly that the tippet does not do up in front, and that it has a three-inch-wide collar. The white cap has undergone a little alteration, caps always tending to be the most flexible item of the attire (Fig. 65). The other important change is that the blue is now navy. In the twentieth century traditional dress was worn only ceremonially, but it was thus preserved as a relic until the end of the school's life in 1962.

ROYAL MASONIC SCHOOL FOR GIRLS

This famous school, called in early days "Royal Cumberland Freemason School" after its Patron, later "The Royal Masonic Institution for Girls", may be taken as an eminent example of the many which were established by guilds, for the education of children of impoverished members or their widows. As well as board, lodging and education, all necessities were provided, including every stitch of clothing, free of charge.

The school was founded in Somers Town, London, by the Freemasons, in 1788, at the instigation of Bartholomew Ruspini, an Italian-born dental surgeon who acquired the title of Chevalier at about this time. The committee's aims were to "train young female minds ... to virtue and social and religious duties" and to "qualify the children to occupy a useful though not menial station in life."[13] Thus some book-learning was given from the first, and the minimum leaving age was fifteen.

Among the detailed rules, laid down in January 1789, no description of the first uniform is given; but it can be pictured with the help of three sources: there is a list of the outfit to be given to "every girl who shall have behaved well" on leaving school; there is a painting of the children by Stothard *c.* 1802 (Fig. 66 and compare Fig. 29) and there are records of purchases minuted by the Governors and the house committee.

The children's "gowns" were made of a coarse woollen camblet; this was replaced for a time in the 1820s by bombazette, a cheap mixture of wool and cotton, and, in the last part of the nineteenth century, by "stuff". The colour, adhered to to this day and now called "Masonic

66. Girls of Royal Freemasons' School, conducted into Masonic Hall by the
Founders. The front girl on right appears to show the blue sash which
they all wore. 1802 (Detail from engraving by Bartellozzi after Stothard, 1802,
inscribed as a "Print representing the Distinguishing Characteristic of
Masonry, Charity exerted on Proper Objects" Courtesy: Royal Masonic
Institution for Girls)

blue", was a deep azure shade. In Stothard's picture the dresses have
the high waistline of their period.

There was a long apron, a mob cap and, for outdoor wear, probably a
cloak and on leaving school a "Teresas hat" (1789). This hat preceded
what is listed, in 1828, as a straw bonnet. It was tied under the chin with
blue ribbon. "Hats" reappear in 1832.

Since gowns, until the second half of the nineteenth century, tended
to be low-necked, the children had to wear the usual linen or muslin
neck-covering. Stothard shows this as a frilled kerchief crossing over in
front. In 1789 the matron reported having in stock "a Pinbefore" for

each child. It is uncertain what this was like, but in all probability it was a simple form of pinafore like a pincloth (see Fig. 105). (The earliest use of "pinbefore" recorded in the *Oxford English Dictionary* is in the 1820s.) Being only for everyday wear, to keep the dress clean, it does not appear in Fig. 66.

The same matron reported in October that nightcaps and worsted mitts were wanted for warmth; and because frocks were all short-sleeved, the doctor suggested in March 1828 as a "measure . . . against the children catching cold that sleeves of nankeen [strong cotton fabric of yellowish colour], made removeable by pinning and unpinning them to the dress for the purpose of washing them should be worn by all the girls from the month of October to . . . April and also that Tippets should be worn . . . when they go into the garden." (Minute of House Committee, 20 March 1828.) This idea was not unique. A pair of separate sleeves of fawn-coloured cotton, with matching tippet, belonging to an unknown little girl in the 1820s may be seen in the Gallery of English Costume, Manchester.[14]

An 1845 portrait, now at the school, of the matron, Mrs Crook, with a little girl shows that by then the children's frocks had followed the fashion in having a lower waistline. For the special occasion of the painting the low decolletage was left uncovered. The frock, now of serge, shows on the left sleeve an interesting badge (see below).

On an August day in 1853 a new school building was formally opened in Wandsworth, and a contemporary print shows the girls in procession at the ceremony. As was still usual even for small children, their skirts reach the ground, but the popular crinoline was, of course, not allowed. And moreover they now all wear a white tippet, not for warmth but rather for its overtones of modesty and charity-child status.

Soon afterwards the governors decided on a "modernization" of the dress, and our Fig. 67 illustrates the result: long-sleeved frocks without tippets, and now the true pinafore, which was to be a feature of the uniform for many years to come. These pinafores were of white or, for workaday purposes, brown holland. A former member of the staff tells us that these last, in the 1920s, were still being "made entirely by hand in the needlework classes and used in teaching various stitches and processes".[15] Fig. 67 also shows the blue sash which was always part of the uniform until it gave place, in 1875, to blue petersham belts for best, and black leather ones for everyday.

In the twentieth century there were changes in the style of the uniforms and a lessening of the charity look, but the first thirty years saw amazingly little concession to comfort. In a photograph of a picnic in

67. Girls of Royal Masonic Institution, in 1875, wearing pinafores and the traditional blue sashes which were abolished later in that year (*Illustrated London News* 24 April 1875.) Courtesy: Radio Times Hulton Picture Library)

1913 the attire looks both ladylike and cruelly stiff. The girls wear long, tight-waisted dresses, and stand-collars trimmed with starched lace tuckers; all have enormous hats. The pinafore, which might have been useful here, is missing for an interesting reason.

Although in the nineteenth century this garment was worn on every imaginable occasion, from the Centenary Prize-Giving at the Albert Hall in the presence of the Prince of Wales down to the drilling class (where it went with lace-up boots), in the twentieth century it was used only at times of formality. It became *de rigueur* to put on the pinafore for tea, as others "dress for dinner": once a humble protection from dirt, then a livery for ordinary wear, it had finally become a mark of special decorum. As we have seen, the apron at Christ's Hospital Girls' School had a somewhat similar history.

At the new Masonic School at Rickmansworth in 1934 enormous changes took place. The tuckers and even the belts disappeared. Though Masonic blue was retained and all garments were still strictly uniform, the designs became much like those of other girls' boarding schools. As regards the pinafores one cannot do better than quote, with his permission, from R. M. Handfield-Jones's history of the school.[16] He remarks: "It is incredible that this humiliating garment could have persisted after 1914, by which time the school had become an admirable one, besides which the laundering of these pinafores must have been an unnecessary expense in war time". Is it possible that being a near-apron it persisted as a sort of masonic symbol? Note Ruspini's apron in Fig. 66.

Exactly when the end came is evidenced by a letter to Mr Handfield-Jones from a former acting headmistress: "The much detested garment was worn very little after the move to Rickmansworth [but] the Battle of the Pinafores was a hard fought one". When at last the pinafore disappeared in 1939: "So great was the delight of the school that every girl managed to embroider for herself a linen envelope for the table napkin that took its place".[17]

A special mention should be made of the badges associated with the school because of their fascinating connections with freemasonry and symbolism. Fig. 68 shows the design of the one embroidered in red on the little girl's sleeve in the portrait of 1845 mentioned above. In "the modernization" of 1856 the embroidered badge turned into a medallion worn on a blue neck ribbon. Medals as prizes were engraved with the child's name and a reminder of her indebtedness: "Royal Freemasons' Charity for female children".

68. Design of girls' badge at Royal Masonic Institution for Girls in 1845. See text. Crown indicates sovereign's patronage, setsquare and compasses the Freemasons' (Drawing partly based on the portrait "Mrs. Crook with Girl")

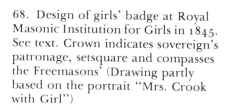

69. Embroidered badge of Royal Masonic Institution for Girls since 1930. See text (Badge lent by Royal Masonic Institution for Girls)

In 1930 a new school badge was designed. The crown is retained but the masonic symbolism is now ingeniously linked with the idea of a girls' school. Thus the motto refers, in Latin, to our daughters being as the polished corners of the Temple; and the centrepiece is a cube, the "Smooth Ashlar" dressed by a mason to act as a corner-stone. This badge is still worn on the blazers of all the girls. An extra "Ashlar" badge, a silver brooch of cubical design, has been awarded since 1960 to girls who have shown a special sense of responsibility. Both badges hark back to the original intention of the founder Masons to "train female minds to virtue".*

* For help with the above we are much indebted to Mr A. A. Huckle, Secretary of the Royal Masonic Institution for Girls, who guided us and allowed us the use of the un-published minute books; also to Miss Dixon and Mrs Rudd of the school's teaching staff for their advice and a tour of their exhibition on the history of the school.

CHAPTER 7

Charity schools: general evolution of the costume

"Charity schools" was the specific term used from the eighteenth century for schools in which social groups rather than single benefactors provided for the care, education and clothing of poor children of the parish or ward. These were mostly day schools and were in other ways distinct from the schools of ancient endowment with which we have already dealt. Many parochial schools did exist before the eighteenth century, and also free grammar schools; but their pupils were not normally provided with clothes and such schools therefore fall outside our subject.

Charity schools proper were largely started by the inspiration and organization of the Society for Promoting Christian Knowledge (S.P.C.K.) which was established in 1698–9. Much support was personally given by Queen Anne. The children were taught reading and writing and the principles of the Church of England.

The schools multiplied rapidly all over the country and all through the eighteenth century. After only twelve years of the S.P.C.K.'s efforts there were some eighty schools in London alone. In these nearly four thousand children were clothed and many others received token uniforms of caps and bands. Steele wrote in 1712 that the charity schools were "the greatest instances of public spirit the age had produced" (*Spectator* No. 224, 6 February), and Addison a year later: "I have always looked upon the institution of Charity Schools, which of late has so universally prevailed throughout the whole nation, as the glory of the age we live in" (*The Guardian* No. 105, 11 July 1713).

Though coarse in material and on the whole plain, the uniforms of charity schools at the time of their foundation resembled in cut and style what was worn by contemporary adults. This was true for children's dress in general, for it was only from the end of the eighteenth century that they wore styles distinct from those of their parents. What is remarkable is the resistance shown to change once a uniform was established, a resistance that was not romantic, as in some of the famous schools, but rather puritanical and disciplinarian. It is interesting to trace, at the same time, the cautious yielding to alterations of fashion and of attitude that appeared as time went on.

Many records kept by people who chose the children's clothing are quoted in the next chapter, where some individual schools are discussed. Records extensively used in the present chapter are the unpublished minutes of the Cloathing Committee of the Clerkenwell Charity School, since these provide good independent evidence, as far as the nineteenth century is concerned. They are referred to below as "Clerkenwell".[1]

The written records can be filled out with much visual evidence, for uniformed charity children were picturesque. The children often featured in illustrated papers and even topographical books; by the end they were being painted and photographed as individuals and even recorded in the form of dressed dolls, of which there are three examples at the Bethnal Green Museum.

70. Blue Coat School, Birmingham, in 1910. Coats, breeches with square falls, bands and caps, all in eighteenth-century style, and thought worth taking by the well-known photographer, Benjamin Stone (Reproduced by permission from the Sir Benjamin Stone Collection of Photographs in Birmingham Reference Library)

71. Statuette showing typical charity boy's dress of the early eighteenth century. Buttons of the waistcoat and tuft on the flat cap are just showing. Entire suit painted brown (Statuette in St Bride's Church, Fleet Street, London, formerly on school in the parish. Photo: Keith Ellis)

The same museum also owns a charity-school doll, made *c.* 1860, whose body is stuffed to form a pincushion.

The popular carved statuettes* have already been mentioned. These date mainly from the very end of the seventeenth to the middle of the nineteenth century. When no longer on school buildings they have been preserved in churches and museums all over the country. Three *caveats* should be entered here. Statuettes were frequently copied one from another, they were often re-erected on later buildings, and their colours may be incorrect owing to inevitable repainting. But on the whole they are a very valuable source, and they are as interesting for what they have in common (owing largely to the S.P.C.K. influence) as for showing the subtle changes that took place.

---

* Early ones were of wood, stone or lead; from about 1770 to 1790 they were often of "Coade stone", a composition imitating stone.

In colour a working-class blue or grey was favoured for the main garments, at first; then, for distinguishing neighbouring schools, also green or brown. Red was rare – perhaps too garish or too military – but it did occur, for example, in the Red Coat School, Stepney, the sister school of the Ratcliff Green Coat, and later amalgamated with the senior part of the Sir John Cass School. And in 1698 William Worrall laid down that the boys of his free school in Cripplegate should wear orange (compare page 95). The girls of St George's School, Hanover Square, were unique in wearing blue with white spots.[2]

BOYS' CLOTHES

For boys the style of coat changes very slowly. Typically it was a single-breasted collarless coat of early eighteenth-century style reaching or covering the knee, buttoned throughout with metal buttons (at first generally of pewter) and having the large flapped pockets of the day. The gentleman's fashion for exaggerated cuffs in the first half of the century was followed only with discretion.

There was a long-sleeved waistcoat which, like that of working men, could be worn as a coat indoors (though the sleeves were of a cheaper material). For gentlemen, the sleeved waistcoat went out of fashion in the 1750s, but it survived much longer for the poor. The little boy's "skeleton suit", fashionable from 1790 to 1830, does not seem to have ever been supplied, perhaps because it needed careful tailoring. The later cutaway, sloping shape for coat fronts, if adopted at all, was a generation late in appearing (end of eighteenth century); eventually in the middle of the nineteenth century some of these small boys were put into square-cut tail coats, with short waistcoats, not unlike those of their fathers. Others continued with the eighteenth-century style for two hundred years.

Another survival was the breeches. Gentlemen went into trousers about 1800, but most working men, even in towns, rather later. Some charity schools allowed the boys trousers in the 1840s, and at least one in 1818 (at Clerkenwell, in corduroy for everyday wear and velveteen for Sundays); but for many it was breeches or knickerbockers into the twentieth century (Fig. 70). At Rotherhithe the boys photographed at the charity school's tercentenary are wearing overalls – a garment that probably came in with the girls' pinafores in the late nineteenth century. Except for being of light-coloured material it resembled the closed, belted, black cotton overall once worn throughout France by working-class schoolboys.

Headgear generally took the form of a cap that was very distinctive

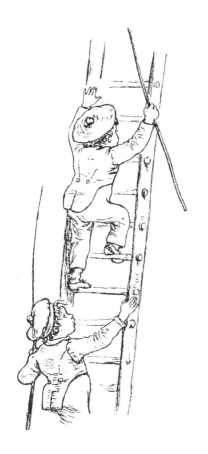

72. Charity boys in tail coats, 1879
(Drawing by Kate Greenaway in *St
Nicholas* vol. VI, 393)

and unlike contemporary fashions even from the first. It had a tam-o'-
shanter-like, nearly flat crown gathered on to a very narrow brim, as at
Christ's Hospital. A string or a ribbon went round the join and,
though the main colour varied, the large bobble ("tuft" or "toff")
adorning the top was almost always red (Figs. 71 and 72). This
headgear was described at first as a "woollen knit cap" – presumably
the brim was stiffened, as at Christ's, by doubling and shrinking. It was
clearly modelled on the "city flat cap" (this term was actually used to
describe it, by the *Illustrated London News* in 1842), i.e. the woollen cap
which, by Act of Parliament in 1571, was enjoined on the lower classes
in order to promote the wool trade. The cap became so much a symbol of the charity boy that when the Vintry Ward School, London, was
refounded as late as 1840 the lads were given typical flat caps, although
their uniform was a tail coat and trousers. However, in some schools

founded in the later eighteenth century the boys wore the black three-cornered cocked hats that had been in fashion since about 1710; and by 1800 the majority wore the round felt hat that had taken its place.

Afterwards various forms of cap were adopted, including "Holland caps" at Saffron Walden and, rarely, the shako, from Waterloo days, as seen on the Bethnal Green Greencoat doll, *c.* 1860. A tall shako was worn by the old Welsh Charity School in London and it had a badge with the Principality's three ostrich feathers in front. This, especially when ornamented with a leek on St David's day, had an exceedingly smart appearance. But the flat-cap shape died hard and was still worn, for example, in Birmingham Blue Coat School (as it was in Northampton's Orange School) until well into the twentieth century.

73. Uniform of a charity school refounded in 1840. Revival of flat cap and of bands, despite the neck ribbon and the contemporary suit. Note the Vintry Ward School badge with the boy's number (Statuette now in Vintners Place, London)

74. Charity schoolboy with tricorne hat, *c.* 1780. Suit in contemporary style. Coat grey, waistcoat red. Note badge (Painted lead statuette from St Luke's Parochial School, Finsbury, now moved to Old Street, London. Photo: Jim Connell)

The most remarkable feature of all, for both boys and girls, was the white neckwear. This seemingly unpractical item was indispensable from the start. Even if the charity provided no other clothing, it almost always gave caps and bands, the bands being white collars which the children wore every day. In shape these were at first like those of Christ's Hospital, a revival of a style that started in the 1640s for "Puritans" and the humble and became fashionable in Commonwealth times. The wide collar had its front ends squared off, the edges meeting in parallel to make a bib shape (Fig. 75). For boys only, soon after 1700 the front lengthened to produce, as at Christ's Hospital, rectangular tabs, like those still worn by clergymen; a band (in the ordinary sense) went round the neck, with the tabs fastened to it in front (Fig. 76). At first the tabs were of better quality material than the "neck". Thus in 1699: "7s. 4d. [was] paid for four Ells of Holland linen to make ye Boys Bands at 1s. 10d: 9s. 4d. disbursed for eight Ells of Holland for necks to ye Bands at 1s. 2d. p. [per] Ell".[3] So essential were the tabs (like his cap) as a mark of the charity boy that in the uniform of the Vintry Ward

75. *Left* Shako worn by Welsh School, London. See text (Lithograph after Robert Scanlon, *c.* 1840, detail). *Right* Square-cut bib-shaped seventeenth-century collar from which the paired tabs on bands of charity boys *et al.* evolved. Described by Randle Holme, 1688, as a "Plaine Band with Bandstrings pendant" made of fine white linen, "Starched, Slickened and Smoothed by the Laundress". (R. Holme: *Academy of Armory* vol. III Chapter II, Pl. facing page 17)

School in 1840, where the boys wore a neck ribbon tied in a bow, the tabs still appeared (Fig. 73). And in the 1890s the Colchester Blue Coat boys wore them under a starched Eton collar!

But there were exceptions. At Clerkenwell, in 1840, for the first time they bought "103 yards of plain black sarsnet Ribbon *in lieu of lawn for neck bands*". Soon afterwards "a gross of bobbins for winding the boys' neck ribbons" and "20 yards of linen for *collars*" (not bands) are

76. Boy's collar worn at Grey Coat Hospital, *c.* 1870. A slot in the neckband allows the opposite tape to pass through and tie in front, ensuring a good fit. Bands (tabs) appear to be overlapping instead of in parallel because the collar is laid flat (Photo: Guy Taylor. Courtesy: the Trustees of Grey Coat Hospital, Westminster)

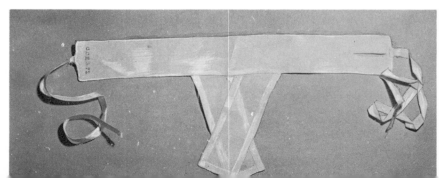

77. Two phases of uniform at the same school, the Colchester Blue Coat. *Left*
c. 1710. *Right* In 1890s. Bands worn even with Eton collar. Echoes of
eighteenth century also in coat, breeches and cap with tuft (*Left* Statuette in
Colchester Town Hall. Courtesy: Colchester District Council. *Right* Painting
by Frank Daniell. Courtesy: Holly Trees Museum, Colchester)

recorded; and apparently at Cam, Gloucestershire, in 1880, the boys sported a white bow tie.

The children's shoes, which for a long time were made to measure and were heavily nailed, tended in their style to move with the times, so that they can be used as evidence in dating, with this proviso, that in the schools that could afford to show their appreciation of tradition an ornamental eighteenth-century shoe buckle was often retained in the uniform beyond its normal period. Boots replaced shoes in the 1860s for both boys and girls.

GIRLS' CLOTHES

Not unnaturally the girls' costumes reflected the fashions of the day more than the boys', though hoops, crinolines and nearly all ornaments were disallowed, and the clothes were largely made by the girls or their mothers from materials supplied. The dresses begin as "gowns" in the open-robe style of the day, that is with a skirt open in front to reveal an underskirt called the petticoat (Fig. 78 and 91). This was a practical plan, since the overskirt was fastened back out of harm's

78. Charity girl in early Georgian period. Overskirt bunched behind, underskirt with apron over; bodice in form of laced stays; cap without the pinched-up frill of Queen Anne's time. (Detail of headpiece of an apprentice's indenture signed and dated 1724. Finsbury Reference Library, London Borough of Islington. Photo: Jim Connell)

way making a sort of bustle behind. The petticoat was generally of the same colour and material as the gown but naturally its shape made it easier to launder. Together they were probably what was meant by a girl's "sute". This style persisted after it was well out of fashion, but about the middle of the eighteenth century it was generally replaced by a single garment, a full-skirted "closed robe"; open robes recurred in the 1780s (Fig. 84) and even later. Very often there was an apron – a coloured "scouring apron" and a white one on Sundays.

As with other girls, gowns were foot length till the nineteenth century and showed little more than the ankles or part of the calf even in 1910, despite the cost in material. They were not called "frocks" till about the 1830s.

Bodices were supported by rather brutal leather or whalebone stays, as we have seen, and were generally laced over a stomacher till the fashion for false fronts came in, in about the 1750s. Stomachers were generally white, but those under the blue dresses at the Cripplegate-Within Ward School were scarlet.[4]

So drastic was the rise in the waistline in the Empire period that even that of charity girls could not be kept down. Their aprons, which were still bibless, shot up too, and the effect of the apron strings tied just below the breasts was rather striking.

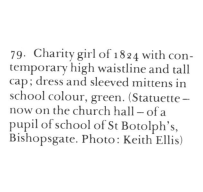

79. Charity girl of 1824 with contemporary high waistline and tall cap; dress and sleeved mittens in school colour, green. (Statuette – now on the church hall – of a pupil of school of St Botolph's, Bishopsgate. Photo: Keith Ellis)

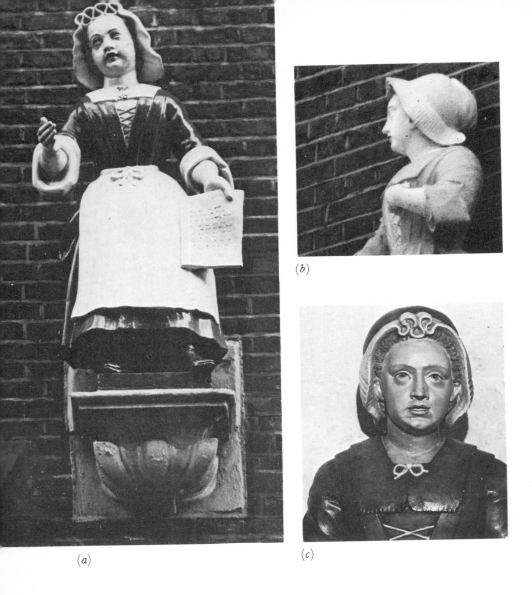

(a)

(b)

(c)

80. (a) Charity girl statuette: "coif" with goffered frill rising in front; square-cut collar; both typical of first quarter of eighteenth century. (b) Side view of similar coif, 1712. (c) Front view of similar coif, c. 1711 (a Statuette on one of the two charity schools in parish of St Andrew's, Holborn – a building in Hatton Garden. Courtesy: Pictorial and Feature Services, b statuette formerly on St Mary Abbots Charity School, Kensington, now on the Church primary school on the same site, c statuette on St Bride's Church, Fleet, Street, London. Photo: Keith Ellis)

Then the waist came down again, following that of the ladies, and made room for a bib to the apron, which is seen in these schools nearly for the first time in the 1840s. However the bibbed apron seems to have been little used, the pinafore being preferred.

When charity costumes had become fully self-conscious at the end of the nineteenth century, the apron was retained, sometimes purely for show, e.g. at Colchester in the 1890s, or in the shape of the muslin aprons which we read were worn at York Grey Coat School till 1881 and the stouter cotton one which persisted there, even out of doors, far into the twentieth century.

A girl's indoor cap, which she always wore, must have meant more to her than most of the uniform, framing her face as it did, and it was allowed to reflect, if discreetly, the changes in ladies' fashions. A good example is the way in which the ornamental headdress rising six or eight inches on top of the head, the lady's "fontange", was hinted at in the caps (called "coifs" or "quoifs" in the records) through the first quarter of the eighteenth century. The starched frill was goffered only in the upper part and in such a way that sometimes two, sometimes three to five extra large folds stood straight up in the centre giving just the impression of a miniature fontange. (Compare the "pinch" in the frill of some ladies' caps in the 1730s – 60s.) The wide side-flaps of the coif were not lappets that could be tied; they remind one of certain Dutch national headdresses and seem peculiar to the charity cap.

The crown or caul varied (Fig. 82). It was mainly close-fitting, yet part of it sometimes bulged out behind, perhaps to allow the wearer a little more hair. The effect is like a cottage loaf. Typical for the schools of Queen Anne's reign, this coif later gave place to a close-fitting cap with low, tightly pleated frill all round except at the mid back. It was like a lady's round-eared cap without lappets. Again, there could be an extra "bun". Near the end of the century a cap with a full caul and broad headpiece came in, often, but not necessarily with a frill or border" (Fig. 81). In 1819 at Clerkenwell the headmistress asked for lawn for making frills to the caps, but this was refused.

81. Pattern of "Schoolgirl's Cap", 1838, labels added (*Workwoman's Guide* by a Lady, Pl. 9)

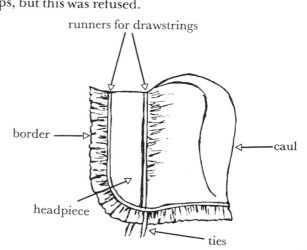

runners for drawstrings

border

caul

headpiece

ties

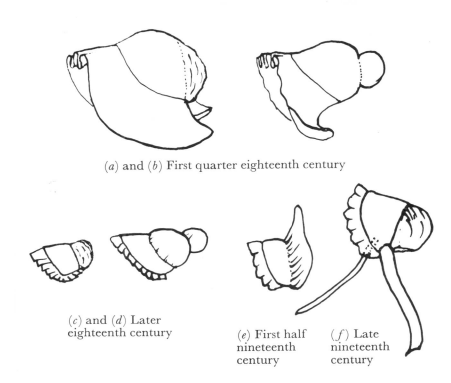

(a) and (b) First quarter eighteenth century

(c) and (d) Later eighteenth century

(e) First half nineteenth century

(f) Late nineteenth century

82. Diagrams (not to scale) based on specimens to show changes in girls' caps (a Statuette, now outside church, from one of the two charity schools in parish of St Andrew's, Holborn, both founded 1700; b statuette in St Bride's Church, Fleet Street, London, c. 1711; c statuette probably from Bridge, Candlewick and Dowgate School, 1775–80,[*] Museum of London; d Statuette of 1759, Stepney Greencoat C.E. Primary School; e charity girls at service in St Paul's, *Pictorial World* 1864; f doll representing Vintry Ward schoolgirl, late nineteenth century, Museum of London)

Then the new fashion took on in the schools for putting height at the back of the head instead of the front, by making the crown (caul) of the cap stand up vertically behind. If tied under the chin, this was a "cornette" style, well shown in some dolls representing Colchester Blue Coat School girls (Fig. 96). In many places the high-cauled cap, or an ordinary mob (Fig. 97), lasted in the schools right through to the end of the nineteenth century – some thirty years after indoor caps had been abandoned by all except widows, nurses and servants.

It is interesting that the Museum of London has a later nineteenth-century charity doll's cap in which long streamers are added to hang

[*] Our thanks are due to Stuart Rigold for this identification.

behind the ties. This reflects a lady's fashion of the 1860s which was retained till the 1880s by parlourmaids.

On any of the caps there was usually a trimming of ribbon in the school's colour, but it had to be "fixed plain around the cap" (1799, St Mary Abbots, Kensington).

Out of doors the girls wore cloaks or "mantles", or, in the later nineteenth century, capes which might match the dresses. An advantage of this type of garment rather than a coat was, of course, that it did not have to fit. It could be made by the girls themselves, could last all through a growing child's time at school and could then be handed down. The other advantage of the loose shape was that it could be worn easily over a starched tippet.

Over the head in the early days the girls would wear a lined hood. This might be stiffened with whalebone so as not to crush the coif underneath. As early as the 1730s there was something called a "bonnet". The period's large bergère hat was worn only by grown-up girls, e.g. in the Magdalen charity in 1761 (see Chapter 9). However, straw hats for the children began in the second half of the century. It was a time when, as Stubbs often shows, even farm women wore elaborate hats. They must soon have been looked on as a necessity; a donor in 1764 left an annuity for the express purpose of providing hats for a school in Middlesex, giving very precise specifications. Every year there were to

83. Girl of Welsh School, London, with cloak over her arm. She carries a leek(?), *c.* 1840 (Lithograph after Robert Scanlon)

84. Girl in large hat, *c.* 1780. Collar rounded and wide – typical for charity girls of the period – blue gown with skirt drawn back, blue underskirt, apron, badge with name of school, shoes with fashionable large buckles (Painted lead statuette from St Luke's Parochial School, Finsbury, London, now at Old Street. Photo: Geoffrey Davis)

be provided "straw hats, green and white such as the girls now have and were made in Dunstable, a pattern of which is preserved; the brims not to exceed $5\frac{1}{2}$ inches; and not to be lined; but to be tied on with a green silk riband such as is now sold for 6d a yard".[5] Similar hats were worn in Finsbury, *c.* 1780 (see Fig. 84), and Stepney, 1786.

But bonnets reappeared in the form of straw "cottage bonnets" in 1814, again in Stepney. These, in their shape and their ribbon bow under the chin, were like the bonnets adopted by ladies in the 1830s, but those of the girls lacked all the ladies' floral trimmings (Fig. 183). Accounts for 1841 mention "the usual supply of purple ribbon for the Bonnets . . . for cleaning 70 Bonnets at 5s. 6d. a dozen . . ."[6] Bonnets continued demurely on till near the end of the century (compare the Green School, Reading, and the Red Maids').

As we shall see, pattens were needed against the mud of Soho. In the same place a few girls were allowed sheepskin gloves in 1704; but the great majority of charity girls knitted their own gloves, in wool for winter (either worsted or "yarn") and linen thread or cotton for summer. Mittens or mitts, often yellow or black, were very common after the earliest and most Spartan days. These, one suspects, were a precaution against the chilblains of a childhood spent in meanly heated rooms (Figs. 79 and 85). The girls wore them from mid eighteenth to the twentieth century and they became almost symbolic. It was said of a London charity girl, in 1842, that she "still exhibits the mittens of 60 years ago" (*Illustrated London News*). But at Clerkenwell in 1818 it was to be muslin gloves or "white cotton gloves instead of yellow mitts". Detached sleeves, tied or pinned up, were probably for the same purpose as mittens; they were not the protective oversleeves of domestic servants since dress sleeves were nearly always short. White lawn cuffs "to be worn for particular occasions only" could be added for elegance.[7]

Perhaps the most interesting story is that of the white neckwear which was the most characteristic part of the outfit. Necessary because of the low necklines prevailing in all dresses, and with all its overtones of chastity, it evolved, nevertheless, through a series of ever more becoming and unpractical forms. First was the band or collar. This was very like that of the boys in its square bib-shaped front, but it was broader all round because of the décolletage and was tied at the chin,

85. Miniature replicas representing children of Frances Hopton Charity School, Cam, Glos., dated "15.12.1880". Girl has purple-ribboned bonnet, large handkerchief crossed over fichu-wise, undersleeves and mittens. Dress and boy's coat both navy blue (Dolls at Hopton C. of E. Primary School, Cam, Glos. Courtesy: the Headmaster)

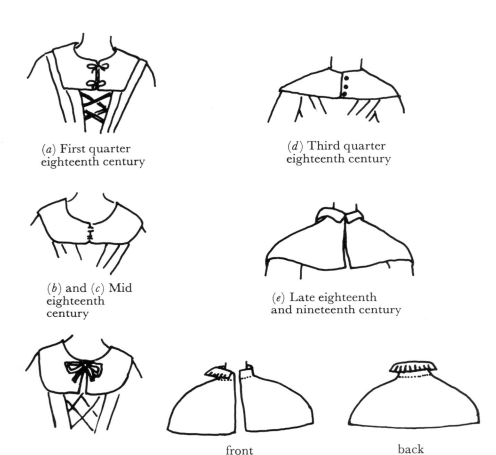

(a) First quarter
eighteenth century

(d) Third quarter
eighteenth century

(b) and (c) Mid
eighteenth
century

(e) Late eighteenth
and nineteenth century

front

back

(f) Nineteenth century

86. Diagrams based on specimens to show evolution of round tippet from collar. (a) to (c) Collar widening, corners rounding. (d) to (f) Tippet enlarging and acquiring collarette – shown on one side in f (a As for Fig. 80a; b statuette at Lady Hollis School, Cripplegate, 1730, drawn after illustration in John James Baddeley Cripplegate . . . 1921; c as for Fig. 82c; d statuette of 1759 at Stepney Greencoat C.E. Primary School; e illustration of charity children processing from church in City Scenes, 1828 edition; f miniature replicas of Vintry Ward School uniform made in late nineteenth century, Museum of London)

and often below, with a tiny bow (Figs. 80*a* and 91). This coincided with the Queen Anne period and accompanied the fontange-like cap and the bunched overskirt. By the 1740s the corners of the band were more rounded (Fig. 86*a–c*) and then spreading shapes appeared (Figs. 87*e* and *f*).

In the last third of the century girls' bands vanished; in their place came a choice of two garments, again strongly reminiscent of seventeenth-century Puritan times; both of these we have encountered in girls' schools: the tippet and the neckerchief, called "handkerchief". Both had been used by ladies, the handkerchief since the seventeenth century, and more recently for undress wear; and the tippet from the 1730s. But with the ladies they were diaphanous and lacy, with the girls more solid. Their teachers wore the same.

The tippet was really a collar so much enlarged as to reach the shoulders and make a small cape, buttoned or tied, usually under the chin but sometimes behind. Of starched linen, it was at first completely plain, as were handkerchiefs (Fig. 88 is unusual). But by 1800 there seems to have been a slight relaxation of standards. A little prettiness crept in (and perhaps more comfort): the girls were sometimes allowed to have a little soft frill of fine lawn at the neck of their tippets, such as had been seen earlier on a few of the wide bands (Fig. 87*g*). This frill increased in popularity and so did the size of the tippet – until in Victorian times it reached the elbows, the limit of practicability. By then most tippets had developed a turned-down "collarette", as though oblivious of their own origin in the collar itself (Figs. 86*f* and 89).

The other alternative to a band was favoured in 1799 by one Mrs Leech who wanted her protégées distinguished from the other girls by wearing "handkerchiefs instead of tippets". The "handkerchief", triangular or rounded behind, covered the shoulders and bosom. This adjunct, in coloured cotton, was universal wear for the working woman through most of our period. With a laced bodice she tucked the corners under her stomacher, otherwise under her apron, or pinned them over it. This is what the charity girls often did too. But with them, pure white was the rule at least on Sundays and festivals. The York Grey Coat girls in 1786 had "2 Blue and 1 white Handkerchief" and also a white "Band or Sunday Handkerchief". In the nineteenth century the handkerchief gradually became less popular.

There was also the hybrid shown in Fig. 87. This was triangular in shape, fore and aft, open in front, like a handkerchief, or sometimes behind. It was really another tippet, being a little cape, often with a collar, usually fastened under the chin and stiffly starched (see Fig. 90). (This was what, in the late nineteenth and twentieth centuries, was called a

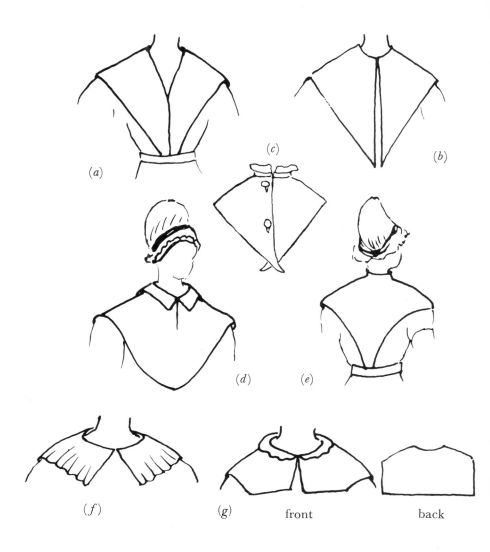

87. Diagrammatic copies. (a) Handkerchief, c. 1805. (b) to (e) Triangular tippets: (b) is front-fastening, c. 1805; (c) back-fastening, c. 1860; (d), (e) closed all round. (f), (g) Unusual collars, 1775–80. (a and b as for Fig. 5; c doll, Bethnal Green Coat School uniform, Bethnal Green Museum; d *Pictorial World*, 13 June, 1874; e *Illustrated London News*, 16 June, 1866; f as for Fig. 82c; g statuette from Farringdon Ward School, Museum of London)

88. Girl with exceptional type of neck handkerchief, typical close-fitting cap, circular badge on right breast, 1760 (Statuette of St John's old school, Wapping. Courtesy: Greater London Council)

"fichu" at the Red Maids' School.) Some tippets were put on over the head, poncho-wise, having only a very short opening under the chin. When triangular they could be held down by means of a waistband attached in front and/or behind; alternatively there could be a loop at the back for the apron string. This is well shown in a uniform of the Liverpool Blue Coat School, now in the Gallery of English Costume, Manchester. A tippet with waistband joined on is shown in *Workwoman's Guide* (1838).[8] In Figs. 87*a* the points are pinned.

Taking the place of apron and tippet, from about the middle of the nineteenth century, the pinafore was often adopted, e.g. at Clerkenwell in 1860, and was also called "pinbefore" as at Stepney in 1854: "Pinbefores each 4d. Aprons each 2d".[9] Compare also Royal Masonic School, page 115. It was made of washing material and was at first for workaday use only. Essentially it was a sleeveless overall, open all down the back and fastened at the neck, with or without a waistband. The author of *Workwoman's Guide* describes the pinafore shown in Fig. 14 as follows:

Pinafores for national and other schools are generally of strong blue linen check with one or two pockets . . . in which their knitting and needlework are put . . . after buttoning up the pockets . . . [the pinafores] are carefully taken off when school hours are over, folded and locked up in the schoolhouse . . .[10]

90. Open triangular tippet with points tucked in, frill or standing collarette. Rosettes worn for anniversary service at St Paul's, 1879 (Original proofs, KG899–903, of illustration by Kate Greenaway for *St Nicholas* magazine, vol. VI 152, 155. Courtesy: London Borough of Camden, from the collections at Keats House, Hampstead)

The same author also recommends a "child's smock frock" or "close pinafore" which is really an overall, not being open behind. "It would be well if, at most large Charity Schools, children attended with these kind of pinafores, which at once give them a neat respectable appearance".[11]

Being more complicated to make, overalls were seldom supplied to girls, but pinafores often had shoulder lappets or "capes", as in Fig. 105*d* (compare Fig. 4).

89. Closed tippets with turned-down collarettes, high-crowned caps, medals on ribbons. Posies for anniversary service at St Paul's, 1870 (Drawing by E. Buckman in *The Graphic*, 1870, page 660)

THE FIRST OUTFITS

From the beginning the S.P.C.K. helped the parish schools as they came into existence by publishing annually a suggested list of clothes for boys and girls and by recommending dealers.[12] Hence, throughout most of the eighteenth century, there was close uniformity in the outfits, apart from colour and, before dealing with our examples, it will therefore be convenient to show what was suggested in the early days. We give two lists exactly as they appeared in the S.P.C.K. Annual Report for 1712.

The Charge for Cloathing a Boy	£	s	d
A yard and half-quarter [1⅛ yds] of Grey Yorkshire Broad Cloth 6 quarters wide makes a coat		3	0
Making the coat, with Pewter Buttons and all other Materials		1	0
A Wastcoat of the same Cloth, lined		3	6
A pair of Breeches of Cloth or Leather,* lined		2	6
1 Knit cap with Tuft and String of any colour		0	10
1 Band [collar; usually 3 supplied annually]			2
1 Shirt		1	6
1 pair of Woollen Stockings			8
1 pair of Shoes		1	10
1 pair of Buckles** [for shoes, transferable from one pair to the next]			1
1 pair of Knit or Wash-leather Gloves			7
The Total		15	8

* The leather was oil-tanned, so it was soft and also washable; the breeches were often lined with the same (e.g. at St Mary Abbots School, Kensington, *c.* 1708).

** Small buckles were necessary, as shoes fastened with a strap (compare Fig. 71). Large ornamental buckles were a later fashion.

Charge of Cloathing a Girl	£	s	d
3 yards and half of Blue long Ells [a woollen cloth], at 16d p[per] Yard makes a Gown and Petticoat		4	8
Making thereof, Strings, Body-lining and other Materials		1	0
A Coif and Band of Scotch-cloth* with a Border** [2 bands annually]			9
Ditto of fine Ghenting*** [for best]		1	0
A Shift		1	6
A White, Blue, or Checquered Apron		1	0
A Pair of Leather Bodice [Stays] and Stomacher		2	6
1 Pair of Woollen Stockings			8
1 Pair of Shoes		1	8
A Pair of Pattens			8
1 pair of Buckles			1
1 pair of Knit or Wash-Leather Gloves			7
The Total		16	1

N.B. The differences in Stature of the Children is allowed for here; and 50 Children between the Ages of 7 and 12 (one with another), may be cloathed at these Rates.

As noted earlier, schools that could not afford to clothe the children completely usually provided caps and bands as essential insignia.

Prices rose, and in 1738 the total was being kept down to about 17s for each boy and girl only by the use of cheaper materials; the composition of the outfits was still remarkably unchanged even in the 1760s.

* Cheap fabric made of nettle fibres.

** Frill to cap or coif.

*** Linen, probably from Ghent.

SUNDAY CLOTHES

Since clothing was given out annually, each new coat and gown could be kept at first for Sundays; so were the clean neckwear and the white apron. The control of these Sunday clothes was a problem, for they must not be lost, dirtied or pawned during the week. A rule for St Sepulchre's Parochial Girls' School, London, in 1846, laid down that: "The Children's best clothes are to remain in the School during the week in a bag provided for the purpose. They are to be given to the girls when they leave School on Saturday and to be returned in perfect order on the Monday after".[13]

BADGES

Besides their distinctive dress, most charity children after about 1717 had to wear badges for reasons already discussed.

Girls were less subject to labelling than boys, perhaps because less unruly in the streets. *The Penny Magazine* of 1837, depicting the combined London schools in anniversary procession to St Paul's, shows all the boys with badges but none of the girls.

In earlier days the boys wore the badge on the breast of the coat or, since coats were not always put on, and in any case were often worn open, on the waistcoat (Fig. 13). Their caps, being of the tam-o'-shanter pattern, did not lend themselves to badge-bearing, but the pill-box shape of the late nineteenth century served this purpose. The Museum of London contains such a cap, presented in 1962 by an ex-pupil of the Cripplegate-Without School. He had worn it himself and so had his uncle before him. Made of a brownish mixed-wool cloth, its badge in bright red depicts the ancient two-towered Cripple Gate itself, in true heraldic style.

When girls wore badges they were fastened to the dress or tippet.

The badge generally took the form of a perforated metal disc, at first of pewter, then of tin, and from 1800 of copper or brass. When embroidery could be done cheaply by machine, we find it being used here and there, as in the Cripplegate and the Welsh School caps, and finally with full splendour in the caps of Sir John Cass schoolgirls in our own time (Fig. 25).

CHAPTER 8

Individual charity schools

As the charity schools had much in common, it is hoped that an arbitrary selection will give a fair picture of their history and the range and causes of variations in their uniforms.

GREY COAT HOSPITAL, WESTMINSTER

This school, almost the first of its kind, and founded at the same time as the S.P.C.K., was established by a group of local worthies. Their first meeting with the children, in January 1699, was mentioned in Chapter 1.

The eight Governors began by ordering boys' knitted caps and a piece of linen which they got their wives to make up into bands; but it was soon resolved, in addition, to give "a paire of Shoes with Buckles and a paire of knit Gloves" and ". . . a Grey Coat to put on and go in order to Church".[1] Further purchases in 1699 were "40 pairs of lined leather breeches", and some grey yarn, to be delivered to the parents "to be by them knit up" into new stockings.

In 1701 the day school was superseded by a boarding school in Tothill Fields nearby.

The "grey cloth" used for the boys' coats was probably of natural colour wool. Most of the schools seem to have started with this, probably to save the cost of dyeing. In the Grey Coat school it persisted, but there were brass buttons to brighten it up. As the girls' gowns were of serge, they were a separate purchase, and the colour blue, as was more usual for girls, was chosen.

The 1701 school building, though much restored, still stands in what is now Greycoat Place. It bears a charming pair of wooden statuettes

91. Girl of Grey Coat Hospital, Westminster, 1701 or soon after. Style of cap, band, etc., typical of Queen Anne period (Statuette on the school, Greycoat Place, Westminster. Courtesy: the Trustees)

which are probably contemporary with the buildings (Figs. 10 and 91). Their repainting has been correct in some points; for example, the boy's cap is black with a red tuft; but the girl's gown and petticoat have, not unnaturally, been made grey. The uniforms are perfect examples of the very early eighteenth-century styles. The boy wears a sleeved waistcoat; a private benefactor did, in fact, present seventeen waistcoats to the school at just about this time. Other donors gave 480 pairs of shoe buckles for the use of the Hospital and forty pairs of pattens for the girls.

On leaving school the children received a generous allowance of clothes, which for girls included "a new gown and pittycoat and their [worn] middle bays pittycoat". Middle bays was a woollen textile of medium weight, resembling thin serge. The bays petticoat was probably an undergarment, the other "petticoat" being the skirt exposed under the open gown.

In the eighteenth century brass badges were designed for the mathematical boys, as at Christ's Hospital, and one of these was still preserved long after the Hospital turned into a school for girls only, in the 1870s.

ST MARTIN-IN-THE-FIELDS SCHOOL

This school and the next were among the first half dozen that owed their origin to the S.P.C.K. Founded in 1699 for poor boys, from 1700 on it accepted twenty to forty girls and, when it began to take in some boarders from 1718, the girls' side became more and more of a separate establishment. In 1894 it was in fact renamed "St Martin-in-the-Fields High School for Girls" (now at Tulse Hill). Miss D. H. Thomas has given us an interesting history of this school based on the old minute books.[2]

We shall therefore discuss here only the clothing of the girls. There are some particulars as to the actual making of the early outfits. The gowns were of "Stuff" and the petticoat of "Blew half thick". "Stuff" was a hard-wearing material made from long-staple wool but coarser and cheaper than worsted; "half-thick" was thinner and made of coarse short-staple wool. ". . . Mr Butler the Taylor was order'd to make them gowns . . . the Parents etc. being to make the Petticoats themselves . . ." and "Mr Honnour the Shoemaker took measure of the said Children and was order'd to make them *shoes* of good Calves Leather at 2/- a pair". "*Orange coloured Yarn*" was bought for knitting into gloves and black yarn for stockings.

On ordinary weekdays, except for white collars and the boys' caps, the children still wore their own rags.

30 January 1700 ... Order'd that the Children do wear their Gowns Petticoats and Stockins only on Sundays and Holy Days, and on such Wednesdays as they do go to Trinity Chappell to have the Sermon, and their Caps and Bands everyday; and that the said Children do constantly bring their Gowns and Petticoats Shoes and Stockins to the School the next day after wearing them in order to be laid up.

For health reasons frequent walks were advised, and in 1705 each girl was given a pair of pattens "to keep her feet clean and tite". Three years later it was decided to give the headmaster a greatcoat and the headmistress a riding hood (a woollen, caped hood, tied under the chin and usually worn in the country or for travelling), "to attend the children in cold and wet weather".

92. Girls of the schools named *c.* 1805: *Left* wearing tippet and bonnet; *right* handkerchief and cap (as for Fig. 5)

The form of the eighteenth-century dress made some sort of under-lying support almost a necessity (and see page 11). A minute of 1748 reads: "The Mistress, informing the Trustees that there are several of the House Girls boarders in great want of Bodice [stays], order'd that 40 pair of Leathern ones be made to supply the present Necessity and the next Whitsuntide Clothing".

In the nineteenth century the girls were still kept walking for their health and we have seen (page 15) that this meant extra shoes and bonnets. We know that they also had cloaks.

Several measures were taken during the century to ensure their being "inconspicuous"; in 1851 their mittens were made to match the dresses, instead of being yellow. The attire evidently conformed to charity-school pattern (Fig. 92). The girls proudly dressed up in this ancient style of uniform to celebrate the opening of new school buildings in 1929.

ST ANNE'S, SOHO

The same year as at St Martin-in-the-Fields a school was opened in the neighbouring parish of St Anne – at first for boys from ten years up-wards, and in 1703 for girls too. Its history, again based on minute books, has been told by J. H. Cardwell.[3] When the boys attended church for the first school sermon in 1699, they wore the grey coats, caps, bands, shoes, stockings and even gloves, that had been presented by the trustees. Not long afterwards they were given the usual leather breeches and brass buttons for their coats, and all the children got shoe buckles, at 2d a pair, presumably for their next pair of shoes. In

1765 a metal badge was added, with the lettering "St. A. WESTMINSTER".

The clothing altered little, except once or twice in coat colour, until in 1845 it was decided that the uniform should comprise: "a Round Brown Jacket and waistcoat with brass buttons and badge instead of the present form of dress and the word 'Soho' be substituted for 'Westminster' on the said badge". The "round jacket" would be a short one like an Eton jacket, normal wear for boys at that time. The change in the badge is an interesting sidelight on the way the Soho area had come to acquire its own individuality within Westminster.

In 1872 the issue of special clothing came to an end with the removal of the school to a new site.

Girls joined the school in 1703 but lived quite separate lives from the boys and spent much time in making and mending their own clothes and the boys' shirts and in knitting stockings for all.

They seem to have been better provided out of doors than girls in many sister schools, for even at the start they had "ash-coloured mantles" and soon acquired not only "pattins" in 1715 but in 1706 hoods.

	£	s	d
[1706] Two pieces of Chamblet for Binding the Girls' Hoods	5	4	0
[1707] Whalebone for ye Girls' Hoods and for making one of them and lineing for one of them		4	6

There were other concessions at the same time. The petticoats had black shalloon borders (frills), and there were already not only white

93. Charity girl wearing rosette and medal on ribbon for anniversary service at St Paul's (Kate Greenaway illustration, as in Fig. 90)

Sunday aprons but "scouring aprons" made of a sort of coarse serge, called cadiz or caddice (misread by Cardwell as "caddue"), in blue or green.

Cardwell tells us little about the nineteenth-century girls' dress but records an actual reminiscence of the annual charity-school festival in St Paul's. At this, our St Anne's girls were "each smartly decked with a green and white rosette on the left breast – a very pretty sight" (Fig. 93).

94. Charity children going to church in typical costumes of 1830s. Over blue
dresses and white bibbed aprons, the girls wear collared tippets; short sleeves
(now unfashionable) with long gloves. Boys wear blue coats and flat caps with
buff, possibly leather, breeches. Suits are in eighteenth-century style contrasting with round jacket and pantaloons of the little gentleman. Note charity
boys' badges, and their bands like the parson's (Hand-coloured print after
T. Richardson of Derby)

ST MARY ABBOTS, KENSINGTON

This school has a special history[4] for it was a parish school grafted on to one that had been privately founded long before. In 1645 one Roger Primble provided in his will "for the maintenance of a Free schoole in Kensington for poore mens children". Then in 1707 the people of the parish decided to increase the endowment of this early school to allow for more children. Aims were to "instruct them in the Principles of the Church of England and to dispose of them to Trades or what their genius [bent] is judged most capable of". Queen Anne was an early subscriber.

The children had the standard outfit, with the addition of riding hoods for the girls, and they were all dressed in blue. The boys had "Blew Woollen Caps with Crimsone Toffs [tufts – sometimes misread as "Toss's"] and Crimsone strings"; also "Briches of Blew leather", though breeches were usually either of buff leather or of blue cloth.

Later the boys, and at times the girls too, had "pewter medals", as the school badge, and for those who owed their places to Roger Primble this was faithfully embossed with the letters "R. P.".

We are fortunate in having the early uniforms portrayed in statuettes, of which for once we know the exact date: 1712. They were made to adorn the building erected for the school by Hawksmoor and can still be seen on the north wall of its successor, the home of the present church primary school, just south-west of the church. In style of costume they are, again, typical examples of the early period, and the boy has the charm of holding a scroll bearing the appropriate words "I was naked and ye clothed me" (Fig. 1).

The girl wears a blue bibless apron such as we know was supplied, but her square-shaped bands, now blue, would have been painted white originally, like her stomacher and the coif with its characteristic pinched-up frill. The children's red shoes are certainly a piece of modern artistic licence. For a good side view of the cap see Fig. 80b.

In 1799 a Mrs Leech made a bequest for the daughters of domestic servants to be taken into the school as boarders, an imaginative charity which must have eased the lives of the mothers as well as the girls. She decreed that they must be dressed differently from the others, who still wore blue. The little girls of the "Mrs Leech charity" were wearing, in 1804:

A stone-coloured camlet gown
A petticoat of the like stuff
The linen and stockings the same as worn by the girls on the School Establishment

A bonet, the same, only distinguished by a purple ribbon fixed plain around the crown
Also a ribbon of the like colour fixed plain around the cap,
A white handkerchief instead of a tippet
Black leather shoes and strings[5]

The "handkerchief instead of a tippet" reminds one of the distinction between older and younger girls' uniform at the Red Maids' School (Fig. 60).

In 1837 a ragged school for the very poor was opened locally. At the same time the parish school ("Bluecoat" as it was often called) began charging a fee of 6d weekly for children and 2d for infants. Soon after this all the free clothing was discontinued.

HAMLET OF RATCLIFF SCHOOL, STEPNEY

This school has very full records[6] and survives to this day as the Stepney Greencoat C.E. Primary School, Norbiton Road, London E.14. Inspired by the church and publicly supported, it opened for boys in 1710 and for girls in 1723.

At the start the boys must have looked exactly like those at the Grey Coat, Westminster, with similar caps and all. The girls' gowns were also grey. All the children received two pairs of shoes a year, a not unusual allowance, but they were certainly more generously dressed than many. The girls already had mittens and, surprisingly, "Leghorn" straw hats with pink ribbons. Later it was bonnets, until 1786 when straw hats reappeared.

The colour of the uniform was changed to brown in 1758 but finally settled down to green, tufts included, in 1763.

A pair of statuettes, now transferred to the modern buildings, are important, since they are of a less well-known period than many of their kind. The receipted bill from Mr Dean, their sculptor, is dated 1759. As might be expected the coat and dress have been repainted green, though at the time that they were sculpted the uniform was still brown.

The boy's coat has the stand collar that was usual in the 1760s and the tabs of his band are much longer and narrower than before. The girl's dress is no longer open, neither the skirt nor the bodice, which has a false stomacher-front. Her neckwear is a very short tippet with three buttons in front, an interesting early form of this garment. The frill of her cap shows no hint of the rise in front that was universal earlier.

In 1782, following the misbehaviour of one of the children out of school, pewter badges were instituted. The treasurer had to provide a set numbered "1" to "35" for the boys and another, "1" to "15", for the girls, all engraved with the word "Ratcliff". From quite early days the school had taken in "unclothed" children as well as "clothed"; it was only the latter who had to wear badges, presumably because they were less easy to distinguish from one another than children not in uniform. Later the whole school wore badges and, as they were always being lost, parents had to put down a deposit of 6d. This was not unreasonable, since the disc was now made of copper.

The problem of pawning was always coming up. In 1757 the mistress was ordered to have all the linen marked "Ratcliff" in full, and legal proceedings were sometimes taken when parents could not produce a child's clothing intact when he or she left the school.

In or around the opening of the nineteenth century there were con-

95. Statuette, Ratcliff Green Coat School, Stepney, 1759. See text (Courtesy: Headmaster, Stepney Greencoat C.E. Primary School)

cessions to fashion and comfort, some of which have already been noticed. The girls' gowns could be of "Camblett", a fine worsted, instead of the rough serge. As it was a thinner fabric, a flannel "coat" (petticoat) was added, but the girls now had to make their own clothes. They had always learnt sewing. A receipt, signed in 1757, records the purchase of "3 dozen iron needles at 3d each". All the children were given pocket handkerchiefs for the first time.

As at St Anne's, the twentieth century saw the dawnings of a pride in the old school tie. As mentioned before, page 32, replicas of the later eighteenth-century uniforms are worn by some of the boys and girls on state occasions to this day.[7] See photograph (1976) at Bethnal Green Museum.

COLCHESTER BLUE COAT SCHOOL

Among charity schools of the early vintage in the provinces, a few that turned into public schools have already been noticed. As regards the others, two must suffice – a typical one at Colchester and a less usual one at Birmingham.

For the school at Colchester subscriptions were coming in well by the end of 1709[8] and it probably opened in the next year. The uniform seems to have been blue from the beginning, including the boys' caps. When this Blue Coat school amalgamated with the Colchester National School in 1811, its boys continued to wear their own uniform until 1927 when the issue of free clothing as such came to an end.

The school has an interest for us in that, as with the Beckett and Sergeant School, there is satisfactory evidence for three chronological stages in the children's dress.

A pair of statuettes, now in the Town Hall, gives an excellent example of the costumes for the boys and girls in the Queen Anne period. The boy is illustrated in our Fig. 77 (*left*) and the girl, who has a long white apron over her blue dress, wears a cap and band very like those in Fig. 80c.

The next stage is illustrated by a quaint set of dolls thought to have been made in the first half of the nineteenth century. The boys' long blue coats are still eighteenth century in style and their legwear suggests either long narrow grey breeches or three-quarter length trousers of a style common in the first two decades of the nineteenth century.

The girls, in their high-waisted blue dresses, are interesting for their white detachable sleeves. The hands are in white mitts, the round tippets (at least as arranged now) fasten at the back and the white caps with a frill continued as a tie under the chin, as in cornettes (see p. 132). In all, the style would correspond with that of charity girls from 1810 to

96. Replicas of Colchester Blue Coat School uniforms,
?1810–1830. See text (Holly Trees Museum, Colchester)

1830. A list of the clothing, which may date from about 1811, was still in existence in 1940.[9]

Finally we have a pair of oil portraits showing the compromise effected between normal and traditional dress in the teenage pupils' uniform *c*. 1890.

97. Portrait of Colchester Blue Coat schoolgirl, 1890s. Traditional dress including undersleeves (Painting by Frank Daniell. Courtesy: Holly Trees Museum, Colchester)

The boy's colour scheme is exactly as before, even to the white bobble on his blue cap and the grey of his breeches (Fig. 77*b*).

Except for the cut of her dress and the mob shape of her cap the girl is dressed much like the dolls (Fig. 97). Beside her is a blue-ribboned straw hat. True to charity-school tradition she is engaged on a piece of knitting.

BIRMINGHAM BLUE COAT SCHOOL

This establishment, now a preparatory-cum-middle school, is somewhat rare in having been a boarding school from its very foundation in 1722. Its aim was to maintain boys and girls who were in need, to impart the Christian religion and "to produce literate, disciplined children as apprentices and domestic servants".[10]

Records of the clothing provided over the 250 years are varied and relatively complete. Accounts show that the main garments of the first issue were very cheap, and one wonders whether some local clothing manufacturer provided them at cost price as his contribution. The shoes, on the other hand, were no cheaper than in London.

	Birmingham in 1722[11]	*London in 1712*[12]
Coat and waistcoat	1s 8d	7s 6d
Gown and petticoat	1s 10d	5s 8d
Shoes	1s 10d	1s 10d

The costumes for 1770 are well shown in a pair of statuettes made in that year and now, after restoration, standing in the school hall. The boy's long coat and waistcoat must have looked very old-fashioned at this date. Indeed his whole uniform could easily belong to Queen Anne's time except that his tabs are elongated and his shoe buckles large and ornamental.

98. Statuettes, Blue Coat School, Birmingham, 1770. See text. If, as believed, these are of Coade stone, they must be almost the earliest examples of "Charity children" in this medium. The sculptor was Edward Grubb. (Colour photographs in *The Blue Coat School, Birmingham*, 1972. Courtesy: the compiler, V. D. B. Still, and the Headmaster)

The girl is more in the fashion. The dress is now a closed gown, the cap close-fitting with no "pinch" to the frill (its blue ribbon matches the dress), and again the shoes have large buckles. What is unusual is the bareness of her neck and arms. She has neither handkerchief, tippet nor mittens, though her square neckline is very decolleté and her sleeves short. However this immodesty was rectified in Victorian times. An old photograph shows the girls in 1855 all wearing fichu-shaped tippets. They still have white aprons, but no caps. Thus one notices that they all have their hair close-cropped.

Walter Morgan, R.B.A., has given us a clear impression of how the boys looked in 1872, in an oil painting now hanging in the school assembly hall. He was commissioned to paint the school building (and the picture shows it, complete with its statuettes), but streaming out from the front door are the boys themselves. They make a striking contrast to the onlookers – a hungry-looking boy and girl in grey and brown rags and a stiffly elegant lady opposite. For once we see boys in outdoor clothes. All have cloaks, introduced in 1860; also tam-o'-shanters and the working-class low boot called a high-low.

Most of the boys are entirely in blue, except for their buff corduroy breeches and, of course, the long white bands. But the second pair are in green. This is to mark off, just as was done in the Northampton Blue Coat School, boys indebted to a particular benefactor. In 1690 George Fentham, a philanthropic mercer of Birmingham, had bequeathed funds for the poor which were partly used to support and educate children. These beneficiaries formed part of the Blue Coat School from its inception but were always, whether boys or girls, dressed in green, cloaks and all.

Thanks to the famous photographer Benjamin Stone we have several photographs of all the children in 1910. The boys, at a picnic, appear almost exactly as before, white tabs included (Fig. 70). The girls at the same picnic are wearing a very unpractical variety of white starched pinafore. It looks as though it was made by joining on to the front of an apron a closed triangular tippet. Possibly the tippet is separate, and has a waistband of its own, attached in front. Compare *Workwoman's Guide*, Pl. 12, Fig. 34. Another photograph shows that the tip of the rear triangle was either left free or tucked into the waistband.

The girls' black boots and stockings and their stiff straw hats were only what any girls might be wearing at that time, but the black mitts are a relic of the past. Three Fentham girls can be distinguished in the front row by the paler tone of their green dresses and their lack of dark bows. They wore smaller ones, of a buff colour.

The girls had an ordinary kind of pinafore for daily work, probably

99. Girls of Blue Coat School, Birmingham, 1910. See text. (Benjamin Stone photograph, as in Fig. 70)

made of brownish holland. It hung straight down from the shoulders and fastened at the back of the neck.

The school still possesses some complete sets of outer clothing for girls and boys, probably as worn just before everyday uniform was abolished in 1955. The blue garments, like most blue uniforms since the nineteenth century, are navy, but the boys' coats are still long and cut with sloping fronts and stand collar just as they always were. Their six buttons and those of the waistcoats are embossed "Blue Coat School" on the blue coat and "Fentham Trust" on the green. There is a boy's blue cloak, but no overcoat. The legwear is almost equally antiquated: corduroy breeches with square-fall fronts, and buff in colour, as though to imitate the earlier wash-leather. The cap is like the tam-o'-shanters in Morgan's painting. The neck-band is of white linen, tied at the back with tapes and having typical long tabs.

Of the girls' dresses, the navy blue, being collarless, beltless, short-sleeved and made of serge, seems of an earlier vintage than the Fentham girls' green one, apparently of mercerized cotton. For both there is a white linen, fichu-shaped tippet, free from the bibless white apron. It seems therefore that the elaborate pinafore had been given up. The mitts, unlike those in Stone's photograph, are white and, like undersleeves, extend above the elbows, where they tie with a drawstring. They cover half the palm and have an open-ended thumb. There are two white caps of the simple mob shape and, over the drawstring that gathers the frill, one has a blue ribbon, the other a green. The green ribbon has "21", the child's number, stitched on it in red. There is a girl's navy-blue cloak, like the boy's, except for having a hood.

Finally we have a pair of late nineteenth or more probably early twentieth-century Blue Coat dolls, about a foot high. Their clothes are carefully finished. The brass buttons on the waistcoat must have been specially made — tiny as they are, they are marked "BLUE COAT" — and the knitted stockings fit nicely. The uniforms, indoor wear, correspond with the actual specimens fairly closely and probably give valid evidence on how these were worn; for example the fichu has a fastening in front, under the chin, with a blue bow covering it.

Today the children, in their up-to-date school, wear uniform only on Sundays; but then there are distinct echoes of the past. And the school magazine is still aptly called *The Blue Cloak*.

CHAPTER 9

Homes for children and young women

The present chapter deals with residential homes where the principal object was the occupants' physical and moral well-being; though education was included, admission could be in infancy or, in the case of "fallen girls", in adulthood. These were therefore not typical schools.

Charity homes for destitute and/or delinquent young people have always been numerous. Our aim is to give some examples that are typical and a few others that have features of special interest. To exemplify children's homes started in the seventeenth century, a London home run by the Church, with royal patronage, will be described.

ST MARGARET'S HOSPITAL, WESTMINSTER

From 1624 to 1873 there stood in the Tothill Fields area of Westminster a home for children called the Green Coat School or, officially, "The Hospital of St Margaret's, Westminster, of the foundation of King Charles", also called "King Charles's Hospital". This is often stated to have been initiated by Charles I[1] but in fact what he did in 1633 was to give a charter of incorporation to an existing institution: ". . . the Hospital of St Margarets Westminster in which poor boys and girls of tender age may not only carefully be maintained with meat, drink and apparel, but also be instructed in the manual arts".[2]

It was the churchwardens of the parish of St Margaret's who had applied to the King[3] for a licence in mortmain. They had set up a

"Children's Hospitall" in 1624* (then called St Margaret's), where the uniform was already green, and there is no doubt that the King was giving his name, his financial support and a charter to a Green Coat institution already begun by the Church.** Poverty in Westminster was acute, the Abbey's almoners still being missed after dissolution of the monasteries, and the building of a children's home by the Vestry of St Margaret's had been one effort to deal with it.

Further funds were provided by members of Parliament at their services in St Margaret's church and also by private benefactors, notably the Earl of Manchester, and from fines levied in the parish for drunkenness and swearing. About twenty, mostly very young children were taken in at first.

Extracts from the churchwardens' records for the first year[4] (1624–5) are worth giving in some detail for the information they afford on the dress of small pauper children at this date. Other entries throw light on what is meant by some of these items (italics ours):

	li	s	d
For twoe peece of broad Cloath for the Children's *Coates*	22		
,, two peeces of Cotton		9	14
,, the carriage and bringing them home			12
,, one hundred *muckenders* at ijd a peece and for tape		17	8
,, one hundred and six ells and a quarter of Canvas at xv d the ell to make *shirts* for the children	6	12	10
,, making of a hundred *shirtes* at 2d the peece		16	8
,, seaven dozen and fower *double bandes* at 3d a band [? collar with pair of "tabs"]		22	

* Evidenced by the churchwardens' accounts for May 1624–May 1625, but apparently unknown to London historians such as Strype and Edward Walford. John Nichols, when quoting the churchwardens' first clothing list for the children's home (*Illustrations of the Manners and Expenses in Antient Times* (1797) p. 33 seq.), mistakenly states that "the children" there mentioned were in the "House of Correction" which had been set up two years before.

** John E. Smith, in his *Catalogue of Westminster Records* (1900) pp. 56–7, suggests that the King Charles Hospital of 1633 "merged with the St Margaret's Hospital"; but there seems no evidence that they existed separately at any time.

For twoe dozen of single *Bandes* at 3d a band	6	
,, 24 paire of *shoes* for the children	24	
[40 more later in the year]		
Paid for 40 *Coyfes* at 4d a peece	13	4
For gartering [made of tape] for the children	3	9
,, fustian* and holland *Capps*	2	9

For nine dozen *Stockings*	3	8	
,, making xliiij^tie *Coates* for Children		22	
,, making of Fortie *petticoates*		10	

For three dozen black *cappes* [for boys]	36	
,, three dozen *girdles* for the children	4	
,, twoe dozen yardes of Caddowes** for *girdles*		
for the Girles	3	6
,, twoe dozen of *pointes* [laces]		6
,, amending the children's shoes	4	6

It is at first sight odd that no gowns for girls nor breeches for boys are here mentioned. This is because the "coate" or "upper coate" was the long-skirted dress, open in front, which was worn alike by girls and boys – by all boys until the age of eight, and by boys in schools like Christ's Hospital at all ages. The "petticoat", like that of Christ's Hospital, was a skirt worn underneath. "White Cotton to make pet-ticoats and lynings at 14d. the yard" is cited in 1628,[5] "cotton" meaning at this date a woollen fabric with a raised nap.

The "muckender" was a pocket handkerchief, something of a luxury. Pockets were rare and for children it would be tied on at the waist, hence the tape (Fig. 100).

There were a few distinctions between girls' and boys' clothing. The girls had blue aprons (from 1628–9) and also woven girdles, instead of cord or leather belts. The coifs, white linen indoor caps, would be worn by small children of both sexes, but the black woollen caps were for the boys only and were already characteristic of charity boys.

* Material with a pile, at this date probably of wool and linen mixed, suitable for winter.

** A worsted tape, a substitute for ribbon.

100. Example of costume of small boys in late Elizabethan and Jacobean times, showing "muckender" or handkerchief tied on at waist of long "upper coat". Working-class children would have a collar in place of ruff (Brass effigy, Merstham church, Surrey, illustrated in Phillis Cunnington and Anne Buck *Children's Costume in England 1300–1900*, 1965. Courtesy: Anne Buck)

A good deal was paid to a tailor for mending, suggesting that the girls were indeed of tender age. Shirt collars were "filletted" (bound, where frayed?), coats were given new sleeves, and in 1624–5 17s. was even spent on mending stockings.

There was the usual absence of outdoor wear. Presumably in bad weather the children simply stayed indoors.

The colour green is first mentioned in 1628 – "greene Cloath to make coates". In 1624 "Disbursments for the Hospitall" (now "King Charles's") include one "For xl yardes of grasse greene kersey", for the same purpose.

In 1691 the philanthropic Duchess of Somerset made a bequest that was applied to scholarships, and her beneficiaries were distinguished by wearing yellow caps.

The Hospital was rebuilt, partly by Dr Busby of Westminster School fame, in 1688. Gradually, like many of its kind, it turned into a high-class school. In 1878 it moved and was amalgamated with Palmer's and others as the Westminster City School (not to be confused with Westminster School); but the boys were still remembered in 1890 as having been dressed in a "long green skirt with a red leather girdle, similar in pattern to the attire of Christ's Hospital boys".[6] Thus there were still links with the little paupers of the past. Today the uniform is black, but livened with gold braid.

101. "Asylum Dining Hall", Lambeth, 1808. Orphan girls in uniform, watched by their patrons (Detail of print in R. Ackermann *Microcosm of London*, 1808)

ASYLUM FOR FEMALE ORPHANS, LAMBETH

The famous philanthropist Sir John Fielding, brother of the novelist, had been profoundly disturbed by the problem of homeless and delinquent children while serving as a Bow Street Magistrate, and in 1758 he founded an Asylum for girls in Lambeth. The aim was to prevent delinquency and especially to protect against prostitution.

The girls were taken between the ages of eight and eleven. They were all trained for domestic service from the start and Mrs Trimmer,[7] in 1801, is warm in her praise of the care the committee took to make sure a household was both humane and respectable before a girl was apprenticed out to it. The Asylum rose to fame and is depicted in

Ackermann's *Microcosm of London*; so we know what the uniform was like in 1808 (Fig. 101). The girls' ankle-length dresses are plum-coloured and have the high waist usual at that time, but in moderation. The very full skirt is a working-class style contrasting with the Empire lines of the lady who gawps at the girls. Like charity-school children they have a white starched tippet, of the rounded shape, which they probably wore only for dinner and on Sundays. The white cap is comfortable, lacking any frill or curtain at the back, and resembles one described as "nightcap or a young servant's day cap" in *The Workwoman's Guide*. There are no white aprons, doubtless as an economy. The girls who are serving wear aprons with brown and white stripes.

We are fortunate in that the *Illustrated London News* has recorded what the girls were wearing exactly one hundred years after the foundation. A centenary dinner was held in 1858, in a marquee, and presided over by the Archbishop of Canterbury (Fig. 102). The girls now have white bibless aprons and curious caps where the crown forms a nearly spherical bun on top of the head. Other new features are the half-dozen buttons on the tippets and a neck ribbon tied in a large bow at breast level. This carries neither the badge nor the medal that a charity schoolgirl might have; it appears to be purely an ornament – perhaps compensating for the absence of collar or frill on the tippet. The charity girl's mittens are now in evidence.

102. Girls of Lambeth Asylum at the Centenary Fete in 1858. (*Illustrated London News* Vol. XXXIII, 41)

THE HARPUR TRUST CHILDREN'S HOME

For an example of an eighteenth-century children's home for both sexes we might look at one which, like so many charities, was a twig that grew on an already ancient tree.

Sir William Harpur, one-time Lord Mayor of London, left land in trust, in 1552, for educational and charitable purposes in his home town of Bedford.

The famous grammar school, now Bedford School, was founded immediately, but in 1764 the value of the property had so greatly increased that the trust was able to establish in addition a hospital (i.e. a home) "for poor boys and girls in real need".

The boys' coats and girls' gowns were made of a soft mid-blue twilled woollen cloth, the boys having leather breeches. In 1789 John Byng[8] on a visit to Bedford remarked on the cleanliness of "two fine boys dressed in light blue, the livery of the great Harpur Charity here".

103. "Hospital boy, Sir Wm. Harpur Charity", Bedford, in 1840s. Old-style suit: breeches with square falls, coat like eighteenth-century "frock" (Contemporary drawings by Bradford Rudge. Courtesy: Bedfordshire Archaeological Society)

However, a committee of governors visiting in 1815 was horrified at the prevailing carelessness and dirt – some of the clothes were ragged and the boys had no nightcaps in bed and threw their day caps on the floor at meals. Supervision was then tightened up and, among other improvements, two clean shirts a week were allowed instead of one. There was now a greatcoat or a cape for outdoors and in 1867 boys had tweed trousers for Sundays.

In 1853 the boys' very old-fashioned weekday outfit (Fig. 103) was changed to corduroy trousers with a cloth jacket in place of the longer coat. The girls in 1782 were dressed just like London charity-school children. They wore a blue open gown and petticoat, a "round-eared cap" and a tippet. They also had black aprons, worsted mittens and later black stuff bonnets. In 1825 they were at last given cloaks, in 1843 straw bonnets and in 1854 a woollen scarf for going to church in cold weather – the winter climate of Bedford was raw and very foggy.

When leaving the home for apprenticeship or service, each child was given an outfit and from 1819 each girl had a deal box to put it in.

The home was finally wound up in 1871. For this account we are entirely indebted to Joyce Godber's *The Harpur Trust, 1552 to 1973* (1973).

THE MAGDALEN HOSPITAL

While Fielding was raising funds for the Asylum for Female Orphans, Robert Dingley with Jonas Hanway and others was planning a home for the rescue of seduced girls and prostitutes; indeed Fielding and Dingley discussed the possibility of building a single institution to combine the purposes of prevention and cure. But this was not done and 1758, the year that the Asylum came into being in Lambeth, saw the founding of the Magdalen Hospital for young fallen women in Whitechapel. However, when the latter needed larger quarters, it was moved to St George's Fields between Southwark and Lambeth and shared some facilities with its neighbour.

The Magdalen Hospital was called by H. F. B. Compston (1917)[9] "the mother penitentiary of our Empire". After a century of life it had already become only one, albeit the most renowned, among eight London penitentiaries for the very same purpose (*Quarterly Review*, 1848). While its avowed aim was the moral recovery of its inmates, it had their physical welfare also at heart and the need was often desperate. *An Account of . . . the Magdalen Charity* written by the chaplain, William Dodd, three years after its inception, tells us that "Most of these poor objects, who have escaped from loose houses, have come almost naked or with borrowed cloaths". This was often because they had escaped from brothels and had not dared

104. Magdalen Hospital girl, 1761.
Grey dress with handkerchief crossed
over and tucked under bib of apron,
or of bodice; black sleeved mittens;
plain bergère-shaped hat (Frontispiece of William Dodd *Account of
. . . the Magdalen Charity*, 1761)

to run away in the clothes there provided lest they be arrested for theft. Of
the 281 girls admitted by 1761 several were under fourteen and ten were
lunatic ("a sad and frequent consequence of taking Mercury") or had fits.

In the year 1760–1 the cost of clothing and house linen for 92 new
inmates, together with replenishings for the other 134, amounted to
nearly a thousand pounds.

Rights of the individual were respected in that every girl had the key
of a locker in which to keep her clothes, but it is a little chilling to read
the rules. Matron must see that "all the women are neat and decent in

their cloaths and person. . . they wear an uniform of light grey and in the whole of their dress are plain and neat". The grey material was a coarse linen canvas or sackcloth and probably neither bleached nor dyed. The rest of the uniform is well described pictorially by the frontispiece of Dodd's book (Fig. 104) and verbally by none other than Horace Walpole. He was one of many who were attracted by the spectacle of the girls in chapel and at dinner. In a letter of January 1760 to George Montagu he writes: "At the west end were enclosed the sisterhood . . . all in greyish brown stuffs, broad handkerchiefs [neckerchiefs], and flat straw hats, with a blue riband, pulled quite over their faces". At table they were without their hats, but it was a rule that their day caps must likewise be demurely worn "forward near the forehead".[10]

Compston could still write, in 1917; "the costume is of uniform pattern". He describes it thus: ". . . for work-a-day use a blue print, with thick shawl for winter; the best dress is of a delicate, light brown with a snowy white tippet folded across the bosom. A neat white cap is worn. This tasteful and becoming costume is an improvement on the original one".[11] We have already noted Compston's view that the style of this outfit was an attempt to suit the girls. To the wearers it must still have seemed antediluvian.

THE FOUNDLING HOSPITAL (THOMAS CORAM FOUNDATION)

Probably the best known of all children's homes in England is the Foundling Hospital which owes its existence to Captain Thomas Coram and received its royal charter in 1739. It was established for the "Maintenance and Education of Exposed and Deserted Young Children". The general rule was to admit only illegitimate babies, who had to be less than a year old.

Coram's scheme received nationwide support. A wider variety of great names has been associated with it than with almost any other comparable charity. Handel raised funds by publicly playing the organ (his gift) in the Hospital chapel. Hogarth was a close friend of Coram's, whose portrait he presented, and he established a long-lasting association between artists and the Hospital; hence its famous paintings.

The dedicated way in which the organizers worked has left us a great wealth of records.[12] The moving scenes these bring to the imagination and the fact that most of the material has never been published have tempted us to deal with the Foundling more fully than with other such institutions.

Admission — Numbering — "Tokens"

The babies were first received at the Hospital in London* and immediately placed out to wet-nurses and foster mothers in the country until their fifth year. Then they returned, were reared till fifteen years old and were finally sent out, the boys to apprenticeships, to the sea or into military bands, the girls mostly as domestic servants. The child's clothing at all stages was provided by the charity, including an outfit when he or she left the home.

A vivid account is given to us by the Daily Committee's minutes of that evening on 25 March 1741 when, at 8 o'clock, the door of the Hospital was first opened. It was all the porter could do to control the crowd of desperate women with their wailing infants. Taken one by one, each baby was very carefully "inspected, Numbered and the Billet of its Descrip[tio]n enter'd by three different Persons".[13] By midnight thirty had been admitted and the Hospital was full.

The "Billet" was a paper on which were entered the date, the child's number, its sex and estimated age, any "marks on the body" and an account of the clothes it was wearing. For this purpose the Committee soon had a form printed on which every item of clothing a baby might have was duly listed, "leaving room for description of each article". Many of these forms, filled in, have been preserved by the Foundation and are interesting documents for students of infants' dress. There were no less than twenty-three, later twenty-six, possible items. Even the babies of the poor tended to be overclad.

To maintain secrecy for the "fallen" mother's sake and at the same time to enable her to reclaim the child, if ever she wished, without confusion of identity, two arrangements were enforced: numbering the child instead of recording its own or its mother's name** and ruling that persons depositing children should "affix to them some particular writing or other distinguishing mark or token".[14]

The first rule was fulfilled by the child's number practically becoming part of its costume. Foster mothers and nurses were to see that the number "was to be always visible that the child may be easily known by it".[15]

---

* Temporarily in Hatton Garden, 1741–7, then in the Bloomsbury purpose-built Hospital till 1926, and now at Berkhamsted. Several branch Hospitals were also built in country towns from 1760 onwards.

** The baby was baptized with an arbitrarily chosen name. Many were called after a benefactor of the Hospital, even in the person's lifetime; alas, child No. 2, "Eunice Coram" died within a month, and Nos. 18270 and 18346, both "Thomas Coram", were reported simultaneously for misbehaviour in 1812.[16]

The first attempt at attaching the numbers was far from satisfactory. The Daily Committee minuted, sixteen days after the first admissions: "Made some progress in affixing and stamping the Number of each child on a Piece of lead pendant on the Neck by red tape". Three days later: "Visited the children remaining in the House. We find the leaden mark of Lucretia Folkes is come off, and that on Jonathan Belcher is coming off". The use of lead however continued for some time. In 1755 we read of a do-it-yourself economy. "Mr Whatley presented a Mould and Ladle ... to cast the Leads whereon are impres'd the Numbers ... which leads now cost ½d each."

By 1799[17] another method was used, and Dickens, who lived in Bloomsbury, describes it in an account of a visit he paid to the Hospital himself in 1853, when he saw two babies admitted:[18]

A parchment ticket inscribed with the figure 20,563 was sewn upon the shoulder strap of the male infant and a similar ticket was attached to the female infant denoting that she was 20,564 – so numerous were the babies that had been there before them.

An identity "token" was brought with each child on admission – a small object, tied round the neck, or it might be "a paper pin'd on the Head"; this last was sometimes a moving document. For no. 11,179 it read: ". . . if you plese to giv the Barrer [bearer] a Tiket for I in tend to take it out a gane In so Doing you will obblige your umbell sarvent".[19] By contrast, with no. 1,116 there was a letter, in an educated hand, from the baby's "unfortunate mother who to Preserve a reputation is obliged to part with it though it is Almost dearer than Life".[20]

The Under-Fives

Each foster mother received with the baby "a bundle of clothing" which was replaced annually.

It is interesting that the Hogarths themselves acted as foster parents. One of his receipts for expenses has survived:[21]

Disbursements to 29 Sept. 1760	**£**	*s*	*d*
No. 8150 To nursing Mary Woolaston	6	10	0
No. 10,889 To Ditto Susan Windham	7	0	0
To Shoes, Stockings for them both		3	6

Recd . . . . .

[Signed] Wm. Hogarth

Until the 1830s the clothing was mostly provided, not in cash, but in kind. In April 1741, when the first bundles were made up, the Sub-Committee (all men: one of them was the Earl of Abercorn) were in some doubt about what to include. "Woollen sleeves", "rowlers" and "flannel waistcoats for some" had all been originally intended. Finally, after two women were called in to advise, these items were omitted at first. Swaddling bands or rollers were never included at any time. It is noteworthy that it was Dr Buchan, physician to the Hospital, who was a major influence in suppressing the common practice of swaddling (see page 16).

As a study in infants' wear, a table of accounts drawn up in 1751 is interesting.[22] A simplified version of it is given here.

Clothes supplied for the first year of the child's life		Second	Third	Fourth
Outside Coat*	1	1	1	1
Bodice Coat*	1	—	—	—
Petticoat*	1	—	—	—
Linsey Mantle	1	—	—	—
Pr of Stockings	2	3	3	3
Pr of Shoes	1	2	2	2
W. Bayze Blankets [white wool wrap]	2	—	—	—
Pilches [flannel wrapper covering nappy]	2	—	—	—
Pincloths [simple pinafore; larger size each year]	2	1	1	1
Biggins [probably woollen caps covering ears]	4	—	—	—
Long Stayes [stiffened with buckram or quilting]	4	—	—	—
Caps [linen]	4	3	3	3
Neckcloths	4	—	—	—
Shirts [of Scotch linen (being softer than Irish) because next the skin]	4	3	3	3
Pr Linen Sleeves [detachable, tied to short sleeves of dress]	2	—	—	—
Clouts [nappies made of Russia huckaback]	12	—	—	—
Annual cost	£1 7s 6d	11s 2d	13s 5d	17s 1d

* These items, all outer garments, were supplied only after the first three months, i.e. at short-coating.

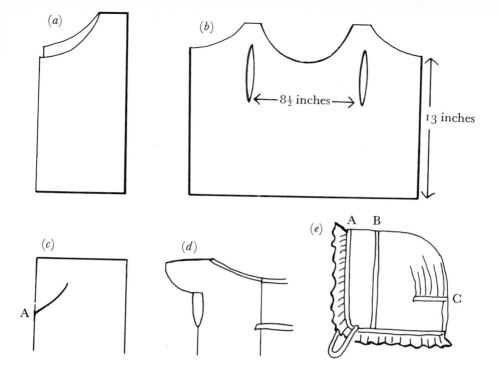

105. (a) Pattern for cutting out a pincloth for a newborn baby, 1808. (b) Same opened out to show armholes. (c) and (d) Pattern for "Waste-not Pinafore" with "shoulder cape", 1838. (e) "Foundling's Cap", 1838. A and B mark "runners for bobbins" and C the position of a "backstay" to smooth over the gathers. (a After *Lady's Practical Assistant*, page 33, 1808, b diagram, c, d and e *Workwoman's Guide* by a Lady, Pl. 3, Figs. 20, 21, and Pl. 2, Fig. 4, 1838)

Fifth year (boys)

Jacket and Breeches	13s	
3 pr Shoes @ 2/4	7s	
4 pr Stockings	5s	3d
1 hat	1s	
Buttons and Buckles		3d
[? Shirts]	6s	4½d
	£1 12s 10½d	

In the early 1750s demands for admission had overstepped resources and the clothing was slightly reduced. Possibly economy was somewhat in mind when the Court of Governors in December 1753, "desiring to bring the children up healthy and hardy ordered that no shoes and stockings be allowed children until their return to the Hospital", in their fifth year. By 1799 this rule had been changed. Inspectors of the foster "nurses" were "desired to take care that no child be permitted to wear shoes or stockings till they are 7 or 8 months old".[23]

While the infants were at nurse, they were already in uniform, their· outer garments being of "grey linsey", a cheap fabric of mixed wool and linen, until they were four years old. They then went into the brown serge of the older children. There was no provision for summer wear. In June 1759 a Mrs Searle wrote that it would be to the benefit of the children "running about" in her care if they were "allowed thinner Garments in Hot weather, for their present Clothing is too thick and I should think if they could have a kind of frocks made of the same sort of Check'd Linning their Pin Cloths are of that would be full as cheap to the Hospital and much more cooler for them".[24]

All little boys up to the age of four were dressed, as was usual at the time, like girls. In 1761 "skirts" were wanted for "66 Girls and two Boys too little to be breeched".[25]

In the nineteenth century there is no obvious change for the infants, except that they now have, for the first time, "Bedgowns" (like a long-sleeved nightdress but open down the front) and "fancy print" or pink "frocks".

About the middle of the century the term "pincloth" drops out from the records and "pinafore" takes its place. The pincloth seems to have been a pinafore as we know it, but in its simplest guise. For new-born Foundlings it was made from a piece of "check" measuring approximately $18 \times 13\frac{1}{4}$ inches[26] (Fig. 105*a* and *b*). In 1838 *Workwoman's Guide* describes infants' pinafores which have a little "cape" or "lappet" (flap) overhanging the armhole – "a shape much used by the poor as it protects the sleeves".[27] Those of the Foundlings were like this (compare Fig. 4).

In the same book we find a baby's cap specially called the "Foundling's Cap", relatively plain and easy to make (Fig. 105*c*). The "chin stay" can be made to button on at each end, so that when slobbered over it can be washed separately, to save laundering the whole cap.

Little boys continued in female attire, and in 1819 and 1820 we find them wearing the same "white tuckers and cuffs" as the girls. Even in 1858 they still had frocks and pinafores.[28]

106. Thomas Coram, with charter, at his Foundling Hospital, 1739. See text (Engraving by F. M. La Cave after William Hogarth. Courtesy: Mary Evans Picture Library)

Children in the Hospital

EIGHTEENTH CENTURY. Coming into the Hospital from the country, the children went into a new uniform. What he thought this would be like is delightfully shown by Hogarth (Fig. 106) in a design he made as the heading of a document giving the Hospital a power of attorney in 1739. (This was several years before any of the children were old enough to be there.) From imagination he depicts the boys (some on the steps, others in the right half of the group backing us) as wearing long coats exactly like those of Christ's Hospital, an institution with much more glamour than an ordinary charity school.* The collar or band with rectangular tabs was now traditional in both sorts of school. However, in the event, because its roots did not go back so far, the Foundling Hospital felt free to choose a more or less contemporary style of coat and collar. Neither does there seem to be any record that a typical charity flat cap with tuft, such as Hogarth depicts, was ever supplied.

The group facing the ships are in sailors' clothes, with which the boys who went to sea on leaving would be fitted out . Note the trousers instead of breeches.

* Deference to Christ's Hospital was again shown when its advice was sought as to whether the Foundlings should be allowed to bathe when taken to the seaside.[29]

As for the girls, Hogarth's guesses were nearer the mark but, since he presents them as typical charity-school girls, he puts them into square biblike collars which in fact they did not wear.

The true appearance of the first generation of Foundlings, as seen through the eyes of a curious contemporary, is described in the *Gentleman's Magazine* for 1747 (p. 284). The occasion was the annual festivity, the "Breakfast for Ladies" (Fig. 107). The boys' and girls' uniforms were, as they remained, a very workaday brown, but this was relieved with touches of red.

The boys have only one garment [i.e. no waistcoat] which is made jacket fashion of Yorkshire [coarse] serge with a slip of red cloth across their shoulders [an epaulette], their shirt lapping over their [coat] collar resembling a cape [i.e. the shirt had a wide turn-down collar unlike that of a man, yet not a charity schoolboy's "band"]. Their breeches hang loose a long way down the leg [to allow for growth?]; instead of buttons [at the knee] is a slip of red cloth, furbelow'd [ruched].

In the magazine's illustration both boys and girls are depicted in straw hats: this was in May; in winter it was still a hat for the boys, but probably of felt, and an outer cap or a bonnet for the girls. Trimmings of these were of red ferret or ribbon, to match the epaulettes.

The boys' suits were cut out by a tailor and accounts show how

107. Girl and boy of Foundling Hospital, with flowers "to present to the ladies" at May Day festivities, 1747 (*Gentleman's Magazine* vol. XVII, 285, detail)

108. Foundlings in the original dining hall, 1773. Close-fitting caps, blue and white check bibbed aprons over brown dresses with red edgings and waist-bands (Watercolour by John Sanders on loan to Foundation, detail. Courtesy: Thomas Coram Foundation)

carefully made they were, with "Buckram, Mowhair, List, Stay tapes etc." For the coat there was a bright red shalloon lining, for the breeches a linen one, "canvas for strengthening the inside Band" and "Russia drab for the pockets".[30]

In 1772 the waistcoat, long since worn at some charity schools, was at last added, for warmth. In 1788, we read, a sub-committee complained about "two Pieces of Lambskin, a sort of Baize used for the Boys Waistcoats . . . the Quality is not as good . . . and the colour [probably red] not like the last".[31]

Regulations had it that the girls in the Hospital must be "dressed plain and neat . . . cloathed in a manner proper for labour and differing from that of children at Nurse".[32]

But the girls' brown serge* dresses were cut in the style of the day (Fig. 108), the bodice stiffened and provided with a "bib" pinned up in front.

---

* In the nineteenth century the woollen cloth called "ell' or "long ell", typically made in Devon, was substituted.

Like the boys, the girls had a little red trimming on the shoulders. For work there was the usual coloured apron made of "check",* with a bib, and always a white linen cap with a border of lawn.

The Gentleman's Magazine reporter already quoted writes: "The girls petticoats are also Yorkshire Serge and their stays [bodices] are cover'd with the same . . . their cuffs, bib and apron are white linen . . . The shift is gathered and drawn with bobbin lace in the manner of a close tucker". At a time when dresses were very decolleté it was usual to show a white frill at the neckline. This was the "tucker", and a lady's was usually lace-trimmed. Had the writer known it, the girls made their tuckers separately from their shifts and of fine linen, not lace. Matron's careful reports make this clear.

In 1797 some change was made in the older girls' outfits but the minutes of the Sub-committee (always, alas, written by a man) do not record what it was.

NINETEENTH CENTURY: GIRLS. No new items appear in the records until 1816: "in future a clean pocket handkerchief be delivered on Sunday morning to each child".[33]

For some fifty years after charity school girls had begun wearing neckerchiefs or tippets, the Foundling girls still had open necks and tuckers. Then in 1841, when an era of primness was dawning even in the fashionable world, it was decided: ". . . to direct the Matron to provide the girls with Linen Tippets to be worn in addition to their ordinary dress".[34] The tippet was open, and triangular fore and aft, like the earlier handkerchief and the later fichu. The points in front were often tucked under the apron string, and the tippet fastened with a button under the chin. Once begun, the starched white tippet lasted, for Sunday and festive wear, right till the end of uniforms. But it is no surprise to learn that, only two years from the start, poor Matron had to report "that the white tippets at present in use become after two or three days wear unsightly and . . . occasion more work in the laundry than could conveniently be performed". From then on, for weekdays the girls wore brown tippets made of holland or of orleans – garments never seen in illustrations since these always portray the children in their Sunday best.

The Foundlings adopted and retained to the end an indoor cap like the cornette cap of 1800, having the caul (crown) very high and flattened behind.

---

* A linen and/or cotton material which was not necessarily checked – often striped or plain.

109. "Foundling Restored to its Mother", 1858. The older Foundling girl wears a triangular tippet and tall-crowned cap; younger one appears to have a round tippet. Presiding is John Brownlow, Secretary of the Hospital, himself a one-time Foundling (Painting By Emma Brownlow, daughter of the above, at Foundation, detail. Courtesy: Thomas Coram Foundation)

Outdoors they had brown capes lined with red and from the mid nineteenth century were allowed thread gloves. Skirts rose to calf length but otherwise the uniform remained entirely unchanged, except for the introduction of pinafores and bare heads for the youngest (Fig. 11).

NINETEENTH CENTURY: BOYS. Bigger alterations took place for the boys. By 1821, ahead of many charity schools, they had gone into trousers and socks, in lieu of breeches and stockings. The eighteenth-century coat gave place to a short, almost Eton-style jacket, worn over a red flannel waistcoat, and by 1855 the neckwear on Sundays was a true starched Eton collar and black tie. By now the Hospital was aspiring to the status of an important grammar school, but all the boys wore canvas or other aprons when at work. They were allowed linen trousers, "grey imperial double warp Duck", in summer[35], from 1841, and in 1814 a change from hats: "Samples of Hats and Caps having been examined, the Committee approved of the sample of Caps worn by the Boys of the Marine Society and ordered a gross".[36] The Marine Society (see page 198) was friendly to the Hospital and sometimes obstreperous Foundlings were transferred to it for training.

Making the Clothing

The children did a great deal of the making themselves. From 1751 to 1760 one Rev. Trant ran a nursery home in Yorkshire for a group of the infant Foundlings, where he saw to it that between the ages of three and five the boys were taught to knit and spin and the girls to sew.[37] Thus he put them, when only toddlers, on the road to making their own clothes. In the Hospital proper they all knitted stockings. The girls' output of clothes for children and babies, listed every month, was formidable and included everything except suits and dresses. These were cut out by a tailor and made up by the Hospital "coat maker" with assistance from boys who were taught the trade. Lame boys, particularly, learnt "Tayloring and Botching of Clothes".[38] (Compare Fig. 110.)

The detailed records kept for two centuries showing all the fabrics used make quite an interesting study in textiles. For example, in the uniform, serge, drugget, and "brown ell" succeeded one another over the years.

In the eighteenth century even the boys mended all their own clothes, "linen and shoes excepted",[39] the girls everything but shoes.

Special Dress for Special Purposes

Apart from sewing, a moderate amount of the menial work of the Hospital, and even teaching, was done by the older children, some of them after the usual leaving age of fifteen.

The older girls who did domestic work, some of whom stayed on because of physical handicaps, ranked as "servants". In 1771 Matron asked for orders regarding their clothing: "whether they shall have that commonly made for the children . . . or what other the Committee shall think proper".[40] The seven girls then in question included, besides a pupil teacher aged eighteen:

No. 3793 Rachel Painter [aged fifteen] blind of one eye and not strong in the sight of the other employed in sweeping the wards

No. 1804 Rachel Bates [aged fifteen] without teeth but otherwise Healthy . . . combing and washing the Children

No. 8048 Rose Otway [aged thirteen] lame of an ancle works with the Coat Makers

No. 9499 Catherine Candour [aged thirteen] Weak of Intelects, but employed in sweeping.

From patterns of calamanco, an inexpensive worsted fabric generally used for waistcoats and under-petticoats, the Sub-committee chose "the green sort",[41] and special gowns were made for the seven servant girls, giving them a uniform in contrast to the children's brown. Compare the York Grey Coat School, where the ten eldest girls were also distinguished by green dresses.

In 1784 all the "servants" were still in green. As well as having serviceable aprons and sleeves, they were favoured with "two white and one coloured handkerchief" (probably neckerchiefs), a quilted petticoat and even a hat – all extras.[42]

For boys in the Hospital service there were special coats for carrying coals[43] and "Linnen working frocks" [smocks] for outdoor jobs. In 1755 the Sub-committee decided to allow "the Big Boy [who] works in the Garden, Lights the Lamps etc., Cloaths made of cloth of the colour worn by the Children [but also] . . . two Frocks made for him that may wash, to save his Cloaths".[44]

Exceptional dress was also granted, in 1787, for an eleven-year old boy, still in the care of a country home, for a reason other than work: a request came in for ". . . some strong Clothing for Bartholemew Walbroke No. 17,143 . . . who is an Ideot, such as a round Frock [smock put on over the head], a strong Waistcoat and a pair of Leather Breeches as he is grown a great unruly Boy and wears his Clothes out very fast".[45]

A popular occupation for the boys was playing in the brass band. This carried on the musical tradition founded in the Hospital by Handel. In the Foundation's Court Room today can be seen a doll, made probably in the early twentieth century, showing the dress of a little bandsman. To his Foundling uniform suit a special distinction is added by a sergeant's stripes on the sleeve and a forage cap of brown, its upturned brim lined with red to match his waistcoat and adorned with the Hospital's crest, the figure of a lamb. The Hospital was built in Lamb's Conduit Fields.

So successfully did the band develop that, in the twentieth century, most of the Foundling boys passed out, no longer into the apprenticeships of ordinary working men, but into the comparative glamour of regimental and naval bands.

Though the boys in the band were extra smart, the dress of all the children, like that of charity schools, has had a great popular appeal, particularly the uniform of the girls when they carried their caps and tippets into the twentieth century. How much the children were displayed both for the benefit of the Hospital and for the pleasure of the public is told in our last chapter. It must have been with mixed feelings that the decision was finally taken *c.* 1950 to abandon the uniform for good.

HOOKE'S MILLS ORPHANAGE, NEAR BRISTOL

In 1795 an "Asylum for Poor Orphan Girls" came into being near Bristol, in a Tudor mansion known as Hooke's Mills. The girls' blue dresses, and the proximity of the Orphanage to the Red Maids' School, gave them the name "Blue Maids". A writer in 1914 shows us how long-lasting was the original uniform:

The uniform is singularly picturesque and becoming . . . a quaint mob-cap is worn indoors, while a white cotton cape [tippet] of almost ecclesiastical design, white straw bonnet with dark blue ribbon strings, white knitted gloves to the elbow, and strong shoes are worn for walking. To this a thick cloth cloak of blue and black check is added in cold weather.[46]

DR BARNARDO'S HOMES

In 1870, when Thomas John Barnardo was still only twenty-five and not yet medically qualified, his rescue work had progressed so far that, with the help of Lord Shaftesbury and other wealthy sympathizers, he rented a house in Stepney Causeway, London, and undertook to maintain there "wholly destitute lads, barefooted and ill-clad".[47]

The boys were provided with a smart uniform suit of indigo cloth comprising a metal-buttoned tunic with stand collar and scarlet piped trousers; also a cap to match. Progress in this and later projects can be followed in the journal which Dr Barnardo edited, *Night and Day*. In the issue for December 1880 we find him appealing to the ladies who had supplied a plethora of socks to switch from knitting to making flannel shirts: "the only plan by which we can avoid rheumatic and other affections among lads such as we have in our Homes is by clothing them in flannel".[48]

By 1883 the uniforms (in nine sizes) and also boots were being made on the Stepney premises, mostly by the boys themselves[49] (Fig. 110). The work was found specially suitable for the many cripples. In the

110. Crippled Barnardo boys, in working jackets, tailoring, *c.* 1890. Note crutches on the floor. Hung up behind (*left*) is a frogged coat made for the brass band (Courtesy: Dr Barnardo's Homes)

tailoring, printing and other workshops special clothing was supplied.

In 1873 Barnardo opened an institute for girls, which was to train them for domestic service. In two years, when their numbers had reached fifty-four, he suddenly pronounced it a failure. Depravity was spreading rather than declining among the girls, and the institutional atmosphere, especially the uniform, was having a bad effect. He started the alternative and very successful scheme of a group of cottages, each to house girls of all ages under the care of a "mother". There should be no "institutionalism" and they must have "nothing in the way of uniform", but be "clad as working people's children were under ordinary circumstances"[50] and, if simply, "with as much variety as possible".[51]

Accordingly Barkingside Village was created in 1876 with fourteen cottage homes. Clothes were partly supplied by ladies' sewing parties. A group, using its own taste, would sometimes take the occupants of a

111. Barnardo girls with cloaks and scarves, some with straw hats, some out-door caps tied under chin. Front pair shows hob-nailed shoes (Courtesy: Dr Barnardo's Homes)

particular cottage under its wing and make clothes for the children whose sizes, ages and even names were known to them. This, and the absence of a set uniform, resulted in just the desired variety in the villages. One group of ladies trimmed "white straw hats with dark narrow ribbon . . . and two bows in front" which a visitor to the cottage said were hailed "with genuine delight".[52] However, the same lady remarks that "The girls' dress, while sufficiently varied is a delightful contrast, in its quiet neatness, to the cheap finery which abounds".

It was certainly practical. Frocks ("good stout ones for winter") were allowed to be fairly short, pinafores were worn, and for out of doors there were "waterproof cloaks".

If the girls reacted badly to uniform, the boys on the contrary seemed to like it. Its use was extended from the earliest days to Dr Barnardo's group of non-resident lads called the "City Messengers" or "Boy Commissionaire Corps". These were organized to deliver trade circulars and other notices for a small fee. Dressed in the same smart uniforms as his other boys (the cost of which was gradually recouped from their earnings),[53] they were stationed for hire at various points in London's shopping streets, where the uniforms made them conspicuous and gave them a certain respectability. They became very popular and successful and were soon offering wood-chopping and a variety of other services like the "bob-a-job" Scouts of today.

Some of Barnardo's boys became attached to the Limehouse "Union Jack Shoeblack Brigade", founded in 1866, who, working near the docks, affected a sailor-like livery. Other shoeblack brigades wore distinctive colours (see Chapter 10). There was also a uniformed brass band.

A climax in the history of the residential homes came in 1894 when Barnardo staged a mammoth exhibition in the Albert Hall. First, twelve hundred children were paraded in their best, "the [younger] boys in white sailor suits and the girls in pink and blue frocks with straw hats".[54] Then the stage was filled with equipment and boys appeared in aprons, some of them with flat white caps, and set to work sewing, hammering, printing and baking. This was followed by "a melancholy procession of the boys and girls in rags and tatters" who had been rescued from the streets during the previous two nights. Then came "the girls from the Village Home, white-cuffed and with snowy white collars, laying tables, cooking and washing . . ."[55] The return for all this exhibition was a huge increase in funds.

In 1883 the doctor started a scheme of emigration to Canada. Each child went off fully supplied with clothing. Old photographs and drawings record their appearance, lined up on railway platforms ready

112. Smartly uniformed brass band of Barnardo boys in Stepney, *c.* 1890 (Courtesy: Dr Barnardo's Homes)

to depart. In one example little girls are having hoods tied under their chins, but in a later photograph (Fig. 114) hoods are replaced by enormous tam-o'-shanters. They carry gaily stripped bags and all look more cheerful than their escorts.

In the twentieth century there have been many changes. The clothing, even for the boys, has varied with time and place and become less and less of a noticeable uniform. In Edwardian times the littlest wore white sailor blouses, as was the fashion. Frank Norman remembers being "kitted out" on arrival at the home for backward children in 1937 "with a school uniform (such as it was) – a pair of shorts, a blue turtle-necked jersey and an ill-fitting jacket"[56] – a very ordinary outfit for a seven-year-old at that date.

By the time of his death in 1905 Dr Barnardo had admitted nearly sixty thousand children to his Homes and arranged the emigration of more than twenty thousand. Though in Canada it fell into some disrepute, in England the movement never looked back (even in the matter of dress!) and the total who have been cared for is now nearly a quarter of a million.

> By birthright pledged to misery, crime and shame,
> Jetsam of London's streets, her "waifs and strays" . . .
>
> Naked, he clothed them; hungry gave them food;
> Homeless and sick, a hearth and healing care . . .
>
> Sir Owen Seaman, verses on the death of
> Thomas John Barnardo, 1905.[57]

113. Barnardo boy emigrants, 1888. Peaked caps have strings, tied on top, presumably useful in Atlantic gales. Otherwise uniform is like that of Messenger Brigade (Press cutting. Courtesy: Dr Barnardo's Homes)

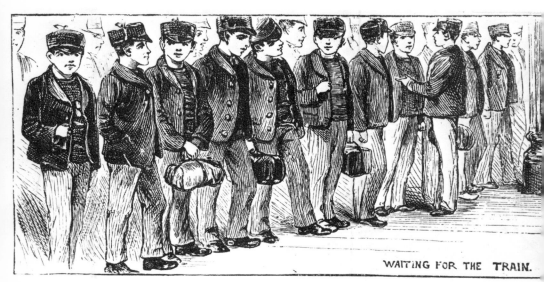

WAITING FOR THE TRAIN.

114. Barnardo girls emigrating to Canada (? early twentieth century).
Uniform varied by different scarves (Courtesy: Dr Barnardo's Homes)

OTHER CHILDREN'S HOMES

We have somewhat arbitrarily concentrated on Dr Barnardo's as an
example of nineteenth-century children's homes, partly because of its
scale and the richness of its records. The National Children's, the
National Society's and the Church of England Children's Homes, with
many others, must inevitably be omitted. Dr Müller's Orphanage at
Ashley Down, Bristol (which, by 1870, was the largest boarding school in
England), and the Royal Wolverhampton School, for the orphans of
cholera victims in 1848–9, are both referred to in other chapters.

The Infant Orphan Asylum at Wanstead, Essex, founded in 1827, is
worth a special mention because it catered for the children of the new
middle class, those overtaken by poverty but "in good social position".

H.W. GREEN Esq
Secretary
H.R.H
PRINCESS
BEATRICE
DISTRIBUTING
the PRIZES to the
Children of the
INFANT ORPHAN
ASYLUM
WANSTEAD
A GROUP of YOUNG PRIZE
WINNERS
A RECITATION
SKIPPING
DRILL

115. Infant Orphan Asylum, Wanstead, Essex. Activities in 1890 (*Daily Graphic* 30 June 1890)

Reminiscences by one of them, who was brought up there from babyhood, in Edwardian times, have come to us through his brother Donald Grist's book *A Victorian Charity*:

When I was five I was removed to the "infant" section of the Orphanage. The frocks of the nursery, in which both boys and girls were dressed, were discarded. The boys were clad in knee-length shorts, long black woollen stockings, boots, jackets cut somewhat in Norfolk style, eton collars with what would now be described as a plug-in tie. Jackets and shorts were made of a coarse material . . . with a fine black and grey check pattern. Yellow flannel vests and linen drawers and shirts completed the outfit".[58]

This uniform expressed the fact that he was a little gentleman by the inclusion of an Eton collar, but ill-fitting boots were a reminder of pauperism. The nurse who issued these was "harassed and over-worked . . . and we were afraid of her . . . If the boots she gave you were too small, you learned to accept them without protest; she had made a rough appraisal of your size and there was nothing more to be said. The effects of the monstrous cramping my feet endured remain with me still".[59]

The orphanage (then "The Royal Wanstead School"), being a charity to serve widows and orphans, became, like many others, to some extent an anachronism in the Welfare State; it closed in 1971.

Young people in training

Samuel Hartlib* in 1649 wrote an appeal for charitable subscriptions (and funds to be voted by Parliament) for the purpose of setting up workhouses. These were mainly to help the miserable poor who lacked even "food and raiment"; but also to train up children in the fear of God and to work. Trades would be taught to the boys, while "Widows or ancient maids" should teach "little children to spin, knit and sow"; the proceeds of their work would more than cover the cost of the teachers. "At 5 years old the children's work will bring in something, though but 4d. or 6d. a week, at six years old 12d. . . . ." and so on. This gives an idea of how easily children could be exploited, though total neglect was even worse (Fig. 117).

The normal fate of a destitute child, if not to live in the streets, was to be put out as apprentice, by his parish's overseer of the poor, to a tradesman or craftsman who was supposed to house, feed and clothe him as well as teach him a trade. The life of these young people was often of the greatest hardship, especially if they were sent from a workhouse to a master in another parish. He could illtreat a lad in every way and, far from clothing him, might "strip him half naked"[1], and there was no one to protest. Crabbe's *Peter Grimes* gives us a picture of the situation.

An obvious motive in charitable projects for children was to improve, for society's sake as well as their own, their chances of earning a living. But at the same time abuses of this kind must be prevented wherever possible; one solution was to set up a free training institu-

---

* Hartlib's tract was in response to one by M[ichael] S[parks], *Poore Orphans Court or Orphans Crie* (1636). Hartlib's frontispiece (our Fig. 117) is based on the title page of that tract.

tion, as we shall see. But many philanthropists made bequests for putting out the poor children of their neighbourhood as apprentices; and for those in homes for destitute children this was nearly always done. The fees would then be paid for a properly indentured apprenticeship to a reliable master craftsman or, in the case of girls, to an approved householder. There was also provided a complete new outfit of clothing to start the young people off and checks on their welfare were often made thereafter.

116. Part of signed indenture of a "Poor Boy of the Charity Schools of St James, Clerkenwell" as apprentice to a brass-founder in 1724. (Finsbury Reference Library, London Borough of Islington. Photo. Jim Connell)

117. "Destitute children who should be rescued and taught to work", 1649
(After frontispiece of a tract, *London Charitie, Stilling the Orphans Cry*, by S[amuel]
H[artlib], 1649)

There was of course another side to the picture. Apprentices were young, and those in comfortable berths, if not as idle as Hogarth's, were at least apt to spend pocket money on sartorial fancies. Rules to limit this frivolity were laid down by the guilds, for example by the Merchant Adventurers of Newcastle in 1554, by municipal authorities, as in the City of London, and even by Act of Parliament.

Thus the endowed apprentice's clothes, though chosen mainly by his benefactor, were subject to restrictions from above, like those of a student. By law, in Elizabethan times in London, he must wear blue, and a woollen, knitted statutory flat cap (which last he must never actually wear, any more than any other headgear, in his master's presence).

BRIDEWELL

One of the early institutions to provide for, as well as train, apprentices was the notorious Bridewell in the City of London. A charity it was, in a literal sense, starting as it did in a former palace donated by Edward VI, and receiving support, with strongly expressed religious motives, from guilds and parishioners of the City and sundry philanthropists. The original aim for Bridewell was to care for, and keep off the streets, the "thriftless poor", the vagrants, drunks, strumpets and what we now call "inadequates". Their children came too, or were born there, and juvenile beggars and delinquents were also brought in from the streets. Bridewell turned gradually into a prison where punishment and forced labour went on in the presence of a large child population.

The youngest children were often sent to Christ's Hospital, but the older, who concern us here, were trained by appointed "art masters" who taught trades, many of them in textiles: spinning, knitting, felting, fustian- and glove-making, "the making of apparel for the house" and the "thicking of caps by hand and foot".[2] Some of the materials used were presented by charitable city magnates.

A blue livery was given to all occupants, though it was gossiped that some of the lewd women, who "supped with the masters . . . flaunted brave apparel" in its stead.[3] The boys had blue doublets and/or jerkins with upper stocks or breeches to match, and from an early date they wore white hats. They attended the annual Spital sermon, after which a number of them would abscond, having just been supplied with new clothes.[4]

At times, the records show, the tailor would save costs by making the boys' suits on mass-production lines with consequent glaring misfits. He would also be willing to make a bargain with a boy who was near the end of his course whereby his suit would be made of a cheaper material but in a colour different from that of the uniform. In this way the boy left without the stamp of Bridewell upon him – thus going one better than the absconders at Easter. The uniform evidently did have some unmistakable features, for we read how the origin of a young truant was recognized when he was found dead in a barn at Hitchin in 1589: "William a little boy in a blew jerkine and a blew paier of gaskins [wide breeches], being the livery of Bridewell, buried, out of William Swillinghurst his barne . . . Oct. 19".[5]

In 1671, in the new buildings erected after the Plague and Great Fire, a proper industrial school was set up. A year later this event was celebrated by past and present Bridewell apprentices who processed through the City, all "decked in blue livery, white hats and stockings", to attend a sermon and a dinner in their new school.[6]

Although the school was organized separately from the prison, they were under the same roof, with the result that even now "the inmates were lowered in the public estimation".[7] The apprentices themselves did nothing to improve their reputation. The evil influence of the prison and the fact that the apprentice could come and go freely led to much disorder, which reached a peak in the early eighteenth century through their excessive enthusiasm as members of the Bridewell Hospital fire brigade. This attended fires all over London, providing excitement in their otherwise dreary life and scope for all sorts of mischief. The public grew to dread the sight of the Bridewell uniform. Hone in his *Every Day Book* . . . (1826) tells us that the boys' behaviour at Bartholemew and Southwark Fairs in 1755 was so scandalous that some of them were "ordered to be stripped of the Hospital clothing and discharged [therefrom]. The Bridewell boys were, within recollection, a body of youths distinguished by a particular dress, and by turbulance of manners".* By Hone's time the uniform consisted of a fustian coat and waistcoat, corduroy trousers, tam-o'-shanter and neckerchief.[8]

In 1830 a "House of Occupations" was set up in St George's Fields in a building belonging to Bethlehem (Bedlam) Hospital. (Bridewell and Bedlam had been administered jointly since 1557.) At first it was for adult ex-prisoners, but in 1836 it became a "Reformatory" for young people only. Thus the objects of four kinds of charity were assembled in the limbo south of the Thames – the mental patients of Bedlam, delinquent apprentices in their Bridewell blue, protected girls in their Lambeth purple and fallen girls in Magdalen grey. The Reformatory's name was happily

---

* Copeland quotes a passage where the uniform is described as "blue doublets and white hats". He gives no source but dates it "*c.* 1792", which seems impossible. "doublets", by then, would be fancy dress.[9]

changed to "King Edward's School" in 1860, and for the boys (orphans or destitute but now mostly innocent) there were, in 1867, new buildings at Witley in Surrey. Thenceforward, though technical classes continued, King Edward's gradually emulated the public schools.

In 1922 the girls' school in London had closed down, but after the Second World War the Governors pioneered by converting King Edward's into a coeducational boarding school. In 1952, with some trepidation on all sides, thirty-seven girls arrived. They did their best to fit in, for wearing their "grey suits and light blue blouses, with darker blue cardigans, they matched the boys' uniform".[10]

Today the uniform and sportswear are smart and modern but the pupils are still all children in some kind of need, and they receive gratis all essential school clothing.[11]

Once a year a fascinating commemoration takes place in St Bride's

118. A monitress at King Edward's School, formerly Bridewell, 1898 (Gordon Humphreys *Goodly Heritage, 1553–1953*, 1953. Courtesy: the Governors of King Edward's School)

Church, close to the original site of the Hospital. A splendid procession of church and civic dignitaries represents five centuries of support, and the Governors still carry green wands of office as did their forebears in Tudor days (compare page 290). On each wand are painted the arms of the City and the historic word BRIDEWELL.

THE MARINE SOCIETY

A massive operation for the rescue of indigent men and boys was mounted in 1756. Two great men, whom we have already met, had started working independently at the same time and then joined forces.

Jonas Hanway had been fighting poverty by recruiting its victims into the Navy, which was in equally desperate need. Meanwhile Sir John Fielding had been asked by Lord Henry Powlett (or Paulet) to find thirty boys to act as servants to his officers on the *Barfleur*. Fielding saw that to go to sea might be "an excellent provision for the numberless miserable, deserted, ragged and iniquitous pilfering Boys that at this time infest the streets of London".[12] Hanway thought that the same was true for destitute men, and so the Marine Society was founded to help both boys and men.

The most notable feature of the scheme was its provision, for the half-naked, of clothing suitable for life at sea rather than a cash "bounty". We are fortunate in having very full MS records of how this was done, from the very beginning.[13]

Although there was no distinctive Marine Society uniform, it seems worth while to give an account of the clothing, since it illustrates what were considered the basic necessities for sailors over a period of some two centuries.

The volunteers had to pass a scrutiny of their health, suitability and need at the Society's office. The boys then went to a hostel in Grub Street in charge of a "proveditor" who had them kitted out by the Society's contractors and looked after them until they were applied for by captains of naval, merchant or fishing vessels. See Figs. 120 and 9. (The settings in both pictures are somewhat fanciful.)

Among the wise instructions given to the proveditor was that: "If any lad or boy is delivered [to you] by a Magistrate as a delinquent . . . when he is sent to be clothed, a proper person must attend him".[14]

The men, on the other hand, went straight to ports or to naval tenders in the Thames, where slopmen provided them each with a standard set of free clothing, sorted out according to size. Hanway's scheme must have pleased the ships' captains who had been urging the Admiralty always to kit out the men brought in by press gangs without delay: lice spread while they waited in "receiving ships" and, as a result, there were terrible epidemics of typhus in the Navy. Pepys writes of the "bad condition of the pressed men for want of clothes" (*Diary*, 10 July 1666).

As there was no strict naval uniform at the time, the choice of clothing was that of the Society and was made with great care. In 1758 Hanway wrote:

As it is the constant aim of the Society to preserve the health of the *men* and *boys*, whom they clothe ... they are not contented with such manufactures as they find in the shops, but buy kerseys of the manufacturer in *Yorkshire*. These being well milled, and not stretched, make Pee-Jackets that will last much longer, and resist weather much better than the common sort of Pee-Jackets. The colour is now fixed to a dark blue, dyed with true indigo [an expensive imported dye – see page 13]; which color stands the weather. [In 1757 brown had been substituted as it came to 6d. less.]

And as the Society thinks, that the severity of the *winter* season renders common flannel waistcoats, or even thin kerseys called half-thicks, insufficient, they occasionally make waistcoats of kerseys ... equally soft, and more durable.[15]

A bill for over a thousand pounds for cloth was paid in June 1757, and a separate bill for dyeing. Hanway's discussion of buttons shows that expert advice had been sought.

The buttons are of horn, coloured with blue; which, tho' cheap, look as well as the buttons on a gentleman's coat. They have strong brass wire shanks, and are set upon canvas, the want of which in the seamens clothes, occasions the buttons seldom holding fast. A strip of *leather*, and also a *packthread*, are run through the shanks, by which they are held the stronger; and the more so, because as the one relaxes by being wet, the other contracts. Nothing that is made easy to the body, can be too strong for these *boys*, or indeed for the *men*.

All were obliged to do their own mending, so each of them must be provided with "7 needles, 2 ounces of thread and 5 balls of worsted ...but," Hanway added, "a right good seaman will have a whole jacket" even if he has to "lace it over the seams, with bits of old sails, by the help of a sail-needle and packthread".[16]

In 1786 there was a new venture – the purchase of a ship. Moored near Greenwich, this became a residential marine training school and thereafter each lad enjoyed a corporate life for at least eighteen months and wore the letters "MS" in his cap.

We may now look a little more closely at the actual clothes the Society supplied. A minute of the Committee records its agreement with a slopman in July of the first year, 1756, and gives the rate for each item of a man's whole outfit.[17] For the interest of subscribers, Hanway published two years later the current lists for men and boys and for comparison the "former" list for men.[18] Partly with his help we can annotate some of the slopman's list as follows.

Slopman's List for Men, 1756

		£	s	d
1	Dutch cap [of woven wool]	1	2	
2	Worsted Ditto [knitted]		8	
3	Linen Handkerchiefs [neckerchiefs]	1	6	
2	Striped Flannel Wastcoats [only 1 supplied]	3	0	
1	Kersey Pee-Jacket	4	0	
2	pair of Russia Drab [breeches]	2	10	
	[1 pr. Russia drab breeches and "1 pr. of drawers of brown half-thick" were supplied in 1757]			
1	Settee Wastcoat [see below]	5	0	
2	Pr of Petticoat Duck [trousers, see below]	4	0	
2	Canvas or hessian Frocks [overalls]	3	4	

For all the "stout *Lads* and *Boys* who offer to serve on Board His Majesty's ships", the clothing given in 1757 was only a jacket, breeches and headgear;[19] but the next year they got the same articles as the men and, perhaps to lift their spirits a little, their hats had "quality binding" and a dark blue cockade.[20]

Hanway, who in bad weather would wear three pairs of socks at once, took a special interest in the boys' feet. They were allowed more shoes and stockings than the men, and the quality must be good. He believed that

Stockings of worstead, well-made, are the cheapest in the issue [i.e. in the long run]. They are not so clumsy as yarn [ordinary short-hair wool], nor heat the feet so much . . . In the summer season, unbleached [linen] thread will be best . . . Their shoes should be well made and of such leather as will stand [last] and suited to their condition . . . a bad spungy shoe is an abomination.[21]

Constant charge is given, that the *stockings* be not too short in the feet, a fault which often happens in these coarse goods. The shoes are provided in Northamptonshire, under the direction of some gentlemen of the Society, whose estates are in that county.[22]

Boys with a taste for music were taught to play the fife and then given a new jacket, picked out quite dashingly with a "white sleeve [cuff] and a white cape [collar]".[23] When special uniform for bandsmen was formalized in the Navy in 1874, it too had a white collar to the coat.

119. *Left* Pea-jacket, 1879. *Right*
Seaman's "frock", a blouse, 1850s.
Apart from the square collar, a late
development, it resembles a coun-
tryman's frock or smock, although
tucked into trousers; note set of its
sleeve (*Left* After *Royal Naval
Regulations*, 1879. *Right* After Gerald
Dickens *Dress of the British Sailor*, 1957)

The clothing for all the boys was augmented in the 1760s and there
were changes. In lieu of waistcoats they received two "under jackets",
one striped and the other made of white "swanskin", a material also
used for their underdrawers. This was a thick flannel with a downy surface ideal for extra warmth and was washable.

Before further changes are dealt with, a few notes are needed on
specifically nautical garments. A pea-jacket was one of these. Jackets in
the eighteenth century were worn by few besides sailors, labourers and
jockeys – people whose activities made the long coat of the period impossible. The pea-jacket in the nineteenth century (when an imitation
of it had a vogue with gentlemen) was a hip-length, thick, double-
breasted, lapelled pilot coat; presumably it was not very different in the
eighteenth century. The delineators of Figs. 9 and 120 show the ordinary,
rather long, eighteenth-century coat. They may well have not known the
pea-jacket! The engraver of the heading to the dinner-invitation from
the Society in 1811 depicted a boy wearing the proper short square shape.

120. Rescued boys being equipped by Marine Society with coats, hats and petticoats or petticoat breeches (Headpiece to Marine Society's Fifer's Credential Form, reproduced in Jonas Hanway *Three Letters on the Subject of the Marine Society*, 1758)

As to the "settee waistcoat" (possibly so called after the settee, a sailing vessel with square sails) we only know what Hanway briefly tells us: "1 Settee-waistcoat – N.B. of blue duffil lined with a thin white flannel, and lapell'd".[24] Duffle was a coarse woollen cloth, originally from Duffel in Belgium, which (in the nineteenth century at least) had a thick nap and was traditional for seamen's clothes.

Sailors' legwear has always been distinctive. Hanway again (1783): "There is no dress better calculated for agility, than the *seaman's*; though the jacket being short, exposes the thighs; but these again are covered with trousers [not only breeches] . . . each lad may be supplied with a pair of trousers . . . but not to use them, except when employed about the ship".[25] Thus the Marine Society was conforming to ordinary custom for actual seamen while the boys were still in training. It allowed both men and boys not only the ordinary kersey or Russia drab woollen breeches of working men, but, as an extra, trousers – which seem to have been invented by seamen centuries before they were worn by gentlemen. Their chief advantages at sea was probably protection from wind. Those supplied here would also have been quick-drying, for they were made of "Duck," or "Ravinduck" or "Ravensduck" linens (e.g. lists for 1756 and 1780) or of canvas (1758) – probably undyed. They could be ankle length as in Fig. 9 or to the calf (Fig. 120). Some were so full as to look like a petticoat; the seated boy in Fig. 120 is pulling on a pair over his breeches. These wide garments are what is meant by the rather cryptic entries "Petticoat Duck" (page 200) and "pett-duck-trousers" in Hanway's 1757 list. They would serve well to shed the rain and spray. In the Navy they were called "petticoat breeches" (as with running footmen) or simply "petticoats".[26] Ordinary breeches were given up in 1804 in favour of long trousers, both woollen and linen.

"Suits" consisting of jacket and trousers were for many years ordered from the linen-clothier and sometimes "duck trousers" are actually specified. In 1817 braces appear for the first time ("141 Pair").[27]

Another occupational item was the "frock", a smock-like overall, especially necessary where there was tar about, and also acting in lieu of a jacket in summer. It was made of Ravenduck or cheaper canvas or hessian. After a temporary suspension for economy's sake, we read in a minute for 1777: "It being represented [by a certain sea captain] that Canvass Frocks were of great use to the Boys on board Ships to work in: [the Committee] Ordered that one such Frock be given untill further notice".[28] In the nineteenth century white "duck frocks" recur. By this time frocks were what we call sailor blouses, being tucked into the trousers. There were also "blue Frocks, Galley" for the kitchen.[29] For cold weather there were either "Guernsey frocks" (knitted sailor's jerseys or possibly jackets), or else worsted cloth frocks.

Finally in 1865 the superintendent on the training ship recommended that "each boy have another Serge Frock instead of a Cloth Frock".[30] These blue serge frocks, which were still in use in 1884,[31] must have resembled that worn by John Masefield on the *Conway* at this time – "an awful coarse blue serge shirt" so scratchy that it was only bearable when worn as a "jumper" outside the trousers.[32]

Headgear was adaptive from the start. The wind-catching tricorne hat of the eighteenth century was never supplied. Knitted caps were practical, but Hanway remarks: "Dutch caps of woollen stuff wove, though thick imbibe much water unless it be pitched . . . hats of long hair in a short brim, to turn the water, may do better".[33] A round felt hat was provided, from 1758 on, as worn by other sailors; and this, like the pea-jacket and trousers, was adopted later by the gentry.

A special item for the men, in the period 1804–10, had the quaint name of "Welsh wig". This was an extra shaggy knitted cap reminis-

121. "Welsh wig" knitted in brown wool. Back part covers the neck and has four rows of twelve-stranded loops on the surface, suggesting an eighteenth-century wig. Dated 1854 (Specimen F. 69.353 in the Welsh Folk Museum, Cardiff. Courtesy: the Museum)

cent of the "thrum" cap worn by sailors, but it had a wig-like shape. A new sun and spray-resisting article, a "japann'd" (i.e. lacquered) men's hat also appeared – as it did on H.M.S. *Tribune* in 1805.[34] Sou'westers were to follow (see below).

Though pocket handkerchiefs seem to have been first supplied by the Society only in 1780 – Hanway wrote in 1783 "cheque handkerchiefs for the pocket, however small, are necessary for cleanliness"[35] – the sailor's "handkerchief" was always in evidence. This was a triangle of material knotted to form a necktie. Conventionally it was black from the eighteenth century (long before Nelson's death in 1805) and the Marine Society supplied silk ones from at least 1778. They must have varied with rank in some way, for in 1813 they were bought at five different prices simultaneously.[36] "Alpaca ties", awarded in 1865 to boys after six months' work,[37] may have been an alternative to the silk neckerchief. In the later nineteenth century "the black silk" worn under the square sailor collar was probably called a scarf, as in the Navy.

As time goes on, a few general trends are noticeable. Some changes in details at the beginning of the nineteenth century suggest that a little glory was reflected on to the lads, from the Navy under Nelson, who had written of the Society's "noble and glorious example".[38] A sub-committee in 1812 even reported that their clothing compared favourably with the Navy's own. More importantly, from December 1801 onwards, a "blue watch coat"[39] was given to the men, and a "greatcoat" to the boys from 1810.

In the course of the nineteenth century, as with many charities, there were changes which suggested higher status and/or yielded more comfort. In 1836 the boys, when passing out into the Navy, got a "Scotch Bonnit" in their outfit and, if apprenticed to fishing vessels:

One Fearnought Jacket and Breeches
Two pair Orkney Stockings
One pair Boots
One South Wester

"Fearnought" was a fabric almost impenetrable by wind and rain, having a very deep nap. The sou'wester at this date was probably of oilskin or tarpaulin.

Boys on night watch on the training ship in 1866 got extra protection

122. Seamen's dress, 1829–30, before the Navy had a uniform. "Round jackets", shorter than the pea-jacket, large shirt collars – preceding square "sailor collar" – neck handkerchiefs (Print, "Mr. Campbell as William in *Black Ey'd Susan*")

M.ʳ Campbell as WILLIAM, *in Black Ey'd Susan*

from the special sort of pilot coat called a monkey jacket and, at long last, from an "Oil Skin Coat".[40] In 1884 there were also "Mittons" and "Worsted Comforters".[41]

In 1877 the Prince and Princess of Wales inaugurated the Society's new ship the *Warspite*, the fifth in a succession of six training ships, each moored in the Thames (Fig. 123). The lads were in their summer uniforms, featuring square blue jean sailor collars. In the Navy, these collars came into fashion in the 1840s, copying those worn on Queen Victoria's yacht.[42] Petticoat ducks were no longer worn (in the Navy they disappeared in the 1820s).[43]

For winter there was now no jacket. The "blue serge" (frock), now worn over a shirt, was more comfortable; still more so was the jumper, which was specially cut to be worn *outside* the trousers.

Caps were like those of the Royal and Merchant Navies; the glengarry style for working, and the hated cheese-cutter for best, were worn on the *Conway*.[44] In 1913, on finally going to sea, the lad was

123. Marine Society boys at Prize Giving, 1877 (*Illustrated London News* vol. LXX, 30 June 1877)

given eight more garments, including a suit of dungarees and another of oilskins.

These thoroughly nautical outfits continued with little change until, during the Second World War, the training ship at last ceased to function. The Society still makes grants or loans towards the cost of the now handsome uniforms required when boys start training for the Merchant Service elsewhere. The founder's intentions are thus still respected, though he would be startled at the scale for each individual. Typical of many letters to the Society is one written in 1973 which says: "I wish to thank the Marine Society for £150 grant awarded to me to help buy my uniform".

SHOEBLACK BRIGADES

The Ragged School Union, promoted for the education of the very poor, flourished in the mid nineteenth century. There grew out of the movement an interesting enterprise by John M. ("Rob Roy") MacGregor, His aim was to find paid employment for boys, aged twelve to sixteen, such as were attending evening classes at the Ragged Schools, and he saw an opportunity when the Great Exhibition was staged in 1851. What with crowds and carriages, there would often be a sea of mud round the Crystal Palace and thousands of people, mostly far from their own homes, all milling about with their feet in it. The boys should clean their shoes. Thus MacGregor established the Shoeblack Society whose funds brought into being a Shoeblack Brigade of boys. They were all equipped with brushes and polish and, what is more, a conspicuous uniform. A trial beginning was made with a rota of lads in Leicester Square, a few months before the Exhibition opened. After it closed many other pitches were set up and were manned so well that a demand was created and grew. The first group was called the Central Brigade or, from their uniform, the "City Reds". It is said that sometimes its members working near Smithfield Market caused a stir among the bulls. The uniform always included a peaked cap, but the main garment was a frock-like tunic. With its bright colour it served as an advertisement. As the shoeblacks were small boys, and always seated, in a crowded street, it was important to give them clothes that showed up. An engraved plate was fastened to the breast or sleeve, giving the name of the Brigade and the boy's number. At the end of the working day he would change his clothes at a headquarters where he was given a meal.

The boys' image became so well imprinted on the public mind that a song by S. Bevan appeared, probably about 1860, called *The Har-*

"BLACK YOUR SHOES, SIR?"

124. Shoeblack, 1864. Tunic with badge, peaked cap, apron (*Punch* 12 November 1864)

monious Shoeblack, with a portrait on the cover. The cheery-looking lad wears a red tunic with belt, a red band in his patent-leather-peaked cap and has a brown apron. On his arm is his badge bearing the words "Ragged School Union" and the number "34".

By that time the Society had organized other brigades in different areas, and the fact that there were local distinctions of colour in the uniforms must have promoted a sense of neighbourhood *esprit de corps* among the boys. The following table shows the colours worn by most of the brigades, with dates of their foundation, where known:[45]

Central London	Red	1850
East London	Blue	1854
South London	Yellow	1854
North-west (Marylebone)	White	1857
Islington (King's Cross)	Brown with red facings	,,
Kensington	Brown with purple facings	,,
West London (Westminster)	Purple	,,
Notting Hill	Blue with red facings	,,

Stratford	?	1857
South Surburban	Red with green facings	Later
"Surrey side of the River"[46]	White	?
Union Jack, Limehouse	Red with blue facings	?

To this list may be added an independent brigade founded mainly for Irish Catholic boys by the Society of St Vincent de Paul. They were based on Queen Square and wore blue.

An important pitch for many years was on the steps of the House of Commons. There, in 1897, Benjamin Stone took a photograph of the established shoeblack, young George Warner.[47] The loose garment has here been replaced by a military-style tunic with stand collar and brass buttons; and the badge, which he wears on the breast, has a central design (perhaps a lion) as well as the words "West London Shoeblack ..." This lad spent years literally at the feet of the eminent and must have been the uncrowned king of his race.

Twenty years later, the Shoeblack Society came to an end. By that time, doubtless as an economy, the boys everywhere were dressed alike – in the original red.

125. Shoeblacks at a Moody and Sankey Service, 1875. One of their badges reads "Licensed Shoeblack 480" (*Pictorial World* 1875)

126. One of Lord
Shaftesbury's "Broomers"
and a shoeblack with apron,
1852. Badges on tunics.
(Detail of headpiece, *Ragged
School Union Magazine* VI)

An offshoot of the shoeblack organization was a scheme proposed by Lord Shaftesbury, at a tea party given for the brigades in 1851. Winter was coming on and would make some of the sites very uncomfortable for small boys sitting still. He suggested that shopkeepers should combine in groups of twenty, each owner paying 1d. a day for a boy to sweep the pavement in front of his shop. The *Ragged School Union Magazine* (vol. III, page 268) reported the results:

Five of the best shoe-blacks were clothed in new red uniforms, having black belts instead of aprons, and hoes and brooms in place of boxes and brushes. They were furnished with oilskin capes, as a protection against rain, and each boy besides his Society badge, had on his breast another bearing the very descriptive name of BROOMER.

Within a month one broomer appeared in the Strand and four in Regent Street.

The scheme was a small example of the social work done by Lord Shaftesbury and was one where clothing played quite an important part.

GIRL TRAINEES

For a girl, until recent times, the training provided by charities was almost exclusively for domestic work. We have seen how it was begun when they were still in children's homes and boarding schools. We will now take a look at provisions made for them when they went out into service, and also at how they fared when prepared in charity training schools for almost the only alternative employment, the textile trade.

In either case, unlike some of the boy apprentices, the girls were given clothing that was nearly as drab as their jobs, and conditions for domestic apprentices, where they lived in, were peculiarly repressive for two reasons. As Violet Frith has pointed out in *The Psychology of the Servant Problem* (1925), residential homes where girls were trained for service could in every sense "keep them in their place". For example, if a girl threw up her job and returned to the institution, being homeless and less able to fend for herself than a boy, she was sure to be treated as a bad penny. Her interests, as opposed to her employer's, were being cared for solely by people who not only had the whip hand but who were themselves of the employer class. The girl was in a cleft stick, for it was not in the interests of her master and mistress to give her any comforts and still less to care for her if she was too ill to work.

It was only the more enlightened institutions that investigated the employing households adequately and used proper indentures (e.g. Fig. 116). Mrs Sarah Trimmer, that expert on charity movements, published in 1801 her views on how a young servant should be dressed, and these were liberal for her time. She conceded that servants should be "plain dressing", but in view of the rising standards in the attire of their mistresses they "cannot reasonably be expected to keep to the very plain and homely dress of former days". If they overstepped propriety in any article of dress,

Care must be taken not to give reproof . . . with that severity of censure which may be construed by evil minded people as proceeding from a desire to tread down the poor . . . And even those, who . . . have had no better garment than the uniform of the Charity School, should on their going into respectable families, be permitted to dress a little above their former condition. The *callico gown* and its suitable appendages may now take the place of the *serge* or the *camblet*.[48]

The edge is taken off this magnanimity, which in any case was lost on the public, when the lady goes on: "but it were much to be wished that *stuffs* were as heretofore the every-day dress of common maid servants, and that the *scarlet* or the *duffel cloak* might be their defence against the cold of winter."

127. Apprentices in domestic service, formerly Ragged School pupils. Teacher receives certificates, on their behalf, from Lord Shaftesbury. 1865 (*Illustrated London News* 25 March 1865)

Scarlet cloaks bespoke a humble station in life, as exemplified in the Red Maids' School or Castle Rising almswomen. Severe restrictions as to what a servant might wear, even out of doors, survived into the twentieth century. (See Frank Dawes *Not in Front of the Servants,* 1973.)

At the Foundling Hospital, as we have seen, a lot of domestic training was given, and when the girls left to continue it as apprentices in selected households, they set off in a complete new outfit with a change of linen as well. The clothes were not all like the children's; for example, there was no tippet and the outdoor clothes were better: in the nineteenth century there would be a shawl or else a "mantle" (mentioned in 1858 – ?a scarlet cloak) and always a new bonnet. Matron's Ledger enumerates, in 1840, the following:

Articles of Clothing for Apprentices, in Store

Book Handker^s	12
Print Dress	12

Shawls	6
Check muslin	10 yards
Sarsnet ribbon	12 yards
Net	5 yards
Nainsook	6 yards
Pocket Handker^s	24
Net frilling	50

The "Book Handkerchief" was probably a neckerchief. The muslin nainsook and ribbon would be for making indoor caps and the net for their frills and for tuckers.

Appropriate dress for domestic apprentices in the 1860s is shown in Fig. 127. Ex-pupils of the Ragged School Union are being rewarded for "keeping their places in service with good characters for 12 months".[49] Their outfits, being uniform, had evidently been given them. By this time the society was clothing, as well as teaching, a number of its pupils. Note that in this period, when the crinoline was at its zenith, their skirts spread out only moderately. The cap is typically that of a mid Victorian lower-ranking domestic servant. All is extremely demure.

THE SPINNING SCHOOL IN YORK

Charity girls were trained in textile skills long before the local authorities set up industrial schools in the nineteenth century. Two schemes for promoting this alternative to domestic work were organized in York in 1785. Mrs Faith Gray, who had married into an influential York family, and Mrs Catharine Cappe, a minister's wife, were women of remarkable common sense, dedication and drive. Besides reorganizing the textile work, which had proved more profitable to the teachers than to the girls themselves, in the Grey Coat School, these ladies raised subscriptions and launched a highly successful experiment, the "Spinning School".

This was a day school for the education, both general and technical, of girls whose parents could give them a home but could neither afford to have them taught when they were little, nor do without their earnings when they reached the age of ten. The younger ones learnt knitting and the rest spinning and dressmaking. The novelty lay in allowing the girls to take home the profits made by their labour. They were also "decently clothed" by the charity, being provided with materials cut out for them by a "Patroness" and made up by themselves. Mrs Cappe[50] lists their outfits as follows:

Clothes allowed to the Spinning Girls, in proportion to their labor

Spinners from four to six Hanks per day	*Six Hanks*	*Seven Hanks*	*Eight Hanks*
	In addition	Additional	Additional
A stuff Gown	A checked	A Cap	A green
Two linen Bedgowns	Apron	A coloured	Ribband
Two Shifts		Shawl	round
Two pair of Shoes		A pair of	the Hat
Two checked		Pattens	A pair of
Handkerchiefs			worsted
Two blue Aprons			Mittens
A straw Hat			
Two pair of Stockings			
Three ounces of Worsted			
Shoes mended twice			

Spinners of Ten Hanks	*Eleven Hanks*	*Twelve Hanks*
Additional	Additional	Additional
A better Shawl	One Cap	One checked Apron
A wolsey Petticoat	A stuff Petti-	A black bonnet
One Shift	coat with the	
	Gown	

The girls had to spin seven hanks a day regularly for a whole year before they qualified for a pair of stays. This may have been not so much to discourage vanity about the figure as to save on the only garments, barring hats and shoes, that were not home-made.

Finally (and rather parsimonious it sounds): "Cloaks are lent, and when the girls go to service, are given to them, if they have behaved well in the School and leave it with the approbation of the Ladies who superintend it."[51]

On leaving, the girls were encouraged to join the newly founded Friendly Society and so to receive another five shillings' worth of clothes after three years' good work as apprentices.

When the twentieth century brought more variety of opportunity for women, a high proportion of such girls as still did go into domestic service came to it complete with their initial outfits, straight from children's homes.

CHAPTER 11

University scholars

Just as schools were founded for the maintenance as well as the education of poor children, so university colleges were established, from the thirteenth century onwards, often in the wake of monastic foundations, to help older students and their teachers in similar ways. Indeed King's College, Cambridge, was founded specially for needy youths who had been on the foundation of Eton, and William of Wykeham, working the other way round, established Winchester mainly as a nursery for his New College at Oxford.

The Bishop of Ely's endowment of the Fellows and Scholars of Peterhouse, Cambridge, in the 1280s, came from his "having a tender regard for their notorious indigence".[1] Although the prime object may have been the promotion of sound doctrine and learning rather than charity, this poverty and the fact that clothing was provided bring many college endowments within the scope of our book. The costumes supplied have a special interest, since they play a considerable part in the development of "academic dress".* It should be added that after a time the clothing was generally not given in kind, but as "livery money".[2] However, as late as 1682 the Duchess of Somerset expressly stated that the scholars she supported at Cambridge must be given an actual cap and gown at the beginning of their first, third and fifth years.[3]

It is proposed to limit the account to Oxford and Cambridge and, from the Reformation onwards, to deal mainly with what we should

---

* Though in the fourteenth century the colleges composed numerically only a small proportion of the entire university, they wielded a special influence, from the eminence of their founders, upon the non-collegiate teachers and students (May McKisack *The Fourteenth Century* (1959) pp. 506–7).

rank as undergraduates, namely the equivalents of the "probationers" or "scholars", and the "junior Fellows" or "Bachelors" of medieval times. In the early days, the first degree was usually taken when a youth was still in his teens so that in age, standing and dress the bachelors were more like undergraduates than graduates.[4] At Cambridge, after 1380, the nearest equivalents to our undergraduate scholars were the "portionists" and "Founder's kin".

In the Middle Ages the whole body of the college was dressed by its founder. At New College Wykeham decreed that the Warden and all the Fellows should have livery from the same cloth, a carefully chosen wool, which was doled out each Christmas time. The Warden received twelve yards, as at Winchester, and the Fellows shared a twenty-four-yards piece between three. It took the Warden and three bursars to do the distribution fairly, since not only did the form of the garments vary with the men's degrees but "the stature of the recipients, more or less" must be taken into account. Each Fellow had 6s. 8d. for the making up and for fur.[5] Livery for probationers or "scholars" Wykeham does not seem to have allowed for, but he permitted Fellows to hand down their own livery when it was five years old to these youths and also to first-year Fellows. Like quiristers at Winchester they were clothed at second hand.

Academic dress has had a long history, the details of which would be out of place here;[6] but the main characteristics were, first, that it was so powerfully resistant to change as to be early medieval in style up to the Reformation and partially Tudor ever since (and the dash of puritanism that came in with Cromwell survived the whole of the eighteenth century); secondly, that the dress was ecclesiastical in its roots. Because of these two features it has, incidentally, much in common with ceremonial mourning (see P. Cunnington and C. Lucas *Costume for Births, Marriages and Deaths*, 1972).

Medieval university teachers were clerics, mostly in holy orders, and a high proportion of their pupils were destined for the Church, if not already ordained.[7] Therefore the costume, except for the tabard described below, had naturally a clerical appearance. A fourteenth-century statute of Peterhouse with regard to "dress, demeanour and carriage" decreed that

The Master and all and each of the scholars [here meaning all the members] of our house shall adopt the clerical dress and tonsure . . . and not allow their beard or their hair to grow contrary to canonical prohibition, nor wear rings upon their fingers for their own vainglory . . . and the scandal of others.[8]

Non-liturgical ecclesiastical dress of the Middle Ages was based on the

128. William of Wykeham presiding over New College, Oxford, drawn *c.* 1463.
The central group, in back view, are scholars and possibly Junior Fellows
or bachelors: hoods with pendant liripipe and no shoulder piece; tabards
with cape-like sleeves; long outer tunics. Nearest to Wykeham are Senior
Fellows (doctors) wearing the "pileus" cap, like his, and closed cloaks.
The foreground group on each side is the choir, in surplices, boys
kneeling. Between choir and doctors each side are Fellows, probably masters,
each wearing a hood with shoulder piece, over a tabard – note its cape-like
sleeve on two leading men on left. All heads are tonsured except choirboys'
(MS C. 288 fol. 3v. Courtesy: New College, Oxford)

Benedictine habit,[9] and this in turn reflected an ordinary man's wear of the thirteenth century except in being longer and black.* A Fellow or a scholar, as shown in Chaundler's drawing of New College, *c.* 1463, wore an outer tunic (*supertunica*, *roba* or *toga*), later the gown, which would be dark in colour and of ankle or ground length, "befitting their state of being clerks".[10] Under this went a long tunic, later called a cassock. The only headgear permitted was a monkish hood of black cloth which, in the fourteen and fifteenth centuries, had the elongated apex that was fashionable in the layman's *chaperon*; but students were not allowed to twist this *liripipe* round their necks as he did his. It hung down behind (Fig. 128). Nor might anyone except masters and doctors line the hood with expensive furs or silk.[11] At All Souls the exact dimensions of the liripipe were laid down in the statutes of 1443 – twenty-seven inches long and six inches wide.[12] (This hood must have been exactly like the one preserved as funeral wear by heralds for the next two and a half centuries.) Joined to or free from the hood itself was a shoulder piece or small cape, fur-bordered for higher ranks, e.g. the masters in the middle distance on each side in Fig. 128. The shoulder piece seems to have been lost to the junior grades (central group in the figure) by the end of the fifteenth century and even the hood itself became, by Elizabeth I's reign, the prerogative of graduates only. It evolved into the academic hood, a curious relic that still shows a vestige of the liripipe.

For all except doctors, who could wear a *cap[p]a clausa*, the tabard was the characteristic outermost garment. This was like the tabard of a layman in the thirteenth century, or of heralds ever after – a garment put on over the head with sleeves typically in the form of a cape-like flap overhanging the upper arm. Sleeves of this shape are well seen in the central group in Fig. 128** but are almost covered by the above-mentioned shoulder piece in the group of masters. Wykeham insisted the tabard should be long (*talaris*), but at Queen's College, Oxford, the "poor boy's " *collobium* (probably tabard) had to end at the calf instead of the heel[13] – another sign of humility *vis à vis* his elders.

---

* Authorities are undecided about the form and even the English names of some of the garments that feature in medieval Latin documents. Furthermore the interpretation of drawings and brass engravings often leaves doubt: for example, whether a shoulder cape is part of a hood or a separate item. It is worth recording that the garments made from the livery cloth for each Fellow of New College were: *subtunica, supertunica, tabarda talaris* or *capa* and *caputium*, but who wore what depended on their degrees.[14]

** A garment of similar shape and with exactly the same sleeves is the "tunicle" worn, for example, by the cross-bearer at Canterbury Cathedral today.

Though members on the foundation of Queen's are called "taberdars [sic]" even today, this already antiquated garment was apparently given up in the sixteenth century[15] and the gown (*supertunica*) thus became the outermost dress. Just as happened at Winchester, the gown was soon to be open down the front like that of ordinary men in the Tudor period and in this form it has remained, with variations of cut, right down to the present.

For ranks below master any headgear other than the hood was frowned on at first. However, at Oxford by 1565 undergraduates on the foundations were allowed black cloth caps (of which more anon) but they had to wear their black hoods at academic functions.[16]

As the Middle Ages wore on, an increasing number of wealthy undergraduates who paid their own way attached themselves to the colleges. Unless they were "Noblemen", they were called at Oxford "Commoners" (paying for their "commons") and at Cambridge "Pensioners" (*"en pension"*).* Students who were supported by the foundations, for whom we shall use the term "scholars" in the modern sense, were distinguished from the others in their dress.

Before dealing with these distinctions, which of course specially concern us, it is worth noting the ever recurring pressure from above to control extravagance or modishness of dress and coiffure at the universities, reminding all that respect for religion demands humility, and respect for learning requires decorum.

Wykeham himself laid down that no one at New College should wear red or green hose, gold-ornamented belts, swords or the excessively peaked shoes so fashionable at his time, and so unsuited to long robes.[17]

For walking in Oxford, or within a mile of the town, he insisted that members of his college should create the right impression. Except in heavy rain, hail or snow they were not to wear a *cloca* or an *armelausa* (i.e. lay-type cloak or side-fastening mantle).[18]**

Wykeham had cause for apprehension. Already, at Cambridge, both teachers and pupils had come under the university's censure in 1343 for "the gay and unclerical appearance of their garments . . . they wore their hair hanging down on their shoulders in an effeminate manner or

* In Harraden's time (1805) scholars, though their clothes were gratis, paid for their food and were therefore likewise called pensioners.

** But at All Souls a brass effigy of Thomas Baker, a non-graduate student, shows the *armelausa*.

curled and powdered . . ."[19] Long hair was again prohibited at Cambridge in 1560 "under payne of 6s. 8d."[20]

We now come to the distinctions observed by custom, or statute, between the garb of students on foundations (scholars to us) and that of other undergraduates.

A royal statute of 1570 shows that endowed scholars came under stricter sumptuary control than the aristocracy, because they were easier to control and moreover ought to show extra modesty.

We wish besides that no one who is supported at the expence of any college . . . shall wear . . . a plaited ruff about his neck [unless it was moderate and had no silk interwoven], or plaited ruffles at his wrists. Provided nevertheless that the above regulations . . . shall not bind in any way the sons of lords, or the heirs of knights.[21]

At Oxford, further rules were made in Elizabethan times. Whereas scholars must wear clerical gowns with long, full sleeves (or at New College, still the tabard), the unendowed "commoners" were allowed a lay style of gown, having a flap collar and the elbow sleeves of the period with pendant strip attached.

129. Henry Dow, undergraduate scholar, who had been supported by Queen Elizabeth, 1578. Gown very long. Head and shoulders emerge through the large opening in the now academic hood (Brass effigy in Christ Church, Oxford. Courtesy: the Precentor)

A good example of a scholar's correct dress at this period is shown in a brass effigy* of Henry Dow (Fig. 129), a scholar supported by Queen Elizabeth I. He was a son of the Robert Dow or Dove whose charities we have noted elsewhere. While studying for his bachelor's degree, he fell ill and died in 1578 at the age of twenty. He is shown with the short hair and moderate ruff that complied with regulations. The tabard is no longer worn over the gown. The hood has a very wide opening, like those of today, and its liripipe is now too short to show.

By 1565 at Oxford[22] and 1549 at Cambridge,[23] it was ruled that scholars should have square caps somewhat like the *pileus* of the clergy – flattish, soft, and made of black cloth, imitated in the cap of Oxford University women in the present day. Commoners were to wear round caps ("bonnets"), also flat, but with a narrow brim which could be of velvet; this was in keeping with lay fashions of the period. Archbishop Whitgift confirmed the distinction in 1602[24] and for over two hundred years it held: square caps for scholars, round for the rest – except that noblemen could wear hats when not in ceremonial dress. Sons of noblemen formed another privileged class, called at Cambridge "Hat-Fellow-Commoners", because they were allowed to wear hats and took meals with the Fellows.

The early seventeenth century saw an interesting change in the form of the square cap. It evolved into a unique structure which was to become one of the insignia of the academic world. The soft four-cornered cap turned into a stiff square board and this, to keep it on, was fused to a black cloth skull-cap: result, a "trencher" or "mortar-board". Higher dignitaries of the Church and judiciary had long worn under their *pileus* a separate skull cap or coif, an arrangement which must have inspired the inventor of the mortarboard. Until the next century scholars were forbidden to sport the little spherical tump in the middle, which was the privilege of the graduates.

Hogarth records for us the three main classes of undergraduate attending a lecture in his day (Fig. 130).

The mortarboard eventually became a coveted object. In 1769–70 the fee-paying students applied for and were granted, in both universities, permission to exchange their round caps for square ones.[25] This marked the beginning of the reversal whereby the privileged group sought to be assimilated to those who were once looked down on as "the poor boys". Even so it was felt proper that fee-payers should have

---

*The costume in this brass has been incorrectly described in more than one publication.

a tassel on the mortarboard – a gold one for noblemen – while some of the scholars had to keep to their (now permitted, but less ornamental) tump until the end of the century. The gold tassel was called a tuft; hence probably the meaning of the expression "toff".

The differentiation in the form of the gown, as well as the cap, between the four categories of students – noblemen, sons of nobles, ordinary undergraduates and scholars – is beautifully illustrated by David Loggan for Oxford in 1675[26] and Cambridge in 1690.[27] Glorification of the aristocracy was soon to be at its height, and already the gowns of noblemen and of their sons are gorgeously decorated with gold, and all are shown wearing hats. (In the nineteenth century

130. "The Lecture", 1737. Scholars and graduates in mortarboards, other undergraduates in round caps, noblemen in hats. All wear bands like those of clergy and charity boys (Engraving by William Hogarth in the British Museum)

Publish'd by W. Hogarth January 20th 1737   *Gratis six pence*

they could rejoice in the top hats of their day, even when wearing gowns; see R. Harraden's engravings of Cambridge, 1805.)

Loggan's ordinary commoners have gowns with flap collars and various ornaments of black velvet. There has been a diminution in the awkward sleeves and by now these have become a mere strip or streamer hanging from the shoulder* (Fig. 131). In many colleges the sleeves disappeared altogether during the eighteenth century, leaving a debased form of gown, nicknamed a "curtain", which however was still lavishly trimmed.

Compared with even the ordinary student, Loggan's scholar, whether at Oxford or Cambridge, is a somewhat forlorn figure. His voluminous black gown has the dignity of excessive length – it actually trails on the ground – but somehow it only looks too big for him. Its enormous funnel-shaped sleeves recall a surplice. There is not a shred of ornament, and even his coat underneath is soberly dark while the other men's are light. His small mortarboard is perched precariously on his head. It contrasts with the bonnet of the "pensioner" who has managed to turn up its brim to give it the air of a hat. The scholar's hair is neatly neck length while that of all fee-paying students is a wavy mass well covering the shoulders and longest of all on the noblemen. While scholars wear the now statutory white band or collar, with perfectly plain rectangular tabs, like those of charity children, for other undergraduates the tabs are made of lace to look as much like the fashionable but forbidden cravat as possible. (Even Charles II's bastard son, the Earl of Southampton, was refused leave to substitute a cravat, to the astonishment of a contemporary student.[28]) The bands (compare Fig. 94) are an interesting reminder of the clerical origin of academic dress, for, after being in vogue in the 1650s, they were by now a relic confined, outside the universities and certain schools, almost entirely to the clergy. Their further history completed the pattern so commonly seen in such symbolic garments: first fashionable (seventeenth century), then other-worldly (eighteenth), then ceremonial (nineteenth) and finally, in a special form, also funereal (today). Another reminder of ecclesiastical origins was the revival in

---

* Called a "leading string" from its resemblance to those survivals of a Tudor fashion which were used as reins on children's dresses in the seventeenth century. Hence the rhyme of 1770:

> Behind our gowns (black bombazeen)
> Are seen two leading strings. I ween
> To teach young students in their course
> They still have need of Learning's Nurse.[29]

1603 of the compulsory wearing of surplices in chapel by all who were on college foundations.

It is interesting that by the later eighteenth century we come full circle. The whole of the scholar's solemn dress was being coveted by his confrères. As we have seen, his cap was snatched by the fee-payers in 1770 and in the same year, at Christ Church, "servitors", a lesser form of life that earned its keep while studying, had to be rebuked by the Vice-Chancellor for "usurping" the foundationer's gown. However he did allow them to exchange their round cap with a button on top, which by now was matched only by the headgear of a charity boy, for a mortarboard; but their mortarboards were not to have the tump that was allowed, by that time, to the scholars.

131. Dress at Oxford University in 1675. *Left* Scholar on foundation: mortarboard, without tump; very long gown with wide sleeves; dark coat. *Centre* "Commoner" with round cap; sleeve reduced to decorated strip hanging from shoulder. *Right* "Gentleman Commoner" with more ornament (David Loggan *Oxonia Illustrata*, Pl. 10, 1675. Bodleian Library)

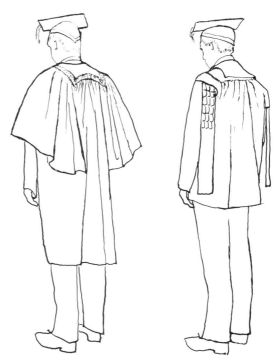

132. Undergraduate gowns worn at Oxford today. *Left* Endowed scholars: clerical style, long with wide sleeves. *Right* Others, commoners: the vestigial hanging sleeves are ornamented and winged (After photographs in D. Venables and R. Clifford *Academic Dress of the University of Oxford*, 1972)

In Cambridge there developed several ways of distinguishing the scholar that were peculiar to individual colleges. Those on the foundation of Trinity College in the Middle Ages wore violet, which was changed to blue in the eighteenth century. Westminster scholars going to Trinity had black gowns like most students but showed their college allegiance by having a violet button and loop on the sleeve. In Oxford the Duchess of Somerset insisted in 1682 that her scholars at Brasenose and St John's should wear "gowns of fine costume cloth with open sleeves like the students of Christ Church, Oxon and square caps without tassels";[30] this special dress was not given up until 1860. At Jesus College, while ordinary students' gowns began having their sleeves adorned with pleats and velvet, the Rustat scholar went soberly on in his traditional plain garment.[31]

Except for this last one, in the present century the distinctions in the scholar's dress have nearly all disappeared, despite (or possibly, in these egalitarian days, not to emphasize) his enhanced prestige. However, at Oxford there is a marked difference in the form of his gown – a scholar's has the loose sleeves of the fourteenth century while other undergraduates have gowns with the turned-down collar and hanging false sleeve (Fig. 132) that go back only to Tudor times. And even the woman scholar stands out among her fellow students. Her gown (for which now, alas, she has to pay) approaches more nearly than theirs, the "ancle length" of old.

CHAPTER 12

People in almshouses

GENERAL FEATURES OF THE DRESS

While the proportion of old people in the population was at no time as great as now, the poverty of those unable to earn through geriatric infirmity (often setting in early) was never properly alleviated, Poor Laws or no. To provide them with a home, food and clothing was one of the major charities, resulting in the setting up of almshouses in every part of the country.

Rotha Clay's *Medieval Hospitals of England* (1909) shows that a number were founded by individuals or guilds, even when the monasteries were doing their work, and of these forty to fifty survived at least in part into the twentieth century. In London alone there were nearly a hundred almshouses in the eighteenth century and 150 in 1901.[1]

We propose to restrict ourselves mainly to the establishments of which clear traces exist today, from beautiful architectural remains to fully occupied dwellings, and especially to those of which manuscript records exist. Most of the purely monastic houses are omitted, for little is known of the clothing there provided.

The inmates were selected not only for poverty and old age (the minimum often fifty!) but also good behaviour. Lord Marny, who died in 1523, laid down in his will that his almsfolk in Essex "shall be such as canne say at lest their pater noster, Ave and Crede in Latin".[2] More usual were William Doughty's rules, 1687, for his Hospital in Norwich: the "Poor People" must "live peaceably with the Master and with one another, as becomes *Christians*, neither cursing, swearing . . . nor being Drunk'.[3]

Lady Dacre's Hospital (see below) precluded also any "hedgbreaker or scould",[4] and Holy Trinity Hospital at Clun, 1618, any "taker of Tobacco".[5]

When the community had a collegiate form, with its "tutor" or "master" a priest, it seems natural that the inhabitants – brethren, sisters, bedes people – should be dressed according to a rule. But this uniformity applied in foundations of all kinds until the twentieth century. So indeed did the obligation to practise religion. This gave the old people an aim in life and a timetable – and for us the extra interest of comparing what they wore every day with the clothes they went to church in on Sundays.

The commonest form of community was a dozen brethren living in adjoining rooms or little houses with a master and a "poor woman" to do the domestic work. All inhabitants were given clothing.

The almshouses sometimes evolved from a medieval hospital where other forms of need had also been taken care of. If children were included, there might grow up an almshouse and a school side by side, the old and the young often wearing the same badge or colour.

Later establishments sometimes followed this plan too, for example, Charterhouse. Again, Lady Dacre, a cousin and favourite of Queen Elizabeth I, when she founded Emmanuel (later spelt Emanuel) Hospital in Westminster, said in her will of 1594 that each of the old people, if willing, might bring up a foster child; and the statutes ordain "that every of the poor in the Hospital and every of their children shall dayly wear upon their right shoulder the connizance [badge] of the Hospitall". The badge bore the initials "A.D." for Anne Dacre. In the late nineteenth century separate quarters were provided in the country for the alms people and "the Brown Coat School". Emanuel is now a well-known day school in Wandsworth. No trace of the old uniforms remains.

At Frome in Somerset, the Blue House, built in 1728, is also a home where young and old were supported, as symbolized by two statuettes on its walls. One is of old "Nancy Grey" in gown, cap, kerchief and apron, the other, "Billy Ball" in the typical uniform of a charity Blue Coat boy. In the dual charity at Clipston, Northants, *c.* 1670, it was the old folks who wore blue, and at Robert Aske's Hospital, Hoxton, young and old alike wore light blue gowns. The Aske Hospital was for "poor decayed Freemen" of the Haberdashers' Company and also for the sons of such. This is an example of the many charities specifically for members of a given Livery Company and their families. The almsmen still wear blue gowns at the Company's ceremonies, and so do the prefects at the now famous Haberdashers' Aske School at Elstree, Herts.

In 1672 William Shelton, who had already set up a day school for

133. Statue of almswoman on the
Blue House, Frome, Somerset, 1728
(After David J. Grapes. Courtesy: the
Trustees)

the poor in St Giles-in-the-Fields, London (mentioned under Green
Coat Schools in Chapter 5), bequeathed the wherewithal for continuing
the salary and the annual present of a gown for "an able and fit
schoolmaster to teach . . . 50 children" and for "a coat yearly for each
scholar at 6s." But there were to be at the same time a gown at 15s. for
each of thirty-five "poor old men and women" belonging to three
parishes, in this case as out-pensioners. And, Shelton added, "The
aforesaid gowns and coats all to be of a green colour".[6]

In keeping with their religious life almsfolk's, usually dress in colour
like that of monks and friars. At the pre-Conquest house in Pontefract it
was white, symbolic of purity, and at medieval Alkmonton it was white
and russet (a poor man's brown) in alternate years. At St Giles' Hospital,
Norwich, the men and women have worn grey; in 1294 it was grey cloaks
over white and the women's veils were black.

The expression "sad colour" was used as late as 1692 at Storey's
house in Cambridge, and the statutes of Whittington's College, 1424,
(see below) state firmly that the almsmen's outer clothing must be

"Derke and broune of color not staring ne blasing and of esy prised cloth".[7] His fellow Mercer, Ellis Davy, used the same words in 1447 for his own endowment at Croydon, the Ellis Davy almshouse which still functions there.

For men's best gowns blue was often permitted; in later times, for every day too, for example at Clipston, Northants, in 1667. Blue was always an ordinary choice for the women.

Custom was defied by Doughty at Norwich, who put his men and women into liveries of purple. (No wonder he wanted to be sure they wore them.) Still more startling an exception is found in the fifteenth-century almshouses at Heytesbury, Wiltshire, where, at least in the twentieth century, on Sundays the men changed from blue coats into red.[8]

Red, as we have seen, is a rare colour for charity clothes but there is another signal exception to this rule. A red cloak has been what Alma Oakes in *Rural Costume*[9] calls one of our "two distinctive garments in Britain", one worn nationwide by working-class women from the seventeenth to nineteenth centuries. So well established was this that Mrs Trimmer, in 1801, while writing about domestic servants' dress, goes on

134. Almsmen, nearly a century apart in time, wearing similar gowns. *Left* "Poor man" at Queen Elizabeth's funeral, 1603. *Right* Typical "Beadsman", 1688 (*Left* British Library MS Add 5408, *right* Randle Holme *Academy of Armory Book* III Chapter III, Pl. opp. page 41)

to remark, as was quoted in Chapter 10: "but it were much to be wished that *stuffs* were as heretofore the every-day dress of common maid servants, and that the *scarlet* or the *duffel cloak* might be their defence against the cold . . ."[10] It is not surprising therefore that, like the Red Maids, certain charity women were given this red cloak. At Sherborne, Dorset, they wore it till recently, and at Castle Rising (see below) they still do.

As is to be expected, almsfolk's uniforms have always been conservative in style and some were purposely old-fashioned, even when first introduced. We have seen William of Wykeham's insistence on the wearing of tabards at New College, Oxford, and this outmoded garment must have been well associated with academic dress by 1437. It is therefore perhaps no coincidence that when, in that year, the Earl of Suffolk and his wife (a granddaughter of Chaucer) founded an almshouse at Ewelme, twelve miles from Oxford, the unworldly dress chosen for the thirteen old men and their chaplain was a tabard with a hood.

What followed the tabard was a long gown open in front, of late-fifteenth-century or early Tudor style, and this has been thought appropriate for academics and for almsmen ever since. Thus the gown, which came to mean "university", also, in time, symbolized a bedesman. Did not a king embrace humility with the moving words:

> I'll give my jewels for a string of beads* . . .
> My gay apparel for an almsman's gown.

> Shakespear *Richard II*, Act III, iii, 131, 133)

Hoods did not survive in almsmen's dress, but their headgear was Tudor in style for centuries and academic-looking to our eyes. In 1688 Randle Holme[11] published an engraving of a man in a flat cap and a gown with hanging sleeves, which was to illustrate not a scholar as one would think but a "*Beads-man* or an old man, in an** Hospital Gown (or Poor Man's gown) with a Bonnet or Cap". While Holme shows a cap, many almsmen had a Tudor bonnet: a cloth hat with a flat crown gathered into a narrow brim just like that of a university doctor today. Trinity Hospital (Abbot's Hospital), Guildford, where these are still worn, was founded as late as 1619. They must therefore have been old-fashioned from the very first.

Finally there are the top hats for men and straw bonnets for women. Where these were eventually allowed as a concession to fashion, in the nineteenth century, they proved just as difficult to get rid of as the caps

---

* A rosary.　　** Misprinted "and".

135. Brother at Abbot's Hospital
(Hospital of the Blessed Trinity),
Guildford, 1973. Tudor-style
bonnet, mitre badge on sleeve of
black gown (After photo:
Chadwick Foster-Smith)

and gowns. We even meet with a top hat on almsmen in the 1960s (see Holy Trinity Hospital, Greenwich, below) combined with a Tudor gown, for all the world as though aping a well-off Victorian undergraduate. The top hats and their leather boxes are still cherished at Greenwich and at Jesus Hospital, Rothwell, Northants.

Early Victorian bonnets survived into the 1890s for many almswomen and are seen in a photograph of 1929 on those at Guildford.

An attractive feature of the uniforms was the badge that they often bore. Some of these were directly religious symbols which we have already noticed. Others were emblems of the donor's office or of guilds, many having a religious connotation too. The ten old men at Thomas Bond's Hospital, Coventry, were members of his own guild, the Trinity Guild of Coventry, and bore its religious symbol; and when in 1553 the Company of St George wanted to help St Giles in Norwich they resolved "to buy as much Freese, as would make thirteen Gowns to be given to thirteen of the 40 Poor People in God's House, and each Gown to have the *Conysance* of the Gild on them (viz a Red Cross)".[12]

Even today, members of the Jesus Hospital at Bray, Berks., (two men and sixteen women) attend the annual dinner of their patrons, the

136. Funeral at Jesus Hospital, Rothwell, Northants., 1888. Brethren's dress old-fashioned (breeches, etc.) but top hats worn (*The Graphic* XXXVIII, 689)

137. Front and back views of badge of Fishmongers' Company's almsfolk at Bray, Berkshire. Heraldic notion of dolphin, "King of Fish". Note rings for sewing badge on to gown. In current use (Badge lent by Fishmongers' Company)

Fishmongers' Company, wearing badges that depict a crowned dolphin, which is one of the charges on the Company's escutcheon.

Personal emblems, such as the donor's initials or his family badge, were (like portraits of individuals in the world of painting) more in evidence after the Reformation. For example, the ten old widows in Bootham, York, who owed their keep to Sir Arthur Ingram, of the early seventeenth century, went about labelled with his crest, a lively cock. (Compare Fig. 21.) These silver badges were still worn until very recently.[13]

But family badges were sometimes used much earlier. A fourteenth-century example occurred in Bristol where the Gaunt family founded a religious community, the Hospital of St Mark. This maintained, besides clergy and an almonry, twelve poor scholars who were to serve

138. *Left* Part of sleeve of gown similar to that in Fig. 135. Mitre of Archbishop George Abbot, founder of the Hospital, 1619. *Right* Badge worn at the Gaunt family's Hospital of St Mark, Bristol – white gants on a red shield (*Left* Photo: Harry Pascoe, *right* after Elizabeth Ralph and H. Evans *St Mark's, the Lord Mayor's Chapel, Bristol,* a pamphlet, 1961)

in the choir wearing surplices and the black copes usually seen only at funerals. But on their habits there was embroidered a red shield with three white birds, and these represent either ganders or crested grebes called "gants" – a play on the founders' name.[14]

Clothing other than outer garments and headgear was less often given in kind but, despite the problem of fitting, shoes sometimes were. At Heytesbury in 1472 the men even received the wherewithal for mending them: "2 paire of shone with lether and hempe to clowte them".[15]

An unusual provision was one made for the almshouse at Saffron Walden when the Guild of Our Lady founded it in 1400. At a time when poverty was so extreme that many could not afford a shroud, the inmates were to be respected even in death and "buried in clothing such as they, and all others in Walden who own no goods, lack . . ."[16]

SOME MEDIEVAL AND
SIXTEENTH-CENTURY FOUNDATIONS

HOSPITAL OF ST CROSS, WINCHESTER

Probably the oldest charitable institution in England, certainly its best-known almshouse, is the Hospital of St Cross, still fulfilling one of the traditions of medieval hospitals in dispensing charity to travellers in the form of bread and ale. It was planned by King Stephen's enter-prising young brother Henry, Bishop of Winchester, mainly as a per-manent home for thirteen humble folk, poor men unable to fend for themselves. When finally established in 1151, the custody of it was handed over to the Knights Hospitallers of St John of Jerusalem of crusading fame.

In 1446 Cardinal Beaufort, Henry VI's uncle, took pity on a group who were seldom the objects of charity, namely aristocrats who had fallen on evil days. He accordingly obtained a charter for a "House of Noble Poverty" to be added to the Hospital. The new community came into being with six members in the 1480s and has existed side by side with the old one ever since.

Clothing was provided for all, but the two groups were sharply dis-tinguished. The ordinary pensioners wear black and probably always did. Their gowns today are of fifteenth or sixteenth-century style, fastened down the front and with full sleeves gathered in at the wrist. We know that in 1694 the gowns were made of black cloth rash, a smooth fabric of wool and worsted mixed. The headgear is a typical

140. Badge of the "noble poor" at
Hospital of St Cross, Winchester: a
cardinal's hat and "Maltese" cross
(After photo: John P. Lucas)

flat black bonnet. Fastened at the left breast is a silver "Maltese Cross",
the emblem of the Knights of St John. The badge of the Order came to
be called a "Maltese" cross, because their base was in Malta from the
year 1530 onwards. It is an eight-pointed cross: the shape of the
almsmen's badge is the popular version. When a pensioner dies this is
laid on his coffin (as would be a duke's coronet) until the burial and is
then passed on to his successor.

The "noble poor", though wearing the same style of gown and cap
as the others, have a different colour and badge. The cap and gown
have always been made in a shade of red, perhaps "cardinal" red at
first, now claret colour. The badge commemorates Beaufort, as it contains a cardinal's hat, originally embroidered in white (see frontispiece
and Fig. 140). This unique class distinction has continued to be observed
down to the present day.

It is fascinating to realize that black gowns like those one sees at St
Cross today have been worn there for over eight hundred years.[17]

WHITTINGTON COLLEGE

That legendary but very real Lord Mayor of London, Richard Whittington, "had ryght liberal and large hands to the needy"[18] and
bequeathed a large moiety of his estate in trust for assistance to the
poor. In accordance with his deathbed instructions, this was used
chiefly to found a set of almshouses for thirteen people, and these were

139. Brothers at Hospital of St Cross, Winchester. Silver "Maltese" cross of
Knights of St John. 1973 (Photo: John P. Lucas)

completed, in the City of London, by 1424. The Mercers' Company, to which he had belonged, were the executors and they have retained an invaluable series of unpublished manuscript records to which we owe much of our material.[19]

The "Goddeshouse" was a purely secular establishment and the almsmen elected their own "Tutor" but until the Reformation they were required to pray for the founder's soul. The Tutor had the duty of ordering their food and distributing their sober coloured gowns (mentioned above) and also their allowances, which were "sufficient to provide all other necessaries, as hose, shoes, linen etc". In 1609 the Mercers' Court ruled that the almsmen should have "gowns against Christmas of some good cloth not exceeding 10/- a yard the lining to be cotton the facing bayes . . . and it is further agreed that they henceforth have new gowns every third year . . . provided that they be enjoined not to go forth in cloaks but in gowns as other almsmen about the town do". This is another proof that an "almsman's gown" was already a received concept.

In 1625 a Mercer presented thirteen valuable silver-gilt badges, and several of this very first issue are still cherished at the Mercers' Hall. The badge replaced an earlier embroidered one, the history of which is interesting. Bedesmen of the Middle Ages always had a rosary and, when not using it, wore it to remind them of their role (Fig. 27). At the Reforma-

141. Silver badge of almsmen at Whittington College, designed after the "maiden's head" emblem of the Mercers' Company. Motto "Thincke and Thancke God". Cast in 1627 (Courtesy: Mercers' Company)

142. Almsfolk of St John's
Almshouse, Sherborne, Dorset, 1960s.
The woman, in the uniform red cloak,
was aged ninety-six (Courtesy: the
Master and Brethren)

tion this had to end, and an alternative means of recognition was devised.
The Mercers recorded in 1547:

Mayden's heades in the steade of beades

Item as consyning [concerning] the bedemen of Whyttington College ...
forasmuche as the sayde Beades be forbydden by the King's Injunciones It is
agreed ... that theye shall weyre in the steade thereof the conysaunce of a
mayden's heade upon theire sayde gownes Lyke as before tyme theye dyde
weare the Beades.[20]

It is startling to find that the old men fastened what was practically a
pin-up girl to their gowns. The explanation is that the figure formed
part of the arms of the Mercers' Company and as such would have
been worn by Whittington himself. At the Lord Mayor's Show, when a
Mercer had been elected to that office, the maiden was portrayed in
one of the floats by a very glamorous young woman.[21] The flowing hair
implied virginity, but the red dress and necklace show that she did not
represent the Virgin, as has sometimes been thought.

The almshouses in the City were replaced by new ones in Highgate
in 1825, by which time old women had taken the place of the men.
Finally, in 1966, they were moved to Felbridge, Sussex, and there the
uniform is no longer worn.

ALMSHOUSE OF ST JOHN, SHERBORNE, DORSET

St John's is worth a mention, for it is a medieval almshouse that still
continues to function in the same beautiful buildings, updated but un-
spoilt; and moreover until 1962 it had a traditional uniform for both
men and women.

Bishop Nevill of Salisbury obtained the royal licence in 1437, and he is accordingly commemorated by a bishop's mitre embroidered on the almsmen's gowns and stamped on their buttons.

The style of the clothes is striking (Fig. 142). Both sexes wear a large cape collar, the man having it on his blue gown, the woman on a version of the countrywoman's red cloak. She also wears a little Victorian-looking black bonnet tied under the chin and had a straw poke bonnet in the summer.

LORD LEYCESTER HOSPITAL, WARWICK

A very different establishment was one devised by Queen Elizabeth's favourite, Robert Dudley, Earl of Leicester, in Warwick. In some beautiful fifteenth-century buildings that had belonged to a religious guild he set up a home expressly for old soldiers, and his intention has been respected right down to the present day. The thirteen brethren are all ex-servicemen.

Queen Elizabeth granted the licence in 1571 and made the Hospital a charming present in the form of thirteen silver badges depicting the

143. One of the original silver badges of the pensioners in Lord Leycester Hospital, Warwick, presented by Queen Elizabeth I. See text (Courtesy the Master and Brethren)

144. Old soldiers, Brethren of the Lord Leycester Hospital, Warwick, 1975.
Badge fastened to the gown sleeve, which is reduced to a hanging strip, here
brought forward over the shoulder and twisted to show the badge (Courtesy: the
Master and Brethren)

earl's family emblem, a bear with ragged staff, surmounted by an earl's coronet. A new and personal touch, perhaps the Queen's own idea, was to have the name of the original recipient engraved on the back of the badge. The Hospital still possesses all but one of the original set. The example seen in our Fig. 143 is marked "BART. HEATH".

The gown still worn is an interesting example of the ecclesiastical and academic style. It is remarkably like the university gowns described in Chapter 11 and also like many vergers' gowns today, the sleeves having been reduced to a strip hanging from the back of the shoulder. Yet, in accordance with the medieval tradition that livery emblems should be worn on the sleeve, the silver badge is fastened to this strip.

As for the "Tudor" hat, this is, and perhaps always was, like that of the Yeomen of the Guard – a quasi military touch rather suitable here. The costume is still worn on special occasions and at church on Sundays.

SOME SEVENTEENTH AND EIGHTEENTH-CENTURY FOUNDATIONS

Henry Howard, Earl of Northampton, who died in 1614, established in his lifetime two important almshouses and made provision in his will for a third. Happily he made the Mercers' Company his trustees, and thanks to their care all three houses have survived, and so have many manuscript records of their history.

HOLY TRINITY HOSPITALS AT GREENWICH AND AT CLUN

Almost coeval and with similar statutes (Greenwich 1615, Clun 1618), these can be dealt with together. The attractive building on the Thames bank at Greenwich (with a contemporary mulberry tree in its garden) is still occupied, and on Trinity Sunday the uniform is still worn. This will be taken as our main example and any differences at Clun noticed in passing.[22]

For the Greenwich Hospital the establishment was to consist of a warden, twenty poor men, a butler, a cook, a poor woman as nurse, a laundress and a barber. At Clun, where there were only twelve poor men, the staff was smaller.

Annually on the founder's birthday each man received "a gowne ready made of good durable cloth [ordinary wool], of a sad colour to wear ... weekdaies of the price of twenty shillings ..."[23] At first this everyday gown was black.

They also had, every fourth year, a best "livery gowne" of "good durable blewe broadcloth [a superior woollen fabric] . . . lined with [blue] baies . . . to be worn only upon Sondaies and festivall daies". It was on this best gown that a handsome embroidered cognizance "being a white lyon", was "sett on the sleeve"[24] (Fig. 145). This was the earl's badge. With the best gowns were issued the "Liverye Hatts of the Price of four shillings, all of one Fashion".

All prices seem to have been lower in Shropshire: the Greenwich gowns were worth 48s. 8d., Clun's 44s.

The sub-warden, chosen from among the men, had a special duty, as we have seen, to look after the Sunday gowns.

There survives a signed statement by an almsman, John Dawson, who entered, aged eighty-five, in 1654, in which he undertakes to fulfil the rules by leaving his final livery to his successor.[25]

Other clothing the men seem to have bought for themselves out of their allowance. To prove that they wore boots (or for the sake of an anecdote) let us quote a case from the old *Book of Corrections*, which is still at the almshouse. The misdemeanour of one Cordell Brewster in 1622 was that "he called the Cooke rogge [rogue] and other foul names because he told him that he must not warm his boots in the kitchen by the fyer (there being a good fyer in Hall) and strock the Cook with his boot".

The warden had livery different from the men's. At Greenwich he had only one gown but it was much dearer than either of the other kinds; he was allowed £5 every two years to buy it. The colour, as at Clun, was "sad marble" and the cognizance the white lion rampant. At Clun the warden did have two gowns, the better one (with the badge) was worth £3.

The cook and butler were given cloaks, using less material and being cheaper to make than gowns, in alternate years. Unlike the "poor woman" they were also given the cognizance. She received only a plain gown.

Changes, though remarkably few, were effected over the years. In 1686 a tailor was making the "gounds" of a "darke" colour (no longer black) and in 1821 we find "brown cloth" being bought for the weekday gown. The garment itself was soon to be called a cloak or a robe and later a coat, although its cut remained the same.

From 1884 the Sunday livery began to be handed out only every sixth year, perhaps because it was less often worn. And at about the turn of the present century the best gown was changed from blue to black, perhaps to go better with the now firmly entrenched top hat.

Embroidered badges came to an end, but in 1835 the Accounts of the Mercers' Court show a resolution that their Wardens and the

145. Badge of almsmen,
Holy Trinity Hospital,
Greenwich: Lord
Northampton's (Howard)
family cognizance; made *c.*
1840 (Courtesy: Mercers'
Company)

Master should "give directions for providing new Silver Badges for the
Blue Gowns given to the Poor Men . . ." There was delay over this innovation and in 1839 the men were paid 2s. 6d. each "in lieu of Silver
Cognizances". Badges were certainly in use in 1859, when it was ruled
that they need not be worn on the "Brown Coat". As they were fixed
on by the tailor, who charged for the job, presumably each man had
had two.

The beautiful badges, of silver repoussé work, are now stored for
safety at the Mercers' Hall and handed to the men once a year for the
Trinity Sunday celebrations.

On 18 June 1962 the Visitation Court appointed by the Mercers

considered the question of replacing the brown cloaks and the black cloaks
worn by the Poor Men of Greenwich Hospital. After examining samples . . .
hearing the opinions of the Poor Men and considering various estimates it
was resolved to recommend . . . that the brown cloaks should be dispensed
with and that the black cloaks should be reserved [retained] but without the
lining, in a faced cloth at a price of approximately £14 each.*

* Even before the 1970s, inflation had thus shown itself to the tune of 1400 per cent (despite
the economy over linings) since the first gown was made.

146. *Left* Pensioner of Holy Trinity Hospital, Greenwich, 1976, in his livery gown and one of the top hats that were worn every Trinity Sunday as late as the 1960s. Gown fastens only at neck. Badge as in previous illustration. *Right* Warden of same Hospital, in Warden's traditional velvet-trimmed gown with hanging sleeve, 1976 (Courtesy: the Warden and the late Stanley Cornish, resident)

It is noteworthy that this is the first example we have come across where the views of recipients of charity have been consulted regarding their clothes. It was not until the 1960s that the top hats were worn for the last time. They now remain in their leather boxes as relics of the past.

A final word on the Warden's gown. This is also black but of a very superior material and is faced with black silk velvet. Although for the first time in history a woman Warden was appointed in 1973, tradition is upheld and she wears this gown, when all the others wear theirs, on the Hospital's great name day.*

TRINITY HOSPITAL, CASTLE RISING, NORFOLK

This almshouse, for women only, was built by the same Henry Howard, Earl of Northampton, during his lifetime, near his Norfolk home, and was probably completed by 1610. The letters patent of the foundation were obtained by the executors in 1615.

There were to be twelve poor and old women from the neighbourhood, under a "Governess", all to be single, "at least 56 years of age" and "of an honest life ... religious, grave and discreet, able to read, if such a one may be had ... no common beggar, harlot", etc.[26] At the present day widows are admitted and presumably it is taken for granted that applicants can read.

Every year each woman "has for their apparel a gown of strong cloth, or kersey, of a dark colour, and every seventh year a livery gown, (and a hat) of blue broad cloth lined with baize, with the founder's badge or cognizance set on the breast, being a lion rampant, argent, embroidered".[27]

The everyday gowns seem for a long time to have been brown (like those of the men in the two sister hospitals at Greenwich and Clun , in the nineteenth century), but black frieze was bought in 1634.[28] The blue livery gowns were kept in the Governess's charge – even women were not trusted with best clothes.

As we have noticed in charity schools, garments for outdoor warmth were slow to appear. The cloak was a practical means of protection and had been worn by all classes from the later seventeenth century onwards. Alma Oakes[29] suggests that the ultimate introduction of serge cloaks at Castle Rising in 1863 was probably due to the sisters having objected to their heavy, old-fashioned, baize-lined dresses ("gowns"). Perhaps dresses were then made lighter (and the house kept warmer?), so that an outdoor garment became necessary. The choice of scarlet is significant, as we have seen. The fact that the bedeswomen's outfit reminds one of a Welshwoman's costume is simply because a country attire previously widespread was preserved in both contexts after disappearing elsewhere. It was exactly the same with the "Welsh" hat – a survival, with modification, of the seventeenth-century "sugarloaf".

* My thanks are due to the Warden, Mrs Simpson, for showing me the treasures of the Hospital, and arranging for the photograph shown in Fig. 146. C.L.

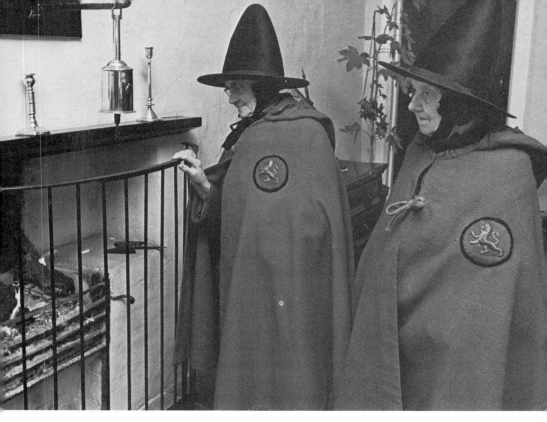

147. Bedeswomen of Trinity Hospital, Castle Rising, Norfolk. Scarlet cloaks bear Lord Northampton's lion rampant (*Eastern Daily Press* 1974)

148. Trinity Hospital, Castle Rising, Norfolk. *Left* Bedeswoman. *Right* Warden (*Eastern Daily Press* 1974)

In the eighteenth century the Castle Rising hats were made in King's Lynn and were later obtained in London from the same makers and materials as men's top hats.

The Warden, like the Wardens at the sister hospitals, has and probably always had, a different uniform from the rest. Her hat is cocked and trimmed with a black ostrich feather and her scarlet cloak has a three-tiered cape which may be an inheritance from its earliest days.

These attractive costumes may still be seen at church services and the annual celebrations on Founder's Day and the embroidered lion rampant, now transferred to the cloaks, still upholds the memory of a noble and large-hearted founder.

STRODE'S ALMSHOUSES, SHEPTON MALLET, SOMERSET

For comparison with the foregoing, it is interesting to see what was thought appropriate for old people right at the end of the seventeenth century in an establishment untrammelled by earlier rules.

Edward Strode opened his almshouses for four poor old men in 1699. As each man had a cottage to himself, it was not to be a collegiate life, but a uniform was prescribed. In alternate years, "against Easter", each man received a quite contemporary, if humble, outfit:

A new grey hat, edged about with red narrow silk galloon lace [braid], the hat so laced to cost 5s. and no more.
One plain neckcloth and dowlas [coarse linen] shirt, both to cost 5s.
A pair of large breeches made of red cloth, at 6s. the yeard.
A large waistcoat made of white cloth or linsey woolsey, of 1s. 4d. a yard.
A pair of blue strong yarn stockings of 1s. 6d. a pair.
A strong pair of tusset [possibly a misreading of "russet"] leather shoes, at 3s. 6d. a pair, with a pair of blue points [laces] to tie the shoes.[30]

Note the plain neckcloth. Unlike charity boys, almsmen were not put into bands; nor of course might they wear the fancy cravat that no gentleman of the time could be without. The Charity Commissioners reported that the outfits were still being supplied in 1820 at a cost of about £13.[31]

The chief garment was no longer a gown but a coat, and this one had a special feature. It was a "loose-bodied coat, with the letter E cut large in blue cloth, and well sewed on the right sleeve, and the letter S on the left sleeve, plain to be seen".[32]

Edward Strode, like others of his family (see p. 35) made sure that his left hand was not the only one that knew what his right hand was doing.

CONINGSBY HOSPITAL, HEREFORD

Finally we come to Coningsby Hospital, left to the last because, occupying as it does quarters built by the Knights of St John, it has links with St Cross, while at the same time, being specially meant for old soldiers, it also points the way to the Chelsea Hospital which we describe in the next chapter.

Sir Thomas Coningsby, a contemporary of the Earl of Northampton, had had wide experience of campaigns abroad and felt a special concern for veterans of war. Building an almshouse for them in 1614, he incorporated the remains of the ancient hospital of the Knights of St John and rededicated it "to the glory of God . . . in thankfulness for his defence . . . in forraigne travels by Sea and Land". The organization was to combine collegiate life (there was to be a well-qualified chaplain) with traces of military government: the head was, and still is, called "Corporall" and there have always been military features in the dress. In this way it is more like Chelsea Hospital than is the earlier Lord Leycester Hospital for ex-soldiers.

Of the eleven poor and old men, the founder laid down that six should be "oulde souldiers of three yeare's service, at least, in the warres . . . in default of them . . . the number to be suplyed by marriners . . .". But it is interesting that the other five members were to be "ould Serving Men of seaven yeares service in one family".

Thus former soldiers and sailors and former household servants mingled and were known collectively as "the Company of Servitors". Almshouses simply for family servants were not unknown, e.g. those of the Paston family at Oxnead, Norfolk, from the fifteenth century.[33] The Corporall was democratically elected from among the pensioners.

Thirty pounds out of the income of two hundred pounds was to be spent on clothes. The first uniform has been described on the basis of the original ordinances, as follows:

a fustian suit of ginger colour [probably the tawney often used in liveries] *of soldierlike fashion, seemly laced*
a hat with a border of white and red,
a soldier-like jerkin with half sleeves and square skirts down to half the thigh [long skirts to doublets and jerkins were typically military in the seventeenth century].
Moncado or Spanish Cap
a soldier-like sword with a belt to wear "as he goeth abroad"
a Cloak of red cloth, lined with red baize and reaching to the knee, and
"A seemely gowne likewise of redd cloth down to the Ankle lined likewise with redd baise" *to be worn in the Hospital and city of Hereford, the cloak to be worn in further walks and journeys.*[34]

149. Old soldiers, pensioners at Coningsby Hospital, Hereford, ?1890–1910
(From booklet, *Coningsby Hospital, 1971*. Courtesy the author, A. K. Beese)

Going to the cathedral or any public place, the men, led by the chaplain, must process two by two in their gowns and "wearing their swordes, *if the law would permit*" – a curious mixture of almsmen's and military attire.

New ordinances promulgated in 1616 reiterate that "each servitor shall constantly, upon every Lord's day, in his proper habit and cloak go along with the corporal to the ... cathedral church".

In the nineteenth century the everyday dress became a coat and trousers worn with a top hat, but it is interesting to note that, if a man is entitled to chevrons when in the Army, he still wears them on his sleeve in the Hospital.

Throughout the twentieth century, there has been only one uniform. The men wear it voluntarily and only on special occasions. (At present a few of them cannot be given one at all as they are too big for the existing coats.) The main garment is a "frock tunic", i.e. a thigh-length

150. *Right* Pensioner and *centre* Corporal Pensioner of Coningsby Hospital. Each man wears on his red tunic the Hospital badge which combines a coney with the cross of the Order of St John of Jerusalem. *Left* Prior of the Order. 1971 (Courtesy: Coningsby Trustees)

close-fitting coat.* It is rather like those at Chelsea in being red, with deep pockets and brass buttons (Fig. 150). A dark-blue peaked cap (based on the Chelsea shako) has taken the place of the topper and has a red band and gilt wire on the peak.

But the most distinctive feature is the embroidered badge that is still worn on the coat. This curious device is Coningsby's own crest, a heraldic interpretation of his name. It depicts (not too aptly for a soldier) a coney, which is nothing more nor less than a rabbit, at his time a comparatively rare creature in England. But who would not be glad to wear it in memory of such a brother-in-arms?

* Early specimens of the coat and cap in the styles still worn, and also a model of the original uniform, may be seen at the City Museum, Hereford. For particulars of the present-day uniform we are indebted to Brig. A. F. L. Clive, Chairman of the Hospital.

CHAPTER 13

Armed forces: hospitals and associated schools

POOR KNIGHTS OF WINDSOR

His helmet now shall make a hive for bees,
And lover's sonnets turn to holy psalms;
A man-at-arms must now serve on his knees
And feed on prayers which are Age's alms . . .

Goddess, allow this aged man his right
To be your bedesman now that was your knight.

Sir Henry Lea, K.G., Retiring from service,
addresses Elizabeth I. Lyric by George Peele, 1590.[1]

The oldest of all establishments for men who have served in the armed forces is that of the so-called "Poor Knights", for whom quarters and all else were provided in Windsor Castle itself, under a plan devised and endowed by Edward III. When the king founded the Order of the Garter in 1348 he planned, in addition, an ecclesiastical college based on St George's Chapel and consisting of canons and other clerics, together with a number of "*milites pauperes*". The statutes of 1352 (translated) describe the position of the pensioners as follows: "Seeing that Alms coupled with Prayer contribute greatly to the salvation of the soul there shall be substituted for those most noble knights [of the Garter] a like number of poor veteran warriors, for the purpose of prayer, who shall moreover have there a means of livelihood".[2] The prayers were to be for the sovereign and the Knights Companions of the Order of the Garter.

The old soldiers were chosen for distinguished service as well as poverty, but the term "Knights" was a courtesy title – they were not dubbed knights nor addressed as "Sir" but had a very honourable

* See also Lord Leycester's Hospital and Coningsby Hospital in Chapter 12.

standing because of their association with the Order. Their number at first was meant to correspond with that of the Garter Knights – twenty six – but, under Henry VIII, it was permanently changed in 1522 to thirteen. The garments provided for them also corresponded to those of the Garter Knights, comprising, as they did, a long ceremonial surcoat, later called gown or kirtle, and a foot-length mantle. Embroidered on the latter was a shield with the arms of St George – a plain red cross on a white ground. The mantles of the Garter Knights were blue, but the first statutes laid down that the veteran warriors should have red mantles. Their surcoats have nearly always been scarlet and those of the Knights crimson.

151. "Alms-Knights" of Windsor in vanguard of procession of Knights of the Garter with Queen Elizabeth, 1575. Ceremonial robes: purple mantle with badge on left shoulder, red surcoat or kirtle (Contemporary coloured print at British Museum, after Marcus Gheeraedts I, detail)

152. *Left* Badge of Knights of the Garter: St George's red cross on white shield, surrounded by the Garter. *Right* Alms-Knights' badge – without Garter. (*Left* Edmund Fellowes: *The Military Knights of Windsor 1352–1944*, 1944. *Right* After contemporary print shown in Fig. 151, detail)

Some changes under Henry VIII's will can be ignored; they affected few individuals, for under Queen Elizabeth in 1559 there were new statutes. By these the colour of the mantle was altered. Each "Alms-Knight" was to receive: "one Gown of 4 yards of the colour Red and a Mantle of blue or purple cloth of 5 yards [a lavish allowance] at 6s. 8d. a yard. The cross of St George in a scutcheon embroidered without the Garter to be set upon the left shoulder of their Mantles".[3] From 1564 to 1637 the colour purple was chosen for the mantles of both the Knights and the Poor Knights; but the Poor Knights were at almost all periods distinguished by having no Garter surrounding the emblematic shield (as do the Knights Companions); moreover their gowns were of woollen cloth instead of velvet.

The mantles of the Knights of the Garter returned permanently to dark blue in 1637,[4] and those of the Poor Knights, probably at the same time, went back to scarlet, so described by Randle Holme in 1688[5] and by Ashmole in 1715.[6]

There was a temporary break with tradition when Cromwell disestablished the College and, while preserving the pensioners, put them all into a dreary almsman's dress without a mantle at all. Each was to have every two years: "a gown of 4 yards of broad cloth of a sad colour at 13s. 4d. a yard, lined with bayes of the same colour at 2s. 4d. a yard, and have the Commonwealth Arms embroidered on the left shoulder of the gown".[7] Charles II lost no time in putting matters right.

In course of time, like so many occupants of charitable institutions, the Poor Knights acquired a prestige of their own and wished for a worthier name. Eventually, in 1833, William IV changed their title to "The Military Knights of Windsor" and gave them military uniforms. The institution bearing this name today is so different from the Poor Knights as to fall outside the scope of our book.

The Poor Knights, forming in a sense a branch of the Order of the Garter, used to play a conspicuous part in the Order's annual celebrations of the feast of St George whenever these were held at Windsor. They headed the sovereign's magnificent procession that made its way through the castle to St George's Chapel (Fig. 151). Ashmole, in his account of the ceremony, gives a detailed description of all the robes, and remarks that "The Habits of the Alms-Knights (a Mantle and Kirtle [the surcoat]) are not unremarkable both for Colour and Materials, which appear suitable to their Age and Degree".[8] He adds that the various costumes, by their juxtaposition "in this grand Proceeding ... entertain the Beholders with a very delightful prospect".

ROYAL HOSPITAL, CHELSEA

Early history and status

Who can have passed the aged soldier in the uniform of a Chelsea pensioner without having felt a sentiment of respect glowing in his bosom, as a pleasing tribute to the defender of his country.*

W. H. Pyne Costume of Great Britain, 1808.

This may be overdoing it a little, but there can be no doubt about the emotive effect of that scarlet coat. And it is matched by the glamour that surrounds the Hospital itself, which was royal not only in name. The brain child of Sir Stephen Fox and John Evelyn in 1666, the scheme was cherished by Charles II, who laid the foundation stone in 1682, and it was earnestly fostered by James II and again by William and Mary. The building finally opened in 1692. Its chief architect was Wren himself, one of its treasurers was Robert Walpole, an organist in its chapel was Dr Burney and an admiring and frequent visitor was Boswell.

The purpose of the Hospital was to provide complete maintenance and a little pocket money for "land souldiers [of all ranks] as are or shall be old, lame or infirm in ye service of the Crown".[9]

* Compare the quotation from the same source on page 63.

Clothing was a first consideration and this was emphasized by the influx of wounded arriving in 1704 after the battle of Blenheim. The Chelsea Board considered giving them a temporary uniform "as they will be quite naked before they can come into the Hospital". But it proved too dear "and only trusses and wooden legs were authorized".

The nation's debt to the Army and the dire need for the Hospital's services were only too obvious, yet its status was, and still is, in an attenuated sense, a charity. Since its inclusion in our book depends on this fact, perhaps it should briefly be explained.

That the Hospital is far from being wholly a charity is clear from the facts, first, that for many years men of all ranks in the Army had certain direct and indirect deductions ("Hospital money" and "Army poundage") made from their pay to support the Hospital; secondly the in-pensioners performed certain guard duties in the Hospital like those of any garrison; then from 1715 to *c.* 1805 they patrolled the highway between Westminster and Chelsea, originally at the inhabitants' request, as a protection against violent footpads; and finally, some of the work in the Hospital itself was, and is, done by resident volunteers.

But as a charity, to a great extent, it has always been regarded. Strype, in his edition of Stow's *Survey of London* in 1720, wrote: "the Royal Hospital ... has been founded for the ends and purposes of a Charitable Relief of Soldiers". Even after first allowing the Crown the full cost of the Army, Parliament was incredibly slow to accept responsibility towards superannuated and disabled soldiers. Sir Stephen Fox, the first Paymaster for the Hospital, gave £13 000 towards the building and was called by Evelyn "This grand benefactor". And Fox himself recorded how much "this great charity" owed to Charles II. Particularly relevant to us is the fact that, for 240 years, pensioners were presented with their greatcoats by Richard, Earl of Ranelagh, for this (otherwise rapacious) Treasurer of the Hospital established a trust in 1707 expressly to supply a "surtout coat" to each man every third year of his life.

Costumes of the household staff

One of the first uniforms to be designed for the Hospital was that for one Thomas Button (something of a character) who was appointed porter in 1687. Much in the public eye, at the main gates, he was given a suit of "Livery Cloathes" designed to impress.* It was green, had a

---

* A miniature model of it may be seen, with many other Hospital uniforms, in the Royal Hospital Museum.

mass of gold lace froggings and with the bicorne hat cost more than a sergeant's uniform.

Caring for nearly five hundred pensioners there was a staff in 1692 of some sixty people. Among the twenty-four men servants the poorer paid, including the surgeon's mate, received a grey uniform suit, the coat having blue cuffs and brass buttons.

The women, who comprised twenty four "Matrons" (mostly soldiers' wives or widows), matched the men, having grey serge open gowns and blue cuffs worn over grey "petticoats". Apart from a change in the facings from blue to black, early in the eighteenth century, the same grey uniform was still being issued in the 1870s.

The "Military Government"[10]

The Hospital was a military organization and it is necessary to say a few words about the hierarchy involved. A pensioner, asked by the authors how he liked the place, remarked tersely "Too many class distinctions". Distinctions of army rank would seem the only ones left today, but his remark would certainly have been pertinent in 1692. Commissioned officers were all "gentlemen", lower ranks were of the lower orders except that, in the Life Guards, they were usually gentlemen and, in the "Light Horse" (Cavalry), they were of at least the yeomen class.

The pensioners were organized in companies of forty-eight men with two sergeants. Each company was commanded by a "Captain" and at first he was naturally a commissioned officer of the Army. But from 1719 till the nineteenth century there were few, if any, commissioned officers in the Hospital except for the Governor, Lieutenant Governor and Major. Since the posts of Captain were considered tenable by gentlemen only, they were filled during this period by Guardsmen. Later in the eighteenth century the Guards ceased to be recruited from the gentry, and then there was nothing for it but to make Hospital Captains out of the more deserving sergeants. These were paid an extra 6d. a week and were known as "Sixpenny Men". Being picked out in a special uniform and yet humble and impecunious, it was said by a contemptuous gentleman of the neighbourhood that "They frequently have more gold and silver *on* their clothes than *in* them".[11] This special class of Captain (they were later called Ward Captains) came to an end in 1850, and once again a commissioned officer, called a "Captain of Invalids", took on their duty. Until that same date, the Light Horse, because of their social class, constituted a company of their own and were paid as highly as sergeants in other companies.

Uniforms of officers and men

The distinctions made according to rank, and the evolution of uniforms in course of time, will be briefly traced.

Of all the articles of attire the one least subject to distinctions and change has been the hat, which can therefore be dealt with here, once and for all. In 1692, the hat was already black and cocked and so it remained for every individual and every period. By 1703 it had settled down, for all but a few, into the typical eighteenth-century three-cornered shape so characteristic of the pensioner's ceremonial dress to this day. The only change has been the addition of a Hanoverian black cockade – that mark of a servant of the Crown introduced in the time of George I. For the highest-ranking officers the shape is a bicorne and to it have been added magnificent white, or red and white plumes.

The undress attire of all the commissioned officers was similar to their regimental uniforms and comprised a gold-braided scarlet coat and blue breeches. The latter were of fine broadcloth lined with white fustian.

The Hospital Captains, when they came into being, were similarly dressed, but the style of their uniforms did not change with the times, as did those of commissioned officers.

For the ordinary pensioner the earliest clothing supplied was the coat that he got in 1685, actually before entry. Like army infantry uniform it was red, not scarlet, but, "as the various regiments had facings of different colours, permission was apparently obtained to put all the pensioners into the royal livery, red and blue". This privilege, otherwise reserved for "Royal Regiments",[12] and enjoyed by the pensioners ever since, must be attributed to James II (and Captain Ingram's economical turn of mind).* In 1692 for lower ranks the "red Cloth Coat" had brass buttons, was lined with "blew Bays" and for a time had "a large Cypher of the King and Queen on the back". The warm lining was important, as at this time there was no overcoat. The blue breeches were markedly inferior to those of an officer. They were made of coarse wool (kersey) lined with "brown Ossenbriggs", the latter being a linen with a rather scratchy texture contrasting with the velvety surface of fustian. Shoes, blue stockings, neckcloths and nightcaps completed the clothing allowance. Some of the garments were supplied only in alternate years, and one pair of buckles was expected to function successively on the straps of two pairs of shoes. "The nightcaps were originally made of wool, but as bald-headed pensioners

---

* Again to simplify, all officers' cuffs were blue.[13]

153. Chelsea pensioners, twentieth century. *Left* Dressing. *Right* In summer
ceremonial attire in eighteenth-century style: tricorne hat, scarlet coat with
blue cuffs, blue trousers with red stripe (Radio Times Hulton Picture Library)

154. Chelsea pensioners, 1814. Black tricornes in everyday use. *Standing left* Light Horse cavalryman: crimson coat with blue cuffs and collar. *Standing right* Infantryman: scarlet coat, its lining and all other garments blue; probably a "Hospital Captain", hence regimental badge on right sleeve, and braided buttonholes. *Seated* Ordinary infantryman (Coloured aquatint by I. C. Stadler, after "C.H.S." in *Costume of the British Army*, 1814)

complained of their prickliness, cotton ones were substituted".[14] Nightcaps were worn informally in day time in the days of wigs, but the pensioners, like others, always dined in their hats.

Sergeants and Light Horse were at first both dressed alike in cavalry uniforms, for the sake of bulk-buying. While, as we have seen, commissioned officers wore "scarlet" and privates "red", this third group wore "crimson". (Thus for all branches of the Army, uniforms were of a bellicose colour without being the same.) The collar, cuffs and lining were of blue serge and breeches were like those of an officer.

Having sergeants and Light Horse dressed alike probably caused embarrassment and already, *c.* 1703, the sergeants had their buttons demoted from brass to pewter and the braid on their cuffs, pockets and hats, from gold to silver. Both ranks, like the officers, supplied their own linen; they probably preferred this, for at that time elegant white cravats were as much a man's personal pride as his necktie is today.

In the early years of the eighteenth century blue waistcoats began to be provided. Till then they had probably been improvised by cutting down and reversing old coats. The waistcoat of this period was nearly as long as the knee-length coat and had sleeves, so it contributed much to the men's warmth. The material and the lining varied according to rank, being similar to those of the breeches.

A splendid portrait of a pensioner, William Hiseland, painted in 1730, can be seen in the Hospital Museum. It displays the uniform in detail, including the waistcoat with its fourteen little brass buttons. As Hiseland was aged 110 when he sat for this portrait, he must have worn, in his time, quite a variety of uniforms – and perhaps could also remember being in rags.

An early change already noted was the provision of overcoats in 1707 – the "surtouts" that were paid for, for all ranks except officers and Light Horse, out of Lord Ranelagh's trust fund. These surtouts and their successors, the lined greatcoats, were blue, with scarlet or crimson facings for upper ranks.

A concession giving further comfort came in 1817 with the introduction of mitts and gaiters. But it needed a visit from Florence Nightingale herself in 1857 for anyone to go deeper. Captain Dean tells us "she was quick to notice that the pensioners' underclothing was limited to a shirt and socks . . .". She sought an interview with the Paymaster General and the upshot was their being issued with flannel vests and drawers.[15]

There was extraordinarily little change in the outer uniform until the middle third of the nineteenth century. Then, when commissioned officers were again installed as "Captains of Invalids", they and the Major and later all commissioned officers were given by William IV what was regarded as a privilege, the right to a Windsor uniform. This dress had been designed for his own informal use by George III and was allowed to members of his household. It comprised a blue frock coat with scarlet facings, blue trousers and buttons having a royal-looking design of crown, star and garter (Fig. 155). By this time all other pensioners' buttons were indented with the letters "RCI" (? for Royal Company of Invalids). The Windsor uniform, which in modified form became the livery of a variety of servants of the Crown (not

155. *Left* Chelsea uniform button. *Right* Windsor uniform button (After C. G. T. Dean *The Royal Hospital, Chelsea*, pages 138 and 177, 1950)

excluding the porter at the British Museum) was a civilian one. Thus at the Hospital "no badges of rank were displayed on it, a peculiarity that persists to this day".[16] However a military-looking tunic in the same colours soon replaced the original frock coat.

The major changes for ordinary pensioners also came in the mid nineteenth century. They had to wait till then to adopt the trousers that had been normal wear for other men for forty years. Somewhat later they, and the sergeants, had their summer coats changed from red or crimson, respectively, into scarlet like those of upper ranks. Possibly this was due to the industrial production of aniline pigments; hitherto scarlet had been one of the dearest of dyes.

Visiting the Hospital today one is struck by the variety in the pensioners' clothes, despite the undoubtedly old-fashioned style they all have in common. One will see a scarlet coat only in summer or on ceremonial occasions. This coat has had its thick blue lining replaced, for coolness, by thin white serge, and a blue collar has been added; but it is otherwise much as it was in Queen Anne's reign. A rather easily soiled garment, it is worn on ordinary days only if a man is in "walking-out order", the dress required if he goes outside a three-mile radius of the Hospital. With it he wears a tricorne only for ceremonies – otherwise an early nineteenth-century military cap, the shako. This is a hard-peaked cap with a high crown (Fig. 156). It bears the red letters "R.H." in the front, true to the tradition that beneficiaries of any kind should be labelled as such.

Within the three-mile radius a little informality is allowed. A man need not wear a coat at all but may go out in his traditional blue sleeved-waistcoat, which is double breasted, brass buttoned and worn like a jacket; but he must still put on his shako.

156. Uniforms still in use by Chelsea pensioners. *Seated* Winter ceremonial: tricorne hat but blue coat. *Standing, left to right* Summer ceremonial, see Fig. 153; undress, inside Hospital grounds: single-breasted sleeved waistcoat, lounge cap with regimental badge; undress, outside but within three mile radius: double-breasted sleeved waistcoat, shako with Royal Hospital badge; walking-out dress, summer: scarlet coat with blue collar and cuffs – this man, a Hospital sergeant or a warrant officer, wears a "cheese-cutter" cap with Royal Hospital badge (Detail of photograph. Courtesy: the Commissioners)

Strolling about the grounds, or indoors, most of the men will be wearing yet another outfit comprising a waistcoat like the first one, but single breasted with black buttons, and a more comfortable little "lounge" cap (Fig. 156). Its badge is not "R.H." but (as the wearer must surely prefer) that of his own old regiment.

In winter, out of doors, the very warm blue greatcoat may be worn on all occasions and under it a knitted "cardigan waistcoat". All headgear is black, and in recent times all blues have become navy.

In everyday wear, a sergeant can still be picked out by more than his chevrons. (Incidentally if he was not a sergeant in the Army but one promoted when a pensioner, his stripes are broader.) His outdoor headgear is a "cheese-cutter", a forage cap which is hard-peaked like a shako but has a low crown.

Dress for special duties and occasions

It remains only to mention modifications of dress for garrisons outside the Hospital, for funerals and for Founder's Day.

As we saw, in 1715 and for nearly a hundred years, the Hospital provided an armed police force to protect travellers on the lonely road between Westminster and Chelsea from robbery with violence. Robert Walpole was doubtless an interested party, since in 1715 he was active both in the House of Commons and as Treasurer of the Hospital. For this dawn-to-midnight duty, in exposed sentry boxes, pensioners were issued with extra shoes, stockings and "watchgowns fitted with hoods" made of Devonshire kersey. The latter were probably like those of the London nightwatchmen or bellmen. Muskets with fixed bayonets were carried.* The Adjutant in command was allowed five pounds a year for an extra "superfine surtout". In about 1805 increased building and street lighting brought the need for armed protection to an end and, as Captain Dean[17] remarks, the patrol "was soon forgotten by everybody except the Adjutant", who continued to claim for his greatcoat every year until at least 1820 – a typical example of the minor abuses to which charities and public services are so vulnerable!

From 1692 for ten years the Chelsea Hospital was responsible for clothing certain "Companies of Invalids", selected from the more able pensioners, to do resident garrison duty elsewhere. Of the company stationed at Windsor Lord Ranelagh reported that: "Their Cloathing is as cheape as wee could make it, Being different from those in ye

---

*They did in fact succeed in killing the robber who attacked the mother of the notorious "Duchess of Kingston" in 1749.

Hospitall, for wee give them Grey Coates lined with blew without Cyphers, whereas the others have red Coates with [royal] Cyphers".[18]

A typical pensioner's funeral is described in vivid, if somewhat maudlin, terms by the Hospital chaplain in 1838.[19] At the gate the guard is turned out, wearing the ceremonial dress of red coat with tricorne hat. The twelve men and corporal are armed with their muskets (every pensioner had a musket until 1854) and the sergeant with his eight-foot-long halberd. The funeral procession then makes its appearance headed by

the firing party, 12 veterans, accoutred for the occasion in old black waist-belts, from which, in the rear, depend old bayonets ... Their muskets, somewhat the worse for wear ... are reversed, not perhaps with nicety ... but after a fashion ... [indicating] that the old men have not forgotten the lessons learned in early youth.

There follow the sergeant of this party, with his halberd reversed, and the drummer and fifer, both greyheaded and feeble old men. Then the coffin is carried by, with the dead man's tricorne hat lying on the pall. At the final interment muskets are fired as a full military honour.

To end on a festal note, we have Founder's Day. The annual celebrations are held as near as possible to Oak-apple Day (29 May)* and the parade is a spectacle indeed. The costumes bring back the Hospital's history of nearly three hundred years: the officers with their military sashes, swords and plumes and their Windsor uniforms might belong to the time of George III; the pensioners with their scarlet coats and tricornes could be soldiers under the Duke of Marlborough. The founder, Charles II himself, is vividly recalled, for every pensioner wears, in tribute, a spray of oak leaves in his coat.

ROYAL HOSPITAL, GREENWICH

Particularly appealing to the sympathy and respect of British people are the men who have been disabled or superannuated after serving their country at sea. Yet through public ignorance they met with neglect until an even later date than veteran soldiers.

At the end of the seventeenth century the numbers and plight of such survivors of recent naval engagements began to be realized, and in 1695 a fund was opened to provide them with a home. Queen Mary II played a heroic part, for she resolved that the palace at Greenwich,

---

*The birthday of Charles II who escaped capture, after the Battle of Worcester, by hiding in an oak tree.

begun under Charles II, should be completed by Wren expressly as a home (called Hospital) for this purpose. John Evelyn, having distinguished himself in the Chelsea project, was probably a moving spirit in this one, and he took on the treasurership of the fund, which was promoted by Lord Godolphin, son of Evelyn's old friend the Countess Margaret. The building was opened in 1705.

The two to three thousand pensioners were naval ratings and marines and at first also merchant seamen. The revenues of the Hospital derived from various sources, including the Treasury and also a contribution of 6d. monthly levied from all active seamen. But, as it owed some of its maintenance to William III, and its very existence to charity, it seems proper to include it here.

Early records are lacking, owing to a disastrous fire at the Hospital, but as regards the uniform of the pensioners we know that it had a strongly nautical appearance. The Governor was always a retired admiral or captain, and the regime was like that on board a man-of-war. Rank was respected, as at Chelsea: "The Coats and Hats of the Boatswains and Boatswain's-Mates are distinguished; the former by a broad, and the latter by a narrow gold lace".[20]

There was no prescribed uniform for ratings in the Navy until 1857, but already by the 1760s blue had become conventional for their jackets, while their canvas frocks, trousers and breeches were blue or white.[21] Certainly by 1789 the coat, breeches and yarn hose given annually to the pensioners were also blue. And there were nautical "Watch Coats for those on Guard". However, in view of their present land-lubberly life, "Great Coats are allowed for the old and infirm"[22] (these being replaced only when totally worn out). Shirts and nightcaps were given to all.

Having a seaman's natural independence the inmates were more apt to abscond than most almsfolk, and advertisements would often appear which incidentally show us what a pensioner's outfit comprised in the eighteenth century. For instance, they would seek information on the whereabouts of a man who had decamped with "a suit of blue clothes, one hat, a pair of shoes, 3 pairs of stockings, a shirt marked G.R., a stock, cap, spoon and towel".[23]

Some facts indirectly involving costume are revealed by an investigation of abuses, made in the late eighteenth century. For example, though the two superintendents and the hundred "nurses" should all have been the widows of lower-deck seamen, yet many of those enjoying the annual issue of "a grey serge gown and petticoat"[24] were the widows of officers or had nothing more to do with the sea than a dubious association with certain Lords of the Admiralty.

157. Greenwich pensioners entertaining Chelsea pensioners, c. 1840. Some of both still wear breeches, some trousers. Greenwich pensioners have dark blue coats with mariner's cuffs and pockets to match. A Hanoverian black cockade, held by gold braid, shows on some of the tricornes (Detail from painting by Andrew Morton, National Maritime Museum, London)

In the 1840s and 1850s the striking feature of the pensioner's attire was its conservatism. He had even worn until recently what the *London Chronicle* in 1762 called "the sailor's enormous pigtail". It had been given up even in the Navy in the 1820s. The uniform coat was still in eighteenth-century style, below knee length, only slightly cut away, with large braided and buttoned pocket-flaps. In fact it was like a Chelsea pensioner's coat except in colour and for one other feature, a very nautical one, the "mariner's cuff" (Figs. 157 and 158). This design was the fashion for gentlemen, and hence for naval officers, in the 1760s. When outdated, it persisted in the Navy. There, by 1787, it was already preserved only in full-dress[25] uniform, ceremonial dress always

158. Three Greenwich pensioners who served in the "Victory" at the Battle of Trafalgar. The one in dress clothes shows mariner's cuffs. All now in trousers. 1844 (*Illustrated London News* 13 April 1844, page 233)

being ultra conservative. Though for different reasons, the pensioners' dress was also antiquated as well as nautical, and so we find a convergence of high and low (just as in the twentieth century the wearing of breeches survived in court dress on the one hand, and in the daily attire of footmen on the other).

The other outdated features were the breeches, worn till the 1840s, the braided tricorne hat and the large ornamental shoe buckles – the last two being fashions that ended abruptly elsewhere near the close of the eighteenth century. The hat supplied to the pensioners in the early days had evidently been, not the sailor's more practical round hat, but the conventional tricorne of the period, and in the 1850s the pen-

159. Greenwich pensioners entering dining hall, 1865. Informal dress
(*Illustrated London News* XLVI 281)

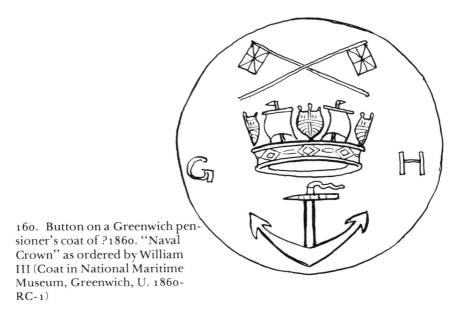

160. Button on a Greenwich pensioner's coat of ?1860. "Naval Crown" as ordered by William III (Coat in National Maritime Museum, Greenwich, U. 1860-RC-1)

sioners were still wearing it, even when sitting about on the Thames bank. It added much to the charm of their appearance, and so did the shoe buckles. In the 1770s everyone wore these and after 1790 almost nobody. Yet the pensioners had them for fifty years after the fashion was dead.*

The *Illustrated London News* in 1865 tells us that (at last) "the knee breeches have been exchanged for trousers and round hats have been allowed for daily wear".

With the ordinary hat for casual wear went a very short double-breasted garment, the true seaman's "round jacket", as seen in Figs. 159 and 122.

The knee-length coat continued, for outdoor and formal use, and an actual specimen from about this period survives in the National Maritime Museum. It is made of a true navy-blue (almost black) dense pilot cloth, lined with wool. The general shape and the pocket flaps still have the old look, but the cuffs are sham turn-ups, represented only by a short strip of braid and four buttons.

---

* It was the same at the Chelsea Hospital. But so completely had buckles been superseded by shoe laces in the world of fashion that in 1791 a deputation of distressed buckle-makers from Birmingham persuaded the Prince of Wales to help them by insisting on buckles being worn at Court, and so they have been, on occasion, ever since. Again the highest and lowest converge!

The buttons are interesting. Whereas in the Navy, from 1812, there would be a royal crown above the anchor, here we have a special crown, the design of which was commanded by William III (Fig. 160).[26]

The *Illustrated London News* shows that there were a few costumes for special duties. The galley staff, in the kitchen, and serving in the dining hall, wear white overalls with flat caps (probably blue). They remind one of their sailing days by having their trouser legs rolled up at the bottom – but they are wearing carpet slippers!

In extreme contrast we have the very elegant drummers and fifers. Their uniform was like that of naval and Marine Society bandsmen in having the cuffs trimmed with white braid. Their hats, though round,

161. *Left* Greenwich Hospital drummer and fifer, 1865 *Right* Pensioners serving in West Dining Hall of Greenwich Hospital, 1865 (*Illustrated London News* vol. XLVI, 280, 281, details)

were stiff and they had large ornamental wings to their coats. A drummer and fifer beat a tattoo every night at the Hospital and all of them had an important role in Trafalgar Day celebrations in London.

And where are all these popular Greenwich pensioners today? In 1869, only a few years after the *Illustrated London News*'s account, they left Greenwich for ever, taking their pensions with them. As the article remarked, they had absolutely no "amusement" in the Hospital except a library, and we have noticed that there had always been a certain restiveness. It was on their own initiative that plans for their evacuation were made. All became out-pensioners and the buildings were finally converted into the Royal Naval College.

SCHOOLS ASSOCIATED WITH
CHELSEA AND GREENWICH ROYAL HOSPITALS

So closely connected with the pensioners' Hospitals that it seems appropriate to mention them here are two homes for the children of deceased or disabled servicemen, one for those of soldiers, the other for those of sailors. Full maintenance and education were given and the boys were encouraged to join the Army or Navy.

The Duke of York founded the Royal Military Asylum in Chelsea in 1801, placing it in close proximity to the Hospital where the fathers of some of the children would be living. (Old boys of the school are known in the Army as "Dukeys".) As the original foundation was a charity we include it here.

Like the Chelsea Hospital, the Duke of York's School was thought well worth a visit by the public and is described in Ackermann's *Microcosm of London* (Vol. III) only seven years after its opening. His plate shows the boys at lessons wearing an attractive uniform. "The clothing of the boys consists of red jackets [with blue cuffs], blue breeches and stockings and black leather caps".

The regime was decidedly military. George Bartley tells us: "The best conducted boys are promoted to be Lance Corporals, Corporals and Colour Corporals . . . The stripes thus earned are highly valued and in some instances the boys are allowed to continue to wear them when they enlist . . ."[27]

The girls' costume had to match the boys' as nearly as possible. In Ackermann we read: "The girls wear red gowns and blue petticoats, white aprons and straw bonnets". When this was written, in 1808, they probably wore an old-fashioned gown with an open skirt revealing the contrasting petticoat. In Fig. 162 a more fashionable one-piece dress is shown, a few years later. It is still red and the cuffs introduce the

162. Children of Royal Military Asylum, Chelsea, 1814. See text (Coloured aquatint by I. C. Stadler, after "C. H. S." in *Costume of the British Army*, 1814, detail of Plate. Army Museum Library)

required blue, as does the bonnet ribbon. There were other military overtones. The sleeve of the girl's dress shows her distinction as a little "Corporal".

Notice the typical charity-girl tippet, this time certainly fastened at the back.

Corresponding to the Military Asylum but very much older was the home and school for sailors' children that formed part of the Greenwich Hospital, practically from the first. It was opened in 1712, and the endowment funds were supplemented by the fines the pensioners paid for drunkenness and other misbehaviour. It is an ill wind . . .

The dress, education and practical training of the boys were all designed with an eye on naval recruitment. They slept in hammocks and learnt to mend their own clothes. Bartley is emphatic that in 1871 it was still "desired that all who leave Greenwich . . . shall be expert in this respect". And the school must have been almost unique in that until they reached the upper grades the boys even had to *make* their clothes.

The outfit in 1811 consisted of a blue cloth suit and blue serge waist-coat with an extra pair of breeches, in leather, "to wear every day". The "small round hat" had a nautical look but not the "black velvet stock". This was replaced by a sailor's black silk handkerchief, when the boy was "bound out",[28] and he was then allowed a nightcap.

Another scheme for fostering sailors' children was the Royal Naval Asylum, set up by private subscription in 1798 at a time of war and known as "The British Endeavour". Early in the nineteenth century the two institutions combined at Greenwich. The girls, who had occupied the Queen's House, were eliminated in 1841.

The *Illustrated London News* shows the Royal Hospital School lined up to watch the old pensioners receive their "Nelson medals" in 1845. The boys wear trousers and what looks like a midshipman's round jacket, with a very wide shirt collar outside it, such as sailors wore at

163. Boys of Greenwich Hospital watching the pensioners advancing to receive Nelson medals, 1845 (*Illustrated London News*, 12 April 1845, detail)

164. "Boys of Greenwich Hospital School inspected by the Shah", 1873.
Summer uniform: white frock (sailor blouse) with square blue collar and
black handkerchief, as in Navy. (*Illustrated London News* vol LXIII, 13, detail)

the time (compare Fig. 122) – the precursor of the sailor collar that
came later. Out of doors at this time the headgear was a curious cap,
shaped like an inverted flower-pot.

By degrees, as we saw on page 62, the school took in more and more
young gentlemen instead of the sons of poor seamen. A Report in
1851[29] showed that there were now two establishments; the boys of the
one invidiously called the "Lower School" were indeed the children
of seamen but did not pass into the "Upper School" which contained
many officers' sons. Leavers from both were expected to go to sea but
with different prospects.

The whole was reorganized more than once but became eventually a
single training school for ordinary seamen. The uniform was naval in
appearance (Fig. 164). The National Maritime Museum has a specimen
of a jacket, with chevrons on the sleeves, which was worn in 1901 by a
"Petty Officer Boy".

Today ordinary trousers and blazers are worn at the school which is now at Holbrook, Ipswich, and, as so often happens with traditional costumes, the nautical uniform is kept for special occasions only. It is an expensive rig-out and is still provided gratis to all the boys.

CHAPTER 14

Miscellaneous charities

FOR VARIOUS SICK PERSONS

In the medieval hospitals where the inmates included the sick, the resident nursing staff consisted of sisters in religious orders and, as such, they depended indirectly on charity themselves (symbolically expressed in Fig. 26). Their dress was simply that of their order, those at St Bartholomew's in London wearing the grey Augustinian habit. After the dissolution of the monasteries the term "sister" and the idea of a uniform dress (now to be called livery) were retained; and, as the hospitals were supported voluntarily, the uniforms, when given, were in a sense still charity costumes. Obviously, however, to discuss them here would be beyond our scope. Suffice it to remark that at Bart's the colour blue was adopted for the re-established sisters in 1555, and so it has remained ever since.

Patients also were sometimes clothed. In the Middle Ages, at the same hospital, if the sick were very poor they were sent away, when cured, with at least a pair of shoes to walk home in. Impecunious long-stay patients, for example at the mental hospital Bedlam, had to be dressed by charity, or at least fitted out when discharged. The churchwardens at St Margaret's, Westminster, recorded in 1612/13 having provided for one "Avelyn Carr at Bedlam . . . Frese, cotton and canvis" to make her a gown and buying her a "smocke" (chemise), a "quoife" (cap), "hoses" and shoes.[1]

FOR LEPERS

Leprosy in England was widespread in the eleventh century and this terrible disease did not abate until the mid thirteenth century. The

furm good my gentyll mayster for god cake

165. Leper in statutory cloak and
hood, early fifteenth century (British
Library MS Lansdowne 451 fol. 127)

leper was thus a familiar figure in the earlier Middle Ages, and a pitiful
sight he was.

The leper was forbidden to go out without the distinctive habit
provided for him, which covered him almost entirely, the main feature
being a cloak down to the feet, generally closed and black, and a hood
covering the bald head. Sometimes over this he wore a hat.

Begging was all he could do for a living and he had either a bell, to
draw attention, and a begging bowl, or else a clapdish which was a
receptacle for money with a lid that clattered.

As soon as a leper was diagnosed he had to go through a strict ritual
called "The Seclusion of a Leper".[2] Though comforting words were
spoken, the service was purposely intended to resemble a funeral. "The
priest must lead him to the church [for Mass] and from the church to
his [Lazar] house as a dead man . . . in such wise that the sick man is
covered with a black cloth". At church he received the sacrament
kneeling under a black pall spread between trestles. He was then conducted to a leprosarium where he would spend the rest of his life, with
all his needs provided by charity. But first some solemn rules for his
observance were read out to him and some of them emphasize the importance of his clothing:

I forbid you henceforth to go out without your leper's dress, that you may be
recognized by others; and you must not go outside your house unshod [lest
you infect the ground] . . . Also I charge you if need require you to pass over
some toll way that you touch no posts or things whereby you cross till you
have first put on your gloves.

Before entering the house the leper was given the leper clothing: "A coat and shoes of fur [probably overshoes, as an extra precaution], his own plain shoes, and his signal the clappers, a hood and a cloak".

The lazar houses were not medical institutions but rather almshouses where the plight of the leper was eased and at the same time the public protected. Their establishment was inspired by the religious movement of the Middle Ages, and a collegiate and religious life was the rule for the inmates.

There now follow some notes on a few of the more renowned leper houses and the further regulations about clothing that some of them imposed.

The Sherburne Hospital, near Durham was a lazar house founded by Bishop Pudsey (or Puiset) *c.* 1181. Here, after the first outfit, "each leper had an annual allowance for his clothing of 3 yards of woollen cloth, white or russet, 6 yards of linen and 6 of canvass; the tailor had his meat and drink on the day he came to cut out the clothes".[3] The statutory black cloaks and hoods, not having to fit and also getting less wear than the other clothing, were probably provided ready made at longer intervals.

Each leper also had four pence a year for shoes and grease was regularly supplied for treating the leather.

There were five resident priest-brethren who were partly self-supporting but who had strict rules as to clothing. When going about on foot, they must wear a black cloak like the lepers.

The Wiltshire Priory of Maiden Bradley ran a hospice of which a few details are given by J.E.T. Rogers for the years 1325–28. Of the women inmates, he says there appear to have been thirteen to fifteen, all lepers. They were supplied with two linen shifts annually and probably, like the sisters and brethren of the Priory, wore gowns of russet or blanket (both cheap woollens) lined with lambskin for winter. English lambskin was the cheapest warm lining available.[4]

In the vicinity of St Albans, Herts., there were two famous leper houses founded by successive abbots in the twelfth century – St Julian's for men and St Mary de Pré for women. At St Julian's, in the matter of the lepers' dress, the general regulations were scrupulously followed and extra precautions laid down. Their russet supertunic and tunic were both to be "cut close and coming down to the ankles, and having sleeves . . . reaching the wrist, and which were not to be stitched up or buttoned", or, as the later ordinances explain it, "were not to be looped up with knots or threads after the secular fashion".[5] This probably meant that the fashionable pendant cuffs, so long that they had to be tied up out of the way, were forbidden. The cape must be of the same full length as the supertunic[6] and have no opening except for the head. This and the hood that went with it must be worn not only out of doors but in the chapel, where daily services must be attended. The lepers were forbidden to wear fur on their supertunics and hoods but were allowed sheep and lamb skins to keep them warm. They had to wear high-cut shoes (really boots) fastened round the leg with three or four ties. If a leper was caught wearing low shoes with only one tie he was punished by having to go barefoot, which meant not only humiliation but, owing to the law, confinement to the house.

Of the Hospital of St Mary de Pré, founded in 1183, all we know, as regards costume, is that by the charter the women were allowed the cast-off frocks and tippets of the monks in the adjoining priory, up to the number of thirteen: a curious example of unisex clothing.

The Hospital at Harbledown provided shelter for both men and women. Over their long supertunics the brothers wore a scapular, probably the monastic style of cloak. They had the usual hood and the women covered their heads with thick black veils, lined with white. Precautions were extreme. Both men and women had long ox-hide boots reaching nearly to the knee and fastened with leather.

Of the numerous leprosaria of Great Britain many were, in course of time, converted into ordinary almshouses. Already by 1434 only two lepers could be found for Sherburne Hospital and the vacancies were filled by thirteen ordinary poor folk. This lazar house and several others are functioning as almshouses to this day.

DOLES; BEGGARS' BADGES

The way in which poverty or exceptional circumstances deprived people even of a decent covering has already been stressed. It drew forth a miscellany of gifts in kind, which was probably a wiser method of relief than doles of money, and yet seems curious to our eyes. Churchwardens distributed actual garments, whether acting as representatives of the parish church, or wearing their other hat as parish overseers of the poor.

Just as a sample of the overseers' work (though not charity in our sense) here are some entries made by those at St Mary Abbots, Kensington, in the reign of William III:[7]

(1697)	Paid Goodey Trevers for nursing a Childe Born under Richard Kirton's Heyrick ye 2d of Feby . . .	2 7 6
	Paid for Clothes for it and a Shroud to bury it.	4 0

(1692) Paid [for a sick man] for a pair of Stocking, Shoes,
Wastcoat, and a Frock for him, and upper Coats   1   1   0

Paid for a Shroud and for burying him . . .   3   6

Paid for a Hat for Francis Jones   2   6

Two rather quaint examples of clothing distribution that were strictly charity were the Petticoat and the Bull Charities. At Stockton-on-the-Forest, Yorkshire, the Charity Commissioners[8] found in 1861 that "a small piece of ground . . . called Petticoat Hole, the property of Mrs Ware, of York, is held subject to an ancient custom of providing a petticoat [skirt] yearly for a poor woman of Stockton selected by the owner . . . Mrs Ware supplies a blue serge gown in lieu of a petticoat, every winter . . ."

The Bull Charity was one of many in Wokingham. George Staverton's will, 1661, provided for an annuity of £6 to pay for a bull which was not only for food: "which bull he gave to the poor of Wokingham town after being baited and the . . . hide and offal to be sold and

166. Beggar's badges. *Left* Of lead, 3-inch diameter, with arms of the town of Kirkcaldy and the number "17". *Right* Of pewter, dated 1772 (Article by E. R. H. Dicken in *Country Life* 20 October 1950)

bestowed upon the poor children in stockings of the Welsh,* and shoes". Women and children were still being given footwear through the sale of bulls' spare parts in 1837.

An alternative to providing clothes for the helpless was to give them a licence to beg. This, from the seventeenth century (fifteenth century in Scotland) involved the use of a beggar's badge, perhaps the saddest item of charity costume we have met, for such it was: it was given and it was worn. At St Margaret's, Westminster, the churchwardens recorded in 1652:

Paid to Mrs White, for fifteene tickets of pewter, for fifteene poore people to take almes, according to the order of the justices of the peace – £1–0–0.
Paid to Mr Morris ironmonger for fifteene yards of brasse Chaine for the said poor people's tickets . . . 9s. 6d.[9]

MAUNDY

One of the best known of all charities is "Maundy", so called from Christ's *mandatum* (commandment) that men should love one another. It was an ancient custom performed

on the Thursday before Easter called Maundy Thursday, wherein the King in a solemn manner doth wash the Feet, clothe and feed as many poor men as His Majesty is years old, bestowing on every one, Cloth for a gown, Linnen for a Shirt, Shooes, and Stockings . . . 30 red and 30 white herrings . . . and a Purse with a 20s Piece of gold.[10]

Maundy was thus described when revived by Charles II after the only break (during the Commonwealth) in the Royal Maundy tradition that has occurred in hundreds of years. It was observed at least as early as 1213, when King John took part.

Clothing was presented in kind, until recent times, so that this act of combined humility and charity concerns us. In the old days sovereigns and the Pope were not the only great ones to perform it. The Earl of Lancaster in 1314 gave 168 yards of russet cloth and twenty-four coats for poor men.[11] Cardinal Wolsey went through the ceremony in Peterborough Abbey in 1530, giving to fifty-nine poor men (fifty-nine being his age) food, money and "three ells of good canvas to make them shirts, a pair of new shoes. . ."[12] The Earl of Northumberland in the same period chose to give hooded gowns and linen shirts.[13]

---

* Welsh wool and/or knitted in Wales. Compare "Welsh wig", a knitted wool cap (Fig. 121).

167. Procession to the Maundy Ceremony, 1733. *In front* Yeomen of the
Guard. One carries a tray with purses, the strings hanging. The two figures in
long robes are the Sub-Almoner and the Lord High Almoner, the Archbishop
of York – note "bishop's sleeves". These wear symbolic towels, stole-wise.
Other figures, officials of the Royal Almonry, wear them as sashes. All carry or
wear nosegays (From drawing by S. H. Grimm. Courtesy: Laurence Tanner,
C.V.O.)

    In the Royal Maundy, it became customary that the sovereigns
should present a garment of their own to one of the poor persons, as
well as the clothing given to each ... Money was substituted for this
garment in Edward VI's reign because his own clothes were those of a
child. But in 1556 Queen Mary not only, on her knees, washed the feet
of forty-one women but gave to one of them, whom she selected
herself, a gown of her own, made of finest purple cloth with ground-
length sleeves and a lining of marten's fur. In 1560, Machyn's Diary[14]
tells us, Queen Elizabeth also gave "her best gowne" to one of the
women. But, perhaps because in her reign the recipients were all
women, so much jealousy was expressed that she soon compounded in
favour of fair shares for all. In 1582, aged forty-eight, she gave forty-
eight women forty-eight pence each, "in a whyt purse ... and in a redd
purse Twentye shillings in lieu of Her M. own gowne".[15] The new-
minted Maundy coins are still given away in red and white purses of
almost medieval design, being made with strings, to be worn on one's
belt – a costume accessory.

    Instead of the ration of clothing Queen Elizabeth gave away lengths

168. In the absence of Queen Victoria, the Lord High Almoner, the Archbishop of York, hands Maundy purse to a poor man, 1867. Observe the nosegay. Each official of the Royal Almonry wears a white "towel" over the shoulder. (*Illustrated London News* 27 April 1867)

of cloth, but apparently garments continued sometimes to be provided as such. In 1724 extra money was substituted for this too, the reason given being that when recipients were women their eagerness to see if the clothes fitted created a most unseemly bustle.[16] George II partly reverted to older practices. When he in his turn was forty-eight years old in 1727, he treated forty-eight men and forty-eight women to shoes, stockings, and lengths of woollen and linen cloth. The dole of cloth came to an end in 1883 when it was found that the poor men often couldn't afford to have it made up.

Another feature of the ceremony today is a curious relic of the traditional washing of feet. It is recorded that, when Queen Elizabeth I carried it out, the feet were washed in advance by yeomen of her Laundry, using sweet herbs, and then by her Sub-almoner.[17] These processes became traditional, though the last sovereign to do any of the washing himself was William III, and it was not done at all after 1754. How the ablutions are symbolized in the twentieth-century ceremony was described in 1923: ". . . today linen . . . towels are worn by all officials connected with the Royal Almonry", those who would be wearing copes having removed them. Furthermore "those who are to take part . . . carry with them bunches of flowers and foliage . . . reminiscent of a preliminary ablution with herbs".[18] Queen Elizabeth I gave to the poor

169. "Children of the Royal Almonry", wrapped in "towels" and carrying nosegays for Maundy Ceremony, *c.* 1900 (Radio Times Hulton Picture Library)

170. George VI and Queen Elizabeth at Maundy ceremony, 1950. Almonry officials wear white towels, "Children of the Almonry" carry posies (Thomson Newspapers)

the towels that she used in the ceremony and the aprons worn by her attendants. Later, and up till 1808, four old men, called "children of the Almonry", were, each year, paid to provide the towels and had the right to sell them afterwards. Subsequently the men were represented by four actual children, generally orphans, who were decked out as in Fig. 169. Since the later 1920s they have been spared the towels, which the little ones were liable to trip over. But to this day they process at the Maundy ceremony bearing flowers, and Almonry officials still wear towels* – a charity costume to recall a happening of nearly two thousand years ago.

* The towels are nowadays kept from year to year. The present ones are already antiques, being monogrammed "V.R.".

CHAPTER 15

Charity costumes on parade

The distribution of Royal Maundy with its attendant procession is an example of the way in which charity costumes (in that case white towels) can be used for decorative display. We will end the book by discussing this unexpectedly happy aspect of our subject.

Charity costumes were particularly pleasing to the eye when the wearers were ranged in rows or massed in groups. Even the sight of a row of pinafored girls might please the public. G.C.T. Bartley, when discussing schools run by the National Society, remarks on the "aspect of the class" where pinafores were worn: "A feature of the Girls' School, which gives it a pleasing appearance to the visitor, is the custom of making each child, while at work, wear a white pinafore".[1]

It was not only for subscribers that the inmates of institutions were exhibited when taking a meal – it obviously gave pleasure to others. In Horace Walpole's day it was evidently quite the thing to visit the Magdalen charity on Sunday for evensong and then to watch what he ironically called "the nuns", in their peculiar uniform, having supper. In 1760 he was one of a party of distinguished lady and gentleman visitors, which included H.R.H. Prince Edward. The girls, having taken off their hats after chapel, "were ranged at long tables ... I was struck and pleased with the modesty of two of them, who swooned away with the confusion of being stared at".[2] The privilege of seeing the Christ's Hospital boys at supper was still being enjoyed in 1819. In Ackermann's *Microcosm of London*, William Combe writes: "The evening meal is displayed every Sunday at 6 o'clock, from Christmas to Easter, and strangers are admitted to it by tickets ...".[3] The Rev. William Trollope in 1834 speaks of "the many who attend with the mere object of *a promenade and seeing the children sup*". It was a spectacle, and those who saw it "were frequently moved even to tears".[4] There is no doubt that the costume contributed much to "this imposing, affecting and unparalleled ceremony".[5]

A favourite Sunday pastime till the end of the Foundling Hospital's life in London was to attend the service in their chapel and then to watch the children at their dinner. Because of the uniform, the scene was so pretty as to inspire pictures in the *Illustrated London News*, and even an oil painting. That great biologist and classicist, Sir D'Arcy Thompson, devotes to it an essay, "Sunday morning, 14 October 1921":[6] "Last Sunday . . . we came, my child and I, to forenoon service at the Foundling Hospital. It was . . . one of the beautiful things of London that I had never been to see". His description of the children's entry into chapel conveys his feelings:

the girls in snowy aprons and little mob caps, the boys in a quaint stiff uniform of brown broadcloth and brass buttons; the boys a trifle heavy of foot [their shoes perhaps still nailed] and stiff in manner like their own little uniforms, the girls on the whole comely, some with gay flower badges which (I rather fancy) mark the chief singers in this great choir . . .

After the service spectators watched "the long procession of small boys troop into the dining room in a winding column so nicely graded, the

171. Gentry enjoy the sight of the Foundlings at dinner, 1872 (*Illustrated London News* 7 December 1872. Courtesy: Old London Ltd)

shorter boys following the taller in so even a descending line that one feels . . . that they should dwindle at last to no size at all." After grace was sung, at the stroke of a mallet, "like one child, the whole company sits down". This regimentation evidently had a great visual charm and, if it strikes us as excessive, we can take consolation from the end of the essay. There the affection spontaneously shown by the children for one of their Governors is heart-warmingly described.

Where the costume had colour to make it striking (this was uncommon), it specially pleased. It will be remembered that in Northampton there were schoolboys attending ceremonies in uniforms of green, of blue and red, and even of blue and orange. The old Blue Coat boy of that town who recalled the 1890s started his article about the schools with the words "Picturesque contributions . . ." and the headline is "Gaily Clad Scholars Gave Town Centre Splash of Colour".[7]

But neither quaintness nor colour were necessary to create an effect. People in uniform provide a rhythmic pattern and in procession they are like a ribbon with a woven design. However colourless, when lining the streets they make a becoming edging like braid or lace. De Mandeville, in 1723, expressed, as clearly as he scorned, the basis of this pleasure:

There is a natural Beauty in Uniformity which most people delight in. It is diverting to see Children well Match'd, either Boys or Girls, march two and two in Order; and to have them all whole and tight in the same Cloaths and Trimming must add to the comeliness of the Sight.[8]

Remarkably similar, a century and a half later, were the words of the Rev. J. Healy: "A long array of stuff frocks, and white aprons, all made on the same pattern, all of the same colour . . . is indeed a pretty sight".[9]

An early example of a quite ordinary russet-coloured livery making an impression by repetition was when the Christ's Hospital children were lined up along Cheapside at Christmas, 1552. That it gave pleasure to the public, not only to the benefactors, is suggested by Stow's account already quoted. Christ's Hospital soon came to feature in many civic ceremonies. Stow gives the impression of having gone to see a spectacle, when he describes the funerals in which these children took part. Of Mellys's cortège in 1562, which was one of the plainest, he says:

there were the Children of the Hospital, two and two together, walking before; and all the Masters of the Hospital, with their green Staves [symbols of office] in their Hands (which is the first time I meet with the Hospital Boys attending a Funeral with the Governors, without Parish Clerks and Heralds).[10]

Governors' green staves still contribute to the decorative effect of "Hospital" processions in London (see Bridewell). In this instance the children were present partly as a tribute to a deceased benefactor.

Machyn's Diary gives many examples of the use made of the same children. He talks of their appearances at the annual Easter sermons, which were given at the St Mary Spital pulpit cross and were always attended by the Lord Mayor and aldermen. The first opportunity was in 1553:

"The iii day of Aprell [there] went unto Saint Mary Spytyll unto the sermon, all the Masters [governors] and rulers and schoolmasters and mistresses and all the children, both men and women children – all in blue coats and [the] wenches in blue frocks – and with eschuceons embroidered on their sleeves with the arms of London, and red caps".[11]

The badge was worn in recognition of the City's support. After marching from the school they were massed on a grandstand made of timber and canvas "sitting like steps". The sea of blue, with rhythmical flecks of red, evidently impressed even such a constant frequenter of ceremonies as Machyn.

The boys were still attending Easter "Spital Sermons" (though now

172. Band of Christ's Hospital making a rhythmical display in the City of London on St Matthew's Day, 1974. (*Daily Telegraph* 21 September 1974)

in Christ Church) in the nineteenth century, and William Trollope writes about the attractive procession that they made in his time. It is interesting that their Easter emblems, mentioned in Chapter 3, were still being worn.

On each day the boys of Christ's Hospital with the legend *"He is Risen"* attached to their left shoulders form part of the civic procession, on the first day [Easter Monday] walking in order of their Schools, the King's Boys bearing their nautical Instruments, and on the second [Tuesday] according to their several wards headed by their nurses [House matrons].[12]

An occasion when Christ's Hospital boys still present a stirring spectacle is when they march through the City of London on St Matthew's Day (Fig. 172).

The most frequent occasions for display were when charity children, even in day schools, processed on Sundays to the parish church, where they often formed the choir.* The spectacle was thought worth depicting, for example, in a coloured print (Fig. 94) and also in the children's guide to London called *City Scenes*.[13] There the picture shows a little crocodile of children, two by two, emerging from church, headed by the parish beadles. Wickham, as a small boy, used to love standing in the avenue to "survey the procession of the municipal authorities of Hertford, who, preceded by the Green Coat Charity Schools, walked in civic pomp . . . to the Church".[14]

This Sunday procession was still to be seen in the rural England of the 1890s and is beautifully recalled at Wilton by Edith Olivier. As a child she climbed on a box at the nursery window when on Sunday morning she heard the "treble pit pat" of the children's nailed shoes.

They were wearing the enchanting suits which had been the uniform of the school since its founding in 1706 . . . The boys wore smart cut-away coats of fine buff cloth, faced with hyacinth blue, and they had little buff caps with black peaks. The Free School boys added beauty and charm to the Wilton streets.[15]

A church attendance surely got up purely for its decorative effect was that of charity children at an important wedding. In 1847 the *Illustrated London News*, reporting that of the Marquis of Kildare, heir to the Duke of Leinster, writes: "the centre aisle was supplied by between 50 and 60 little girls educated at the Duchess' own school all of whom wore white

---

* Anguish, of Norfolk, had in 1617 ordained that on Sundays his small protégés "are to be in their coats and caps and to attend upon the Sword [magistrate]" in the civic procession to the cathedral (F. Blomefield . . . *History of* . . . *Norfolk* (edn. 1806) vol. IV, 407–10).

173. Charity schoolgirls lined up at the wedding of a Marquis, whose mother, the Duchess of Leinster, *right*, is their patroness. 1847 (*Illustrated London News* 16 October 1847, detail)

dresses and straw hats trimmed with a wreath of green leaves . . . All the boys wore white favours". (Alas, either the journalist or the artist must have been absent on the day – see Fig. 173 – but whatever the details the effect was clearly pleasing.)

A different sort of occasion when the children were displayed was at the "beating of the bounds" of a parish. The custom was thus described in *Costume of Great Britain* in 1808:

Once in three years the poor children who are cloathed and educated at the expense of the parish walk in procession and trace and preserve the boundaries of the same. They are preceded by the Clergymen, the Churchwardens and Beadles, each boy carries a white wand and being all dressed in the same livery they make a very pretty and interesting appearance.[16]

In the above-mentioned *City Scenes* (edn. 1853) the reaction is similar: "Well here is a merry sight indeed! Such a troop of little boys, all dressed in their curious school uniforms, with long white wands and gay nosegays in their hands . . ." The boys used their wands to beat the boundary stones as they went round.

174. In procession, to "beat the bounds": parson, beadles and charity boys. Boys wear uniform – badges, bands, etc. – and carry wands. 1853/4 (*City Scenes*, edition of 1853–4, detail)

The order of the procession in the Hamlet of Ratcliff, Stepney, in 1821 was preserved in the school records.[17] The "Charity Children (Boys)" – sharply distinguished from the motley "Public Boys" on the one hand and the dapper "Gentlemen's Children" on the other – surely added much to the scene by the rhythm of their green uniforms. The daughter of a former vicar of St Martin-in-the-Fields, looking back, remembered that there the boys of the charity school still "flogged the boundary stones with long canes" in 1870.[18]

As we saw, the boys of Queen Elizabeth's Hospital, Bristol, had a specially striking uniform and also had considerable dependence on the town. Hence they were drawn into many civic ceremonies. Between 1614 and 1620 they earned £6. 2s. by gracing the funerals of important persons at the rate of about £1 a time. They were paraded at the laying of the foundation stone of the City Council House and at assize services and so on: indeed eventually they came to be called the "City School". They beat the bounds regularly until 1805 and they carried a banner on Queen Victoria's coronation day. Their band was specially effective: it played the Crimean veterans to church in 1905 and gallantly escorted the Red Maids to the girls' Founder's Day Service every year.[19]

Charity folk, as we saw, often wore appropriate tokens on occasions of national importance; they also, by their actual presence, often played an ornamental role at celebrations of these by the public. Here the Chelsea pensioners have been specially effective; for example, they used to be paraded in London on the king's birthday, and in our own time some of them form a splendid splash of colour in the Albert Hall every year at the Royal British Legion Festival on the eve of Remembrance Day.

In 1802, when Nelson, accompanied by Lady Hamilton, made a triumphal visit to Birmingham, it is recorded that "the appearance of the Blue Coat School afforded him much pleasure".[20] And after his final victory, there began in London the annual Trafalgar Day festivities. In these the drummers and fifers of the Royal Hospital, Greenwich, who wore the specially striking costume we have described, played an important part.

Until near the end of the nineteenth century charity children and almsfolk frequently walked in procession at state funerals, not always as a tribute to a benefactor but as a garnish to the scene. Henry VIII's funeral in 1547 was conducted magnificently "to the great admiration" of the "innumerable People . . . very desirous to see the sights". From Westminster, where the King died, to Syon, *en route* for Windsor where he was buried, the procession began with ecclesiastics and choirs. These were very decoratively flanked on either side by: "the Number of two hundred and fifty Poor Men in long Mourning Gowns and Hoods, with [the King's] Badges on their left shoulders, the Red and Whyt

175. Two of the "12 bed[e]-men of Westmynster with long new blake gownes . . . and torches", so described in Machyn's *Diary*, at Anne of Cleves's funeral in 1557 (After contemporary drawing, British Library MS Add. 35324 f.8)

176. "Poor Men" in long gowns in funeral processions. *Left* At George Monk, Duke of Albemarle's, 1670. *Right* At Sir Philip Sidney's, 1587 (*Left* Francis Sandford *The Interment of George, Duke of Albemarle*, 1670. *Right* engraving by T. de Bry after T. Lant in *Funeral Procession of Sir Philip Sidney*, 1587)

crosse in a sonne [sun] shining, the Crown Imperial over that. In each of their Hands a large Torch burning".[21] On arrival at Windsor the funeral cortège was adorned by a contingent from Eton: "all the young children scollers of the colledge in their whyt surplices bare headed, holding in ther one Hands Tapers and in th'other Books, saying the seven psalms . . .".[22]

From their proximity to Westminster Abbey and from their being King's scholars, it seemed natural for the boys of Westminster School to participate sometimes in a royal funeral. We know that they appeared, for example, in 1557, in the cortège of Anne of Cleves, wearing their own long gowns,[23] and passed with it through an avenue of mourning almsmen in the glow of the torches they carried. They also attended Lord Palmerston's funeral in 1865.

At the magnificent obsequies of Sir Philip Sidney in 1588 thirty-two "Poore Men" (thirty-two being his age), led by their "Conductors", headed the procession. Though allowed to vary their headgear and neckwear, all had long black mourning gowns. With sovereigns, and also at the near royal funeral of George Monk, Duke of Albemarle, the number exceeded the age. Monk was sixty-two, but there were seventy-four poor men, all uniformly dressed (Fig. 176). Their Puritan-looking plain bib-shaped collars, already old-fashioned, are in the style retained for charity schools until collars with elongated tabs took their place. At Elizabeth I's funeral there were fifteen almsmen in special gowns with false hanging sleeves (Fig. 134) and no less than 266 almswomen in mourning, making an endless ribbon of black and white that must have been a memorable sight.

At the otherwise disrespectful funeral accorded to poor Caroline, George IV's queen, in 1821,[24] a touching contribution was made by the Latymer School children. She had been kind to the school when living as their neighbour in Brandenburgh House, Hammersmith, and it was there that she died. *The Observer* (19 August), reporting on the funeral procession, actually remarks on the effectiveness of the school uniform:

The spectators were gratified with one of the most interesting sights, we believe, ever witnessed. The children, male and female, ... issued from the school-house in their best dresses wearing crape upon their hats ... Having ranged themselves at the head of the cavalcade ... two and two they proceeded, strewing their flowers [which they had begged from local gardens] in the road as they walked along. The extremely neat dresses of the children, with their earnest manner ... excited the highest admiration and the deepest sympathy.

The eighteenth-century charity schools of London participated in many national celebrations. There were already enough of them to

177. Funeral procession of Queen Caroline, headed by uniformed children of Latymer School, 1821: girls in tippets and bonnets, boys in tail coats and breeches. All carry flowers (Engraving after Banks in R. Huish: *Memoirs of Caroline, Queen Consort of England* vol. II, 1821)

make a splendid adornment to the pageant in 1713, when the Treaty of Utrecht had proclaimed the end of the War of the Spanish Succession, and Parliament processed to St Paul's to give thanks. Here is a contemporary account of the festival:

Upon the Thanksgiving day for Peace, about Four thousand Charity children (Boys and Girls) new cloathed were placed upon a Machine [grand stand] in the Strand which was in Length above 600 foot, and had in Bredth Eight Ranges of seats, one above another, whereby all the children appear'd in full view of . . . the solemn procession . . . who by their singing Hymns . . . as well as by their appearance, contributed very much to adorn so welcome a Festival and gave great Satisfaction to all the Spectators.[25]

The children were arranged school by school so that they made blocks of different colours. The separation of boys from girls added to the neatness of the effect and all the four thousand children wore gleaming white bands. We know from a minute dated 9 April 1713, that our St Martin-in-the-Fields School decided to be present.

So spectacular was this parade that Vertue made, and later presented to George I, an engraving about a yard long giving a panoramic view of the

178. Detail from admission ticket to the "Anniversary Meeting of the Charity Children" at St Paul's. Drawings of charity boy and girl, both with badges, act as decoration; the design dated 1807 (Mansell Collection)

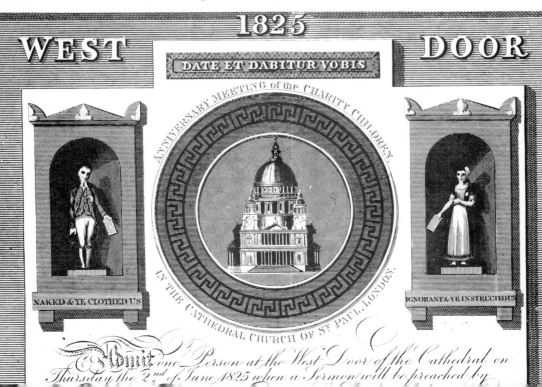

whole scene. A print is in the possession of the S.P.C.K. Another tribute was paid by Joseph Addison: "There was no part of the Show . . . which so much pleased and affected me as the little Boys and Girls who were ranged with so much Order and Decency in . . . the Stand . . . Such a numerous, innocent multitude, cloathed in the Charity of their Benefactors, was a Spectacle pleasing both to God and Man . . .".[26]

In the following year the children were mustered again, this time to line the streets in the City for the ceremonial entry of George I at his accession. The charity school at Camberwell recorded the presence of their green-coated children, and minutes of the S.P.C.K. record that the Prince of Wales (later George II) "was pleased to say that the Charity Children were one of the finest sights he ever saw in his life; and that he only wished his own children had been with him to have seen them".

When the recovery of George III from his first grave illness was celebrated in St Paul's in 1789, an elaborate drawing of the whole scene in the cathedral was made by E. Dayes, and the charity children in their serried ranks form the most striking feature in the picture.[27]

But the most spectacular of all displays was that which took place in connection with the annual church service of the assembled London charity schools. By 1782, after several changes of site, the service was solemnized in St Paul's Cathedral, where it was repeated annually for almost a century. It became a spectacle that attracted enormous attention. The distribution of the children's new clothes was timed for the event and they were shown to maximum advantage in body and in spirit. George Thornby in his *Old and New London* celebrates the recent move to the cathedral with impressions in 1784:

One of the most beautiful and touching of all London sights . . . In endless ranks pour in the children clothed in all sorts of quaint dresses – Boys in knee breeches of Hogarth's school days, bearing glittering pewter badges on their coats, girls in blue and orange, with quaint little mob caps as white as snow, and long white gloves covering all their little arms.

It is clear that costume, as such, contributed much to the effect.

In 1814 the service was attended by the King of Prussia and the Emperor of Russia. (The King of Prussia, Marshal Blücher and "other distinguished figures" expressed great satisfaction at having attended "an occasion at once so grand and so affecting. At one point the Emperor was observed to shed tears".[28]) In fact the whole scene was rejoiced in for a century by spectators of all sorts from Mrs Trimmer to Thackeray, and from journalists to George III.

The converging streams of children from all quarters towards the

179. Picturesque scene as beadles conduct streams of charity children along Cheapside to the anniversary service at St Paul's, 1837 (*Penny Magazine* Monthly Supplement 31 October 1837, page 424. Cutting C.49 P.T. Guildhall Library)

cathedral was a drama in itself. Dr (later Bishop) White Kennett had noted this in his sermon at the third annual (commonly called "anniversary") service in 1706. The sight and sound of the children singing in the church, but also to see them "walk in decent Couples thro' the Streets, led by the Ministers . . . to see them cloath'd with Neatness, and set off with good Manners . . . and Piety . . . Oh what a Christian Entertainment is this! A Spectacle far beyond the Vanities of the Stage or Musicke House . . ."[29]

Thackeray refers to the festival as "a day when old George [George III] loved with all his heart" to attend St Paul's; and Thackeray himself thought "in all Christendom there is no such sight as Charity Children's Day. *Non Angli, sed Angeli*".[30] Many years later, in 1869, the *Graphic*[31] recorded the visual impression made by the uniforms: ". . . The children of each school sit together, the boys being placed above the girls, and the effect of the differently coloured costumes, which are the distinguishing marks of each institution, is most striking and picturesque".

As time had gone on, more and more of the schools had allowed the children those special little fineries for the occasion that were frowned on by Mrs Trimmer and others. At the turn of the century some of the girls had a coloured bow at the neck and boys a feather in their hats. At

180. Boy of St Katharine's School wearing feather in hat for the anniversary service at St Paul's, *c.* 1805 (John Page: *Book of engravings depicting the costume of . . . each charity school . . . in the . . . anniversary service . . . in St Paul's,* Guildhall Library)

181. Children coming out of school to attend the anniversary service at St Paul's, a decorative procession, 1879. Smallest girl is allowed a rosette. Note details of "fichu", sleeve-mittens, etc. (Original proofs, KG 899-903, of illustrations by Kate Greenaway for *St Nicholas* vol. VI, 151. Courtesy: London Borough of Camden, from the collections at Keats House, Hampstead)

Clerkenwell there is a record of buying bows and feathers for boys and rosettes for girls in 1819; later the girls had posies too (Figs. 180, 181 and 89).

In 1879 in *St Nicholas*, a magazine for the young, the writer of a story, "Children's Day in St Paul's", extols the quaint costumes of the girls and questions whether the little "daughters of dignitaries" in the congregation, wearing their highly fashionable hats, were "any prettier than some of the charity girls, in their funny mob-caps".[32] He mentions in passing that the girls' costumes were now prettier than those of the boys, who in the last twenty years had exchanged their antiquated knee-breeches and bands for conventional trousers and collars.

The St Paul's event was so attractive that tickets of admission were required; on the handsome one shown in Fig. 178 the charity boy once again bears the legend "I was naked and ye cloth'd me".

The spectacle inspired countless illustrations and even works of art. Perhaps the earliest is a fascinating small book[33] by John Page, who

182. Charity children entering St Paul's for the anniversary service, 1866. The coloured ribbons, fastened behind, carry medals (*Illustrated London News* 16 June 1866)

183. A selection of costumes of charity schools attending the anniversary service at St Paul's showing pleasing variation within a general pattern (As for Fig. 180)

was Vicar Choral at St Paul's and was also a good observer and a moderate draughtsman. Published *c.* 1805, it is entitled: *A book of hand-coloured engravings depicting the costume worn by the children of each charity school of London taking part in the festival anniversary service.* About fifty children are individually shown with considerable detail (Fig. 183). Uniforms are blue, grey, green or brown.

A magnificent coloured lithograph showing the schools in serried ranks was produced in 1826 and another soon afterwards. (In the latter the girls, rightly or wrongly, are shown wearing tall-crowned hats like the Castle Rising almswomen.) After that, year by year, the illustrated papers would include drawings of the scene, one of the last of which we reproduce in Fig. 182. It will be agreed that the visual charm was again greatly dependent on the costumes.

In the collection at Keats Memorial House, Hampstead, there is a programme for the service in 1877, with some "doodling" sketches of the girls' mob-caps pencilled in the margin by the artist Kate Greenaway. The upshot of her attendance at St Paul's was a series of captivating drawings which were published as illustrations to the story in *St Nicholas,* mentioned above (Fig. 181). The originals are also at Keats House.[34] Among these is a front view of the girls praying behind their raised aprons and making a peculiarly decorative pattern. In 1842 a columnist in the *Illustrated London News* had been enchanted by the same sight, and still more so by the effect of the combined movement afterwards of thousands of aprons coming down again, "like a fall of snow".[35]

184. Charity girls in St Paul's for the anniversary service, aprons drawn over their faces for prayer (As for Fig. 181)

The ceremony at St Paul's illustrates a good deal of what has been said about charity costumes and their significance down the years; it also shows the givers, receivers and even the public at their happiest and best. This seems therefore a good note on which to close.

Though genuine feeling and piety may lie behind some of the quotations we have used, they can easily be mocked for sentimentality. What they endeavoured to express has more happily been put by William Blake.

Holy Thursday

T'was on a Holy Thursday, their innocent faces clean,
The children walking two and two, in red and blue and green,
Grey-headed beadles walk'd before, with wands as white as snow,
Till into the high dome of Paul's they like Thames' waters flow.

Oh what a multitude they seem'd, these flowers of London town!
Seated in companies they sit with radiance all their own.
The hum of multitudes was there, but multitudes of lambs,
Thousands of little boys and girls raising their innocent hands.

Now like a mighty wind they raise to heaven, the voice of song,
Or like harmonious thunderings the seats of Heaven among.
Beneath them sit the aged men, wise guardians of the poor;
Then cherish pity, lest you drive an angel from your door.

William Blake *Songs of Innocence*, 1789

References

Chapter 1 Problems and Practices (pp. 1–19)

1. James Thorold Rogers *A History of Agriculture and Prices* (1866) vol. I, 66
2. Quoted in Edward Geoffrey O'Donoghue *Bridewell Hospital . . .* vol. I (1923) 141–2
3. Mercers' Company's return to Royal Commission (1888) p. 51
4. Quoted in F. Blomefield . . . *History of the County of Norfolk . . .* vol. IV (edn. 1806) p. 409
5. Jonas Hanway *Three Letters on the Subject of the Marine Society* (1758) Letter III, p. 29
6. Foundling Hospital MS minutes of Daily Committee, Greater London Record Office
7. *The Letters of Charles Dickens 1842–1843*, ed. M. House and G. Storey, vol. III (1974) pp. 562–3
8. Norman Wymer *Father of Nobody's Children* (1954) p. 73
9. Sarah Trimmer *The Oeconomy of Charity* (edn. 1801) p. 174
10. Foundling Hospital MS minutes of Sub-Committee: XXIX, 183. Greater London Record Office
11. *Extracts from the Statutes of Ellis Davy's Almshouse at Croydon . . .* (pamphlet) Mercers' Company
12. Mercers' Company MS *Ordinances of Trinity Hospital, Greenwich*
13. Mercers' Company MS 1/116/6
14. Foundling Hospital Sub-Committee: I, 167
15. Ibid. IX, 139
16. Personal communication by kindness of Miss Alice Cox
17. Cripplegate-Within Ward School Rules (nineteenth century) Guildhall Library MS C. 49.1.T 18-
18. Mercers' Company MS 1/116/1
19. A. G. K. Lestrange *The Palace and the Hospital . . .* (1886) vol. II, 252
20. Clerkenwell Charity School "Minutes of the Cloathing Committee", Islington Public Library (Finsbury Branch) MS
21. Mercers' Company MS T.H. 5, book I
22. John Leland *Collectanea* ed. Thomas Hearne (1770) vol. IV, pp. 358–9
23. Cripplegate-Within, loc. cit.
24. Trimmer, p. 238
25. Foundling Hospital Sub-Committee: XVIII, 9 (1785)
26. P. and A. Mactaggart in *Strata of Society* (1974) p. 27 (published by Costume Society)
27. Hanway, op. cit. p. 29
28. *Statutes of the Colleges of Oxford for the Royal Commission* (1853) vol. I, 44 (translated from Latin)
29. National Maritime Museum Library MS MSY/B/2 p. 326
30. Jonas Hanway *Proposal for County Naval Free Schools . . .* (1783) p. 53
31. Clerkenwell, op. cit.
32. Foundling Hospital Sub-Committee: XXIX, 333
33. Clerkenwell, op. cit.
34. Joyce Godber *The Harpur Trust, 1552 to 1973* (1973) p. 140

35. *Report on the Charities of Northampton* (1908)
36. Godber, p. 138
37. D. H. Thomas *A Short History of St Martin-in-the-Fields High School for Girls* (1929) p. 88
38. Quoted in R. H. Nichols and F. A. Wray *The History of the Foundling Hospital* (1935) p. 132
39. Foundling Sub-Committee: I, 111
40. Ibid. IV, 11
41. Mercers' Company MS 4/73/1 No. 110
42. Foundling Sub-Committee: III, 197
43. Loc. cit.
44. Mercers' Company MS 1/116/1
45. Hanway *Three Letters* p. 40

Chapter 2 General Characteristics of the Costumes (pp. 20–39)

1. Sarah Trimmer *The Oeconomy of Charity* (edn. 1801) p. 120
2. D. H. Thomas *A Short History of St Martin-in-the-Fields High School for Girls* (1929) p. 89
3. Quoted in John D. Carleton *Westminster School* (1965) pp. 19, 20
4. Trimmer, p. 121
5. Thomas Boyles Murray *The Children in St Paul's: an Account of the Anniversary of the Assembled Charity Schools* (1851) p. 16
6. Quoted in J. V. Pixell *A Short History of the Hamlet of Ratcliff School* (1910) pp. 17, 18
7. E. J. G. Rich *The Two St Mary Winton Colleges* (1883) p. 84
8. Quoted in E. H. Pearce *Annals of Christ's Hospital* (1908) p. 190
9. H. F. B. Compston *The Magdalen Hospital . . .* (1917)
10. Mrs Barnardo and James Marchant *Memoirs of the Late Dr Barnardo* (1907) p. 121
11. Quoted in *The Reformatory and Refuge Journal* (1888–90) vol. X, 79
12. Charles Dickens *Dombey and Son* (1847–8) chapter V
13. Pixell, p. 43
14. Quoted in *Parochial Charities of Westminster* (1890) p. 66, published by the parishes of St Margaret and St John
15. Pearce, op. cit. p. 185
16. *Merton Muniments*, translated and edited by P. S. Allen and H. W. Garrod (1928)
17. *Cambridge University and College Statutes* vol. III, 444, 446
18. Trimmer, op. cit.
19. Charles Lamb "On Christ's Hospital . . .", originally in *Gentleman's Magazine* (June 1813)
20. George Wickham *A Blue Coat Boy's Recollections . . .* (1841)
21. Charity Commissioners' Report vol. 17 (1828) p. 219
22. William Wheatley *Edward Latymer and his Foundation* (1953) p. 149
23. Quoted in Elizabeth Brunskill *Some York Almshouses*, York Georgian Society No. 7
24. Unpublished thesis by Marie, a Sister of Sion "The Administration of the Poor Law in Kensington" (1967), Royal Borough of Kensington and Chelsea Central Library
25. Charity Commissioners' Report vol. 3 (1820) p. 398
26. Charity Commissioners' Report vol. 20 (1829) p. 703
27. C. G. T. Dean *The Royal Hospital, Chelsea* (1950) p. 187
28. Camden Society NS. No. 17, p. xliii

29. Royal Masonic Institution for Girls MS minutes of the General Committee
30. Francis Blomefield . . . *History of the County of Norfolk* . . . vol. IV (edn. 1806) pp. 407–10

Chapter 3 Attitudes towards the costumes (pp. 40–64)

1. *Parochial Charities . . . of Westminster* (1890) p. 48, published by the parishes of St Margaret and St John
2. *Proceedings of the General United Society for Supplying British Troops with extra Cloathing* (1798)
3. *Statutes of the Colleges of Oxford for the Royal Commission* (1853) vol. I, 44 (translated from Latin)
4. John Stow *A Survay of London* (1603) ed. C. Kingsford (1908), reprinted 1971, vol. II, 82
5. John Lydgate *Pilgrimage of Man*, English metrical version of French poem, British Library MS Cott. Tib. A VII fol. 103 (spelling modernized)
6. J. B. Nichols *Account of the Royal Hospital and Collegiate Church of St Katharine near the Tower of London* (1924) p. 4
7. Henry Dryden *Hospital of St John Baptist and St John Evangelist, Northampton* (1875), published by Northamptonshire Architectural Society
8. Catharine Cappe *An Account of Two Charity Schools . . . in York* (1800) pp. 115–16
9. Foundling Hospital MS minutes of Sub-Committee: XX, 105, Greater London Record Office
10. *Illustrated London News* vol. LXX (1877) p. 618
11. Cappe, p. 5
12. *York Grey Coat Girls' School, Bicentenary Souvenir 1705–1905* (1905) p. 58
13. Ibid., loc. cit.
14. *Parliamentary Accounts and Papers* vol. XLIV, 23 (1851)
15. Charles Lamb "Christ's Hospital . . ." in *Essays of Elia* (1823)
16. Phillis Cunnington and Catherine Lucas *Occupational Costume in England* (1967) plates 49a and b
17. D. H. Thomas *A Short History of St Martin-in-the-Fields High School for Girls* (1929) p. 78
18. Anna Wickham "Compassion" in *Shilling Selections from Edwardian Poets* (1936)
19. Jonas Hanway *Three Letters on the Subject of the Marine Society* (1758) Letter III, p. 3
20. National Maritime Museum Library MS MSY/B/2 p. 328
21. Quoted in R. H. Nichols and F. A. Wray *The History of the Foundling Hospital* (1935) p. 289
22. *Vox Populi*, British Library Thomason Tracts E 146, No. 2
23. J. H. Cardwell *The Story of a Charity School 1699–1899* (1899) p. 86
24. Sarah Trimmer *The Oeconomy of Charity* (edn. 1801) p. 119
25. F. Blomefield . . . *History of the County of Norfolk* . . . vol. IV (edn. 1806) p. 407
26. Charity Commissioners' Report 29 (1835) p. 377
27. Samuel Pepys *Diary*, 21 June 1660
28. Quoted in J. Pinchbeck and M. Hewitt *Children in English Society* (1969) vol. I, 426
29. Cappe, pp. 71–2
30. W. K. Jordan *Charities of Rural England 1440–1660* (1961) pp. 228 seqq.
31. *The Newcomen Education Foundation and Clothing Charity*, Guildhall Library, Pamphlet 3204
32. *Illustrated London News* vol. LX (1872) p. 262
33. C. G. T. Dean *The Royal Hospital, Chelsea* (1950) p. 209

34. Ibid. p. 136
35. Hanway, Letter III
36. National Maritime, op. cit. p. 136
37. H. F. D. Compston *The Magdalen Hospital* . . . (1917) p. 173
38. *Illustrated London News* vol. I (1842) p. 45
39. Charles Lamb "On Christ's Hospital . . .", originally in *Gentleman's Magazine* (June 1813)
40. D'Arcy W. Thompson *Day Dreams of a Schoolmaster* (1864)
41. Charles Dickens *Dombey and Son* (1847–8) chapter V
42. Thomas A. Readwin *Account of the Charities of Wokingham* (1845) p. 21
43. Charity Commissioners' Report 7 (1822) p. 503
44. G. C. T. Bartley *The Schools for the People* (1871) p. 103
45. R. Ackermann *History of the Colleges of Winchester, etc.* (1816)
46. Dickens, loc. cit.
47. W. H. Blanch *The Blue Coat Boys* . . . (1877) p. 62
48. Lamb, art. cit.
49. Extract from *Proceedings in Respect of the Amicable Society School* (1926), Southwark Public Library (Newington Branch) TS
50. V. D. B. Still *The Blue Coat School, Birmingham, 1722–1972* (1972) p. 20, published by the School
51. Blanch, p. 51

Chapter 4 Introduction to schools; Blue Coat Schools (pp. 65–79)

1. Quoted in E. H. Pearce *Annals of Christ's Hospital* (1901) p. 187
2. Ibid. p. 188
3. *Punch* (1864) p. 188
4. *City Scenes* [compiled by William Darton] (1814)
5. George Wickham *A Blue Coat Boy's Recollections of Hertford School* (1841)
6. Ibid.
7. Illustration in Wallace Clare *The Historic Dress of the English Schoolboy* [1940]

Chapter 5 Other boys' schools (pp. 80–99)

1. Quoted in D. L. Edwards *A History of the King's School, Canterbury* (1957)
2. Ibid. (appendix)
3. Ibid. p. 150
4. Quoted in Lawrence E. Tanner *Westminster School* (1951) p. 2
5. A. F. Leach *A History of Winchester College* (1899) p. 92
6. Ibid. p. 173
7. New College, Oxford, MS C. 288
8. H. C. Adams *Wykehamica* . . . (1878) p. 55
9. E. J. G. Rich *The Two St Mary Winton Colleges* (1883) p. 72
10. Ibid. p. 57
11. George Bompas *Life of Frank Buckland* (Nelson edn. first published 1885) p. 31
12. Ibid. p. 39
13. J. D'E. Firth *Winchester College* (1949) p. 67
14. Ibid. p. 115
15. Leach, pp. 169–70
16. Personal communication

17. A. K. Cook *About Winchester College* (1917) p. 451
18. Ibid. p. 455
19. Arthur Bennet in *Old Quiristers' Association Yearbook* (edn. 1936–7)
20. Cook, p. 455
21. L. Cust *A History of Eton College* (1899) p. 83
22. Ibid. p. 182
23. Ibid. p. 223
24. *Bailey's Magazine* vol. VII, 346, quoted by H. C. Maxwell Lyte in *A History of Eton College 1440–1884* (1889)
25. E. H. Jameson *Charterhouse* (1937) p. 24
26. Rowland Dobie *History of the Parishes of St Giles-in-the-Fields and St George's* . . . (1829) p. 252
27. Charity Commissioners' Report 7 (1822) pp. 485–6
28. *Northampton Borough Records* vol. II, 357
29. Personal communication from J. M. Swann, Northampton Museum
30. *Chronicle and Echo*, Northampton (12 December 1967)
31. In the Central Museum, Northampton
32. Charity Commissioners' Report 14 (1826) p. 281
33. *Report of Special Committee on Northampton Charities* (1908)
34. *Chronicle and Echo* art. cit.
35. The account is based on Dora Robertson *A History of the Life and Education of the Cathedral Choristers for 700 years* (1938)

Chapter 6 Girls' schools (pp. 100–118)

1. The source of this and some other quotations regarding this school is W. Lemprière *A History of the Girls' School of Christ's Hospital* . . .(1924)
2. Personal communication kindly given by Miss E. M. Tucker, Headmistress, 1975
3. Ibid.
4. Quoted in W. H. Sampson *History of the Red Maids' School* (1908) p. 22
5. Ibid. p. 38
6. For the particulars regarding recent times we are indebted to the Headmistress of the Red Maids' School and to Miss Janet Arnold whose article on the subject in *Costume* (in preparation) should be consulted for further history.
7. Mrs Edwin Gray *Papers and Diaries of a York Family 1764–1839* (1927)
8. Thomas A. Readwin *Account of the Charities of Wokingham* (1845) p. 121
9. Quoted in John Man *History and Antiquities . . . of the Borough of Reading* (1816) p. 210
10. Quoted in *Hatfield and its People* Part 8 "Schools" (1962), published by Workers' Educational Association, Hatfield Branch
11. Edith Olivier *Without Knowing Mr Walkley* (1939) pp. 28, 29
12. *Chronicle and Echo*, Northampton (12 December 1967)
13. Quoted in R. M. Handfield-Jones *The History of the Royal Masonic Institution for Girls 1788–1966* (1966), a book to which we are much indebted
14. Illustrated in Phillis Cunnington and Anne Buck *Children's Costume in England 1300–1900* (1965) p. 163
15. MS letter from Miss Lilian Atherton quoted by kind permission of Miss M. Dixon, Royal Masonic School for Girls
16. Handfield-Jones, p. 116
17. Ibid. loc. cit.

Chapter 7 Charity schools: general evolution of the costume (pp. 119–144)

1. Clerkenwell Charity School MS minute books, Islington Public Library (Finsbury Branch)
2. John Page *Book of engravings depicting the costume of . . . each charity school . . . in the . . . anniversary service . . . in St Paul's* (*c*. 1805), Guildhall Library
3. J. H. Cardwell *The Story of a Charity School 1699–1899* (1899) p. 106
4. John James Baddeley *Cripplegate . . .* (1921) p. 248
5. Bedfordshire County Record Office MS W3271
6. Clerkenwell (1841)
7. Clerkenwell (1822)
8. *Workwoman's Guide* by a Lady (1838) pl. 13
9. J. V. Pixell *A Short History of the Hamlet of Ratcliff School* (1910) Appendix C
10. *Workwoman's Guide*, p. 135
11. Ibid. p. 131
12. In "An Account of Charity Schools . . . in Great Britain and Ireland" which was updated each year as part of the S.P.C.K. *Annual Report*
13. A printed broadsheet in Guildhall Library, Collection C.49.1

Chapter 8 Individual charity schools (pp. 145–161)

1. Grey Coat Hospital minutes of a Governors' meeting (1698). Most of the particulars given in this section are from E. S. Day *An Old Westminster Endowment, being a history of the Grey Coat Hospital as recorded in the Minute Books* (1902)
2. D. H. Thomas *A Short History of St Martin-in-the-Fields High School for Girls* (1929) pp. 17–18
3. J. H. Cardwell *The Story of a Charity School 1699–1899* (1899)
4. See Judith D. Guillum Scott *The Story of St Mary Abbots, Kensington* (1942), the source of our data except where otherwise stated.
5. Minute book quoted in an unpublished thesis by Marie, a Sister of Sion "The Administration of the Poor Law in Kensington" (1967), Royal Borough of Kensington and Chelsea Central Library
6. See J. V. Pixell *A Short History of the Hamlet of Ratcliff School* (1910)
7. See colour photograph taken in 1910, reproduced in Pixell, and actual replicas kept at the school
8. S.P.C.K. *Annual Report* (1709)
9. Quoted by L. C. Sier in "The Blue Coat School, Colchester" in *Essex Review*, vol. XLIX (1940) pp. 124–133
10. Quoted in a booklet by V. D. B. Still, *The Blue Coat School, Birmingham . . . 1722–1972* (1972) p. 4
11. Ibid. loc. cit.
12. S.P.C.K. *Annual Report* (1712)

Chapter 9 Homes for children and young women (pp. 162–191)

1. e.g. John Strype in *A Survey of the cities of London and Westminster* (his edition, 1720, of Stow's *A Survay of London*
2. Quoted in *Parochial Charities of Westminster* (1890) published by the parishes of St Margaret and St John
3. Churchwardens' accounts quoted in John Nichols *Illustrations of the Manners and Expenses in Antient Times* (1797) pp. 41–2

4. Churchwardens' accounts, Westminster Central Library Record Department MSS E 77, XIV fols. 22–24v

5. Ibid. XV fol. 39

6. *Parochial Charities of Westminster*, p. 46

7. Sarah Trimmer *The Oeconomy of Charity* (edn. 1801)

8. John Byng *Torrington Diaries,* ed. C. B. Andrews (1938) IV, 110

9. H. F. B. Compston *The Magdalen Hospital* . . . (1917) p. 24

10. Minutes of Committee (26 November 1972) quoted by Compston, op. cit. p. 172

11. Compston, p. 172

12. Besides those at the Thomas Coram Foundation's building in Brunswick Square, a huge collection of manuscripts is held by the Greater London Record Office

13. Foundling Hospital MS minutes of Daily Committee (25 March 1741)

14. Thomas Bernard (ed.) *An Account of the Hospital for Exposed and Deserted Young Children . . . with Regulations* (edn. 1799) p. 89

15. *Gentleman's Magazine* (1747) pp. 284–5

16. Foundling Sub-Committee XXIX, 96

17. Bernard, p. 88

18. Charles Dickens in *Household Words* (19 March 1853)

19. Foundling Billet MS Books, Greater London Record Office

20. Ibid.

21. Manuscript at Thomas Coram Foundation

22. Foundling Sub-Committee (October 1751)

23. Bernard, p. 93

24. Foundling MS letter, Greater London Record Office

25. Foundling Sub-Committee IV, 176

26. Foundling minutes of Committee I, 167 (1753)

27. *Workwoman's Guide* by a Lady (1838) p. 31

28. Foundling Matron's Ledger, Greater London Record Office

29. Foundling Sub-Committee (1797)

30. Foundling Clothing Committee minutes (11 August 1757), Greater London Record Office

31. Foundling Sub-Committee XX, 60

32. Bernard, pp. 94, 96

33. Foundling Sub-Committee XXX, 138

34. Ibid. XXXI, 144

35. Ibid. XXXVI, 144

36. Ibid. XXIX, 250

37. R. H. Nichols and F. A. Wray *The History of the Foundling Hospital* (1935) p. 102

38. Ibid. p. 142

39. Ibid. p. 140

40. Foundling Sub-Committee IX, 131

41. Ibid. IX, 135

42. Ibid. XVIII, 11

43. Ibid. XXIX, 368

44. Ibid. II, 138

45. Ibid. XIX, 79

46. Mrs A. F. Green-Armytage in *Bristol Times and Mirror* (21 May, 1914)

47. Norman Wymer *Father of Nobody's Children* (1954) p. 73. To this readable book we owe much of the history of Barnardo's Homes

48. *Night and Day* vol. IV, 85–6

49. Ibid. vol. VII, 18
50. Mrs Barnardo and James Marchant *Memoirs of the Late Dr Barnardo* (1907) p. 121
51. Dr Barnardo quoted in A. E. William *Barnardo of Stepney* (1953) pp. 95–6
52. *Night and Day* vol. V (1881) p. 185
53. T. J. Barnardo *Something Attempted – Something Done* (1889) pp. 158–9
54. Wymer, pp. 220–1
55. Wymer, loc. cit.
56. Frank Norman *Banana Boy – A Childhood Autobiography* (1969)
57. Written for *Punch* and reprinted in *Owen Seaman, a Selection*, ed. R. Clement Brown (1937)
58. Donald Grist *A Victorian Charity* (1974) p. 45
59. Grist, p. 59

Chapter 10 Young people in training (pp. 192–214)

1. *Enquiry into the Causes of Increase . . . of the Poor* (1738) p. 43
2. Alfred Copeland *Bridewell Royal Hospital Past and Present* (1888) pp. 50, 51
3. Edward Geoffrey O'Donoghue *Bridewell Hospital . . .* vol. I (1923) p. 191
4. Ibid. vol. II 70
5. Entry quoted in J. C. Cox *The Parish Registers of England* (1910) p. 98
6. Gordon Humphreys *Shared Heritage – the History of King Edward's School, Witley, 1553–1972* (1972) p. 25
7. Copeland, p. 97
8. O'Donoghue, vol. II 236
9. Copeland, op. cit. p. 149
10. Humphreys, p. 68
11. Personal communication from the Clerk to the Governors
12. John Fielding *An Account of the Origin and Effects of a Police . . .* (1756)
13. The Marine Society records are lodged in the Library of the National Maritime Museum, the most useful being minutes of the Committee's monthly meetings, catalogued MSY/A/1–5 (1756–74) and MSY/B/1–35 (1774–1949), and also Rough Cash Accounts, MSY/Y/11–15 (1801–29)
14. Jonas Hanway *Three Letters on the Subject of the Marine Society* (1758) Letter III p. 40
15. Ibid. Letter III 29, 30
16. Ibid. Letter III 23, 24
17. National Maritime MSY/A/1 p. 11
18. Hanway *Three Letters . . .* Letter III 22, 23, 27
19. National Maritime MSY/A/1 p. 133
20. Ibid. p. 27
21. Jonas Hanway *A Proposal for County Naval Free Schools* (1783) p. 54
22. Hanway *Three Letters . . .* Letter III 30
23. Ibid. Letter III 49
24. Ibid. Letter III 22
25. Hanway *A Proposal . . .* p. 52
26. Gerald Dickens *Dress of the British Sailor* (1957) pp. 4, 5, published by the National Maritime Museum
27. National Maritime MSY/Y/13 (June 1817)
28. National Maritime MSY/B/1 p. 317
29. National Maritime MSY/Y/14 (1820)

30. National Maritime MSY/B/23 p. 10
31. National Maritime MSY/B/26 p. 345
32. John Masefield *The Conway* (1933, 1953)
33. Hanway *A Proposal* . . . p. 55
34. Dickens p. 5
35. Hanway *A Proposal* . . .
36. National Maritime MSY/Y (September 1813)
37. National Maritime MSY/B/23 p. 118
38. Horatio Nelson, letter to Admiral St Vincent after the Battle of the Nile
39. National Maritime MSY/Y (July 1814)
40. National Maritime MSY/B/23 p. 115
41. National Maritime MSY/B/26 p. 345
42. Dudley Jarrett *British Naval Dress* (1960)
43. Dickens p. 5
44. Masefield, pp. 47, 79–80
45. Mainly from Gwyn Lewis *One Hundred Shining Years – a History of the London Shoeblacks* (1951); also material kindly lent by Messrs Reckitt and Colman Ltd, including an extract from *A Hundred Years of Waifdom*
46. *Charles Knight's London* ed. E. Walford (1875–9) vol. I 19
47. National Portrait Gallery
48. Sarah Trimmer *The Oeconomy of Charity* (edn. 1801) p. 40
49. *Illustrated London News* XLVI (1865) p. 270
50. Catharine Cappe *An Account of Two Charity Schools . . . in York* (1800) p. 101
51. Ibid. p. 102

Chapter 11 University scholars (pp. 215–226)

1. J. B. Mullinger *University of Cambridge* . . . (1873) vol. II, 229
2. Christopher Wordsworth, ed. R. Brimley Johnson *The Undergraduate* from Dr Christopher Wordsworth's *Social Life at the English Universities in the Eighteenth Century* (1928) p. 117
3. Duchess of Somerset's Foundation Indenture (a copy at St John's College)
4. Mullinger, vol. I, 352–3
5. *Statutes of the Colleges of Oxford for the Royal Commission* (1853) vol. I, 44–6 (translated from Latin)
6. See W. Hargreaves-Mawdsley *History of Academical Dress in Europe* (1963)
7. Mullinger, vol. I, 165
8. Quoted ibid. vol. I, 233
9. E. C. Clark *The Archaeological Journal* vol. 50, 80–2
10. Hargreaves-Mawdsley, p. 131, quoting T. Rymer *Foedera* vol. VII, 242 re King's College, Cambridge
11. Clark, p. 91, re Oxford Statutes of 1462
12. Ibid. p. 85
13. Clark, p. 141
14. *Statutes . . . Oxford . . .* vol. I, 44
15. Hargreaves-Mawdsley, pp. 96, 195
16. S. Gibson *Statuta Antiqua Universitatis Oxoniensis* (1931) pp. 386–7
17. *Statutes . . . Oxford . . .* vol. I, 46
18. Ibid. loc. cit.
19. C. H. Cooper *Annals of the University of Cambridge* (1842–53) vol. I, 94

20. Ibid. vol. II, 162
21. Quoted in Wordsworth, op. cit., but there slightly mistranslated
22. Hargreaves-Mawdsley, pp. 96
23. N. F. Robinson in *Trans. St. Paul's Eccles. Soc.* vol. V (1901) p. 9
24. Ibid. p. 13
25. Hargreaves-Mawdsley, pp. 94, 99
26. David Loggan *Oxonia Illustrata* (1675)
27. David Loggan *Cantabrigia Illustrata* (1690)
28. J. R. Magrath *The Flemings at Oxford* vol. I, 245–6 (1904)
29. Quoted in Wordsworth, p. 149
30. *Historical Register of the University of Cambridge* (1967) p. 196
31. Ibid. loc. cit.

Chapter *12* People in almshouses (pp. 227–251)

1. Walter Besant *London in the Eighteenth Century* (1925) and *East London* (1901)
2. Philip Morant *The History and the Antiquities of the County of Essex* (1768)
3. Francis Blomefield . . .*Topographical History of . . . Norfolk* (edn. 1805–10) vol. IV, 448
4. C. Scott-Giles and B. Slater *History of Emanuel School* (1966) p. 29
5. John Leland *Collectanea* ed. Thomas Hearne (1770) vol. IV, 372
6. Rowland Dobie *The History of the United Parishes of St Giles-in-the-Fields and St George Bloomsbury* (1829) p. 252
7. Mercers' Company MS: Whittington College admission register
8. Arthur Mee (ed.) *The King's England – Wiltshire* (1939)
9. Alma Oakes and Margot Hamilton Hill *Rural Costume: its Origin and Development in Western Europe* (1970)
10. Sarah Trimmer *The Oeconomy of Charity* (edn. 1801) p. 41
11. Randle Holme *The Academy of Armory* (1688) Book III, Chapter III, plate facing p p. 41
12. Blomefield, vol. II, 736
13. Elizabeth Brunskill *Some York Almshouses*, York Georgian Society Paper 7
14. Elisabeth Ralph and H. Evans *St Mark's . . . Chapel, Bristol . . .* (1961) pp. 3, 4
15. Rotha Clay *The Medieval Hospitals of England* (1909) p. 175
16. C. B. Rowntree *Saffron Walden Then and Now* (1951) p. 59
17. Paul Cave *The History of the Hospital of St Cross* (1972); this booklet has been our main source of written information
18. Mercers' Company MS "Preamble to the Ordinances of the Whittington Hospital"
19. Where other references are not given, the source of data is *The Charity of Richard Whittington* (1968), a valuable history by Jean Imray, Archivist to the Mercers' Company
20. Mercers' Company MS: Mercers' Accounts of Court for 1527–60 fol. 216
21. John Stow *A Survey of . . . London . . .* (edn. 1720) vol. II, book V, 174
22. Particulars regarding Clun are from John Leland *Collectanea* (edn. 1770) vol. IV, pp. 347–383
23. Mercers' Company MS 1/116/1 "Ordinances of the Hospital"
24. Ibid.
25. Mercers' Company MS 4/73/1
26. The early history of Castle Rising we owe to Blomefield, op. cit. vol. IX, 55 seq.

27. Ibid.
28. Oakes and Hill, Appendix II
29. Oakes and Hill, loc. cit.
30. Quoted by H. Edwards in *A Collection of Old English Customs* (1842) p. 107
31. Charity Commissioners' Report 3, p. 404 (1820)
32. Quoted by Edwards, op. cit.
33. W. Jordan *Charities of Rural England, 1480–1660* (1961) p. 124
34. The quotations are all from A. K. Beese *Coningsby Hospital* (a booklet published in 1970) with additions (in italics) from Edwards op. cit.

Chapter 13 Armed forces: hospitals and associated schools (pp. 252–276)

1. George Peele *Polyhymnia* (1590)
2. Quoted in Edmund Fellowes *The Military Knights of Windsor 1352–1944* (1944) p. xvi
3. Quoted in Fellowes, p. xxxiii
4. John L. Nevinson in *Apollo* (1937) and J. Nichols *Progresses of James I* (1828)
5. Randle Holme *Academy of Armory* (1688) book III, chapter III, 54
6. Elias Ashmole *The History of the Order of the Garter* (edn. 1715) p. 472
7. Fellowes, p. xxxvii
8. Ashmole, p. 472
9. Royal warrant, Audit Office, Treas. Acct. 1682–5
10. C. G. T. Dean *The Royal Hospital, Chelsea* (1950) p. 131
11. John Walter's MS from the late R. Blunt's collection
12. Dean, p. 72
13. Ibid. p. 73
14. Ibid. p. 137
15. Ibid. p. 293
16. Ibid. p. 277
17. Ibid. p. 198
18. British Library MS Harl. 4712 fol. 89
19. G. R. Gleig *Chelsea Hospital and its Traditions* (1838)
20. John Cooke and J. Maule *An Historical Account of the Royal Hospital for Seamen at Greenwich* (1789) p. 83
21. Dudley Jarrett *British Naval Dress* (1960) p. 41
22. Cooke and Maule, p. 83
23. Quoted in A. G. K. Lestrange *The Palace and the Hospital . . .* (1886) vol. 2, p. 279 This book is the authority for most of the history given in this section.
24. Cooke and Maule, p. 86
25. Jarrett, p. 44 (illustration)
26. Lestrange, op. cit. Preface
27. G. C. T. Bartley *The Schools for the People* (1871) p. 237
28. Cooke and Maule, p. 42
29. H. Moseley *Report on the Royal Hospital Schools, Greenwich, to . . . Admiralty* (1851), Parliamentary Accounts and Papers vol XIV, 7 seq.

Chapter 14 Miscellaneous charities (pp. 277–287)

1. Westminster Central Library Record Department MS E 77
2. *Office of Seclusion of a Leper* (translated) Surtees Society 63, p. 105
3. Quoted in J. Y. Simpson *Archaeological Essays* (1872) vol. II, 37

4. James Thorold Rogers *A History of Prices and Agriculture* (1866) vol. I, 572, 576, 583
5. Arthur E. Gibbs *Historical Records of St Albans containing . . . Leprosy in St Albans during the Middle Ages . . .* (1888) p. 66
6. Ordinances (translated) quoted by A. Weymouth *Leprosy* (1938) but with an error due to absence of punctuation in the original
7. Judith D. Guillum Scott *The Story of St Mary Abbots, Kensington* (1942) p. 78
8. Charity Commissioners' Report 8 (1861), 720
9. Quoted in John Nichols *Illustrations of the Manners and Expenses in Antient Times* (1797)
10. E. Chamberlayne *Angliae Notitiae* (1669)
11. John Stow *A Survay of London* (1603) (ed. C. Kingsford (1908), reprinted 1971, vol. I, 86)
12. *Chambers' Book of Days* (1863) vol. I, 411–12
13. Ibid. loc. cit.
14. Henry Machyn's Diary published by the Camden Society (1848)
15. This and other particulars regarding Maundy are drawn from *The Pictorial History of the Royal Maundy* (Pitkin Pictorials, 1973)
16. Ibid.
17. *Chambers'* loc. cit.
18. George Williamson *Curious Survivals . . .* (1923) p. 180

Chapter 15 Charity costumes on parade (pp. 288–305)

1. G. C. T. Bartley *The Schools for the People* (1871) p. 509
2. Horace Walpole, letter to George Montagu (January 1760)
3. R. Ackermann *The Microcosm of London* (1819) pp. 18, 19
4. William Trollope *History of the Royal Foundation of Christ's Hospital* (1834)
5. Ackermann, loc. cit.
6. D'Arcy Wentworth Thompson [junior] *Science and the Classics, and Other Essays* (1940) pp. 241–3
7. L. W. Dickens in *Chronicle and Echo*, Northampton (12 December 1967)
8. Bernard de Mandeville *The Fable of the Bees . . .* (edn. 1723)
9. *Conference of Managers of Reformatory and Industrial Institutions* (1884) p. 27
10. John Stow *A Survey of . . . London . . .* (edn. 1720) Book I, p. 259
11. Henry Machyn's Diary published by the Camden Society (1848)
12. Trollope, p. 106
13. *City Scenes* [compiled by William Darton, revised by Ann and Jane Taylor]; edns. 1814 and 1828 have different illustrations of the same subject
14. George Wickham *A Bluecoat Boy's Recollections . . .* (1841)
15. Edith Olivier *Without Knowing Mr Walkley* (1939) p. 27
16. W. H. Pyne *The Costume of Great Britain* (1808)
17. J. V. Pixell *A Short History of the Hamlet of Ratcliff School* (1910) pp. 24–5
18. D. H. Thomas *A Short History of St Martin-in-the-Fields High School for Girls* (1929) p. 108
19. F. W. E. Bowen *Queen Elizabeth's Hospital, Bristol* (1970) p. 21
20. Quoted in *Birmingham Post* (30 October 1961)
21. College of Arms MS I 11 (fols. 92–105v describe this funeral)
22. Ibid.
23. College of Arms MS transcribed in S. Bentley *Excerpta Historica*
24. R. Huish *Memoirs of Caroline, Queen Consort of England* (1821) vol. II
25. Quoted by John Ashton in *Social Life in the Reign of Queen Anne* (1882) vol. I, 20

26. *Guardian* No. 105 (11 July 1713)
27. Reproduced in J. Pinchbeck and M. Hewitt *Children in English Society* (1969) vol. I, 213
28. Thomas Boyles Murray *The Children in St Paul's: an Account of the Anniversary of the Assembled Charity Schools* (1851)
29. *Sermon* by Dr White Kennett, preached at St Sepulchre's at the Anniversary Meeting of Charity Schools in 1706. Published as a leaflet, 1706. British Library 694. i. 16(2)
30. William Thackeray "The Four Georges" in *Cornhill Magazine* (1860)
31. *Graphic* (1869–70) pp. 659–60
32. *St Nicholas* vol. VI (April 1879) p. 135
33. A copy at the Guildhall Library
34. Catalogued by Rodney Engen, author of *Kate Greenaway* (in preparation)
35. *Illustrated London News* vol. I (1842) p. 45

INDEX

Page references to illustrations are normally given in bold numerals; in the case of institutions treated at length the textual references may also be consulted for illustrations.

Individual establishments are entered under place name.

Charity Costumes

INDEX OF TEXTILES

This index includes references to textiles whose nature, usage or name is now unfamiliar.